P9-CRH-742

KITCHEN GYPSY

*Recipes and Stories from a Lifelong
Romance with Food*

by JOANNE WEIR

photographs by THOMAS J. STORY
foreword by ALICE WATERS

Oxmoor House®

foreword

Joanne and Alice in the Edible Schoolyard garden.

×

OVER THE YEARS, many people have come through the doors of Chez Panisse for internships, jobs, and *stages* in the kitchen. Most are enthusiastic and learn from the experience of working at the restaurant. But some of them take the ideas, values, and community of Chez Panisse to heart and truly thrive. Joanne, who first came to us in the mid-1980s and worked here for five years, is among the latter. It seemed as if each time I came to the restaurant during her stay, I would find her flourishing in a new position. There was Joanne helping to unload the delivery of vegetables from the farm and then rolling out pasta. There was Joanne at the salad station in the Café. There she was assembling an apricot galette with Lindsey Shere in the pastry department.

From the start, it was apparent to all of us that Joanne had an endless curiosity about food and where it came from and was hungry to learn everything she could. What I learned— and what you'll learn yourself through the stories in this book—is that Joanne's maternal and paternal grandparents both ran their own farms and that her mother loved to cook. She grew up surrounded by family members who were growing, harvesting, and cooking their own food and passing on that essential knowledge to the next generation. Joanne is proof that when you get that kind of early edible education, it can last your whole life.

In the years since Joanne left Chez Panisse, I have loved hearing about her many projects: teaching, cooking, exploring, filming. She is an incredibly positive spirit. It is rare to find someone with such excitement and passion for whatever work she is pursuing. Joanne is also a true purist: she is always at the farmers' market making friends with the farmers and ranchers, finding out which fruits and vegetables are the ripest—the most alive and vibrant—and using those ingredients simply and beautifully.

We often joke that once people become part of *la famille Panisse*, they never truly leave the fold, even if they move on to other cities—or even other countries—and it is wonderful to have them come back and collaborate on projects. Early this spring I went to the restaurant during the preparations for our annual Parsi New Year celebration, and there was Joanne in the thick of it again, helping our pastry chef Mary Jo Thoresen put together *jalebi* and *falooda*. And not long ago, Joanne and I filmed her television show together here at the Edible Schoolyard in Berkeley, and it was a pleasure to see her deep appreciation for teaching children in the garden and in the kitchen.

What's particularly lovely about this memoir is how brightly Joanne's positiveness shines through in her stories and recipes. After just a few pages, you will understand what I mean. Joanne's infectious enthusiasm for food, farming, and teaching draws readers effortlessly into a new and beautiful relationship to food.　　　　—ALICE WATERS

introduction

I HAVE WRITTEN SEVENTEEN COOKBOOKS, plus countless recipes for my PBS television programs, my restaurant Copita, scores of cooking classes, numerous magazine spreads, and more. And although I feel as if a thousand recipes are swimming in my brain at any given time, I wasn't sure I was ready to write another recipe book. Yet I found myself sitting in the offices of *Sunset* magazine in Menlo Park, California, with the food editor, Margo True, and editor-in-chief, Peggy Northrop, discussing a possible new book project.

"What do you think of California cooking? What does it mean to you?" Margo asked.

I squirmed uncomfortably in my chair and began to fidget.

"Since you were working at ground zero of the California food movement in its early days, how do you see it now?" Peggy chimed in.

I knew from their questions that California cuisine was the subject that they were most interested in pursuing with me. Yes, it's true I was cooking when the California food movement was just beginning. I had gotten my start at Chez Panisse, one of the restaurants that fueled the new style. But did I want that to be my next book? I wasn't sure.

I looked down at my hands and started twirling my ring, a nervous habit of mine since I was a kid. I was searching for the right answer, and I knew that that answer was not in my palms. I could feel my face reddening as I looked up blankly.

"If you could write any cookbook at all, what would it be?" Peggy asked, trying a different tack.

I smiled and relaxed a little. My chair suddenly felt much more comfortable. I didn't recall ever having been asked that question by a publisher. It was so basic, so elemental, that I was surprised to realize I had an answer ready. Thoughts and images swirled in my head. I knew in that moment that yes, I did have another cookbook inside me, and it was screaming to get out.

"Food is my life!" I exclaimed enthusiastically. "I want to write a book about how everything I've done in my life has gotten me to exactly where I am at this moment. I want to write about my path. And I want the recipes to show the way."

I continued, "I want to write about the horrible blunder I made as a kid when I mixed 1½ cups, instead of 1½ teaspoons, of baking soda into a batch of oatmeal cookie dough, and how my mother used that and other mistakes to teach me valuable lessons about cooking and about life. With that story, I could share Mom's recipe for the best oatmeal cookie you will ever eat. I want to write about my love of travel and about how my father anointed me his 'wandering gypsy.'"

I told Peggy and Margo about my family—about how both sets of grandparents owned farms and were passionate about their land and the food it produced. I could hardly cap my excitement as I related my tale of sitting under a big, old maple tree at my grandfather's dairy farm in the Berkshires and eating maple-walnut ice cream that he and I had churned together. "Wouldn't it be amazing to share that ice cream recipe with my readers?" I wondered aloud.

In my next breath, I shared a story I hadn't told in years about finding a fly in a bottle of red wine and jetting off to France for the most unforgettable meal of my life. I explained that I was only twenty-four at the time, yet the trip spawned a serious interest in wine that has lasted a lifetime. I added that recipes from that memorable meal at Château Mouton Rothschild could accompany the story. Margo and Peggy were now leaning forward in their chairs.

I described studying with brilliant cooking teacher Madeleine Kamman, and how although it was one of the hardest years of my life, I would never trade it for anything. That spilled into my account of a job interview with the incomparable Alice Waters at Chez Panisse. Tales of cooking in one of the world's top kitchens would obviously be central to the book. I couldn't wait to explain to readers the ways in which that experience changed my life forever.

Over the years, I had shared these adventures, these stories, with family and friends and sometimes with my students. But I had never gathered them together in a single place. As I continued to brainstorm ideas in the *Sunset* offices, I realized what a wonderful opportunity it would be to tell this tale—this story of my culinary journey.

"And one last thing, this book wouldn't be complete without talking about the trials and tribulations of opening my restaurant Copita—about learning some tough lessons the hard way. Of course, along with that story, I'd have to include my recipe for the perfect margarita and the best pork belly tacos on earth." My mouth began to water just thinking about them.

I took a breath and realized that I'd been talking passionately and rapidly without a pause. I just couldn't stop the avalanche of memories, images, and stories. I hoped that Peggy and Margo had caught my excitement.

"This is the book I want to write," I said, feeling thrilled that I shared something that even I didn't know was inside of me.

"That's the book you should write," Peggy agreed enthusiastically.

When I walked out of the office that afternoon into the bright sunshine, I felt like I was bouncing on a fluffy white cloud. I had learned something incredibly exciting that day: Yes, I had another cookbook inside me, and it would be unlike any other cookbook I had ever written. It would be the story of my passion for food and my pursuit of knowledge about it. I was ready to recount all the tales of my gypsy-like journey through life's kitchens.

CHAPTER 1

UNDER
the
MAPLE
TREE

W HEN I WAS ABOUT SIX YEARS OLD, I remember my mother telling me that she was going to make me a tomato sandwich. My response? I wondered why my mother couldn't be like all of the other mothers and just make me a tuna fish sandwich or a peanut butter and jelly one. But no such luck.

It was the height of summer and we headed out to our garden in search of a perfectly ripe red tomato. We stood among the vines, which drooped under the weight of the plump fruit, breathing in the sweet, tangy aroma. She plucked a juicy sweet beefsteak tomato and carried it inside, warm from the sun and nestled in her hands, almost as if it was a precious baby. I could smell its fresh fragrance. Mom toasted a couple of slices of her freshly baked white bread and slathered the warm toast with creamy homemade mayonnaise. With a small serrated knife, she sliced the tomato, releasing bright red juices onto the countertop. She carefully laid the thick tomato slices onto the bread and sprinkled them with salt.

"Whenever you eat tomatoes, they need a little bit of salt to bring out the acidity and sweetness," she counseled.

from left:
I must've told
a joke to Aunt
Jin, Nana and
Grampa Sears,
my parents,
and Auntie Ann.
Me, eating, my
favorite pastime.

✕

from top:
My sisters Nancy
and Jinny
with me, always
the ham, in
front singing.
In the navy
blue dress with
white smocking
that Nana Sears
made for me.

×

Although I didn't say it, I remember thinking, I'm six years old, what am I ever going to do with this information?

As soon as I took a bite, I realized that this homemade tomato sandwich (see page 12), so lovingly assembled by my mom, was probably the most delicious thing I'd ever tasted. I am convinced that my love affair with food began with that sandwich.

× ● ×

"STAND IN FRONT OF THE REFRIGERATOR, HONEY!" my mother said with a smile.

"Oh, mom!" I looked at her with pleading eyes. "Please don't make me."

"Joey, please? Please sing for everyone? Sing 'Silent Night.' You know that everyone loves it when you sing."

"But, . . . " I said, my eyes begging her. Deep down I knew she had me. Whenever she asked me to do anything, I'd do it for her. Even when she asked me to kiss Uncle Harry, who smelled of Old Spice and stale cigar smoke, or Auntie Ruby, who had moles sticking out all over her face, I'd do it. I knew that my sisters, Nancy and Jinny, and my brother John would never do the things she asked, so I always did them.

With a defeated sigh, I relented. "Okay, I'll sing."

In a navy blue dress with white smocking around the collar—my favorite dress, made for me by my grandmother Sears—and with my head bowed low, I walked slowly toward my stage: the front of the white Frigidaire. Why my mom chose the refrigerator as my stage was a mystery to me, though I am guessing it was because she loved the stark white backdrop. Or maybe it was what was inside?

I looked up but could hardly see through the smoke rising from the cigarette dangling from Aunt Milly's lips. Auntie Ruby, in a red chiffon dress with white polka dots and nursing a stiff martini, sat next to her. My mom stood there with a wide smile on her rosy face egging me on.

It was Christmas Eve, late 1950s, and I was about to make my debut on the Frigidaire stage.

"Si-i-lent night, ho-o-ly night, all is calm, all is bright . . ."

As I looked around, Aunt Milly and Auntie Ruby were grinning ear to ear. I picked up the tempo.

"Round young vir-r-gins, Mother and Child," I could hear giggling, but I just kept going.

"Holy infant so tender and wild." And then, for the finale, I belted it out, "Sleep in hea-ven-ly pleeee-ease, sle-ep in hea-ven-ly please."

Having completed my first live appearance, I stepped away from the stage.

"Ding!" the timer from the stove rang.

"Dinner is served!" my Mom said, as she shoved big oven mitts onto her hands and pulled a pan of bubbling hot scalloped Blue Point oysters, the dish for which she was famous, from the oven. Plenty of oohs and aahs rose from the grown-ups' table, but the kids' table remained silent. Why didn't we give the scalloped oysters a chance? All it took was watching Auntie Ruby slurp up a huge, slippery oyster, guts and all, and my stomach did a flip-flop. Maybe next year, I thought. (It would be years before I appreciated Mom's scalloped oysters (see page 12), the crisp blanket of buttery cracker crumbs a perfect counterpart to the oysters' sparkling salinity. Turns out Auntie Ruby had it right all along.)

mom's tomato sandwich

Don't be fooled by the simplicity of this sandwich. The combination of these few ingredients is flavor perfection. If my mom wanted to gussy this sandwich up a bit, she'd add a few thin slices of cucumber for some crunch.

 2 slices homemade white bread
1½ tablespoons homemade mayonnaise (page 277)
 2 ripe tomatoes, cut into ¼-inch-thick slices
   Kosher salt

Toast the bread. Spread one side of each toasted slice with half of the mayonnaise. Arrange the tomatoes on 1 slice and sprinkle them liberally with salt. Close the sandwich with the second slice, mayonnaise side down. Cut in half on the diagonal and enjoy.

serves 1

scalloped oysters

With only four ingredients, it seems funny to me now that my mother got a standing ovation nearly every Christmas when this simple bubbling dish of baked oysters emerged from the oven.

3½ cups oyster crackers, very coarsely crushed
 3 cups shucked oysters with their liquor
 8 tablespoons unsalted butter
   Kosher salt and freshly ground black pepper
 1 cup half-and-half

1 Position an oven rack in the top third of the oven and preheat to 375°F.

2 Butter a 2½-quart baking dish. Place one-third of the crackers on the bottom of the prepared dish. Top with half of the oysters and their liquor. Dot the oysters with 3 tablespoons of the butter and season with salt and pepper. Pour ½ cup of the half-and-half evenly over the oysters. Top evenly with half of the remaining crackers and then all of the remaining oysters and liquor. Dot with 3 tablespoons of the butter, season with salt and pepper, and pour the remaining ½ cup half-and-half evenly over the oysters. Strew the remaining crackers evenly over the surface and dot with the remaining 2 tablespoons butter.

3 Bake until bubbles appear around the edges of the dish and the top is light golden brown, 25 to 30 minutes. Let rest for a few minutes before serving.

serves 6

MY MOM WAS NO ORDINARY MOM when it came to cooking in the late 1950s and early 1960s. Store-bought prepared foods or anything from a box had no place in our kitchen. My mom made everything from scratch, a fact that was made abundantly clear to me on a shopping trip to the A&P.

As we walked from aisle to aisle and tossed things into the basket, I realized that I was starving. It was the kind of hunger that made my stomach hurt as if it was folded in half and my head feel so light that I felt like I was in the clouds.

"Mom, can we get a can of New England clam chowder?" I begged, as I was about to keel over. She looked at me, her eyes popping out of her head as if I'd said a bad word. I wanted nothing more than to go home, use the electric can opener to open that can, pour that chunky, thick, flour-laden clam chowder into a pan, add some milk, and in seconds have a steaming bowl of soup.

"No, I'll buy a can of clams. I have everything at home to make homemade chowder."

Homemade was a big word in our house. "Mom, please? It will take all day. I'm starving. Can't we please just get a can that's already made?" I asked.

clockwise from left: Mom and Dad on the porch at Papa Jonas and Mama Anna's farm in 1946. My mom with a calf in 1943. Me, on my birthday, licking the frosting off the candles.

She grabbed a can of clams from the shelf, put it into the cart, and we headed toward the checkout. I realized at that moment that I was never going to be like all of the other kids with kitchen cabinets full of Kraft Macaroni & Cheese and Campbell's Tomato Soup or with freezers stacked with Swanson's TV dinners. By being forced to eat only homemade food, I felt deprived. I wondered, is this a form of child abuse?

Once home, and after putting the groceries away, my mom whipped up a pot of clam chowder. In a matter of minutes, she'd combined that can of clams with onions, potatoes, cream, and milk. The aroma was intoxicating. Sure, I was light-headed and about to pass out from hunger, but smelling the promise of creamy soup laden with plump clams and vegetables kept me holding on. As I sat down to an enormous bowl of Mom's rich chowder I thought, maybe this isn't abuse after all. Perhaps I was just a lucky kid.

new england clam chowder

Sometimes, my mom got fancy and added a cup of freshly cut sweet corn kernels to the chowder, which is how I liked it best. More often, however, she preferred the simplicity of this recipe: buttery, creamy, and with plenty of potatoes and clams.

2 tablespoons unsalted butter
⅓ cup chopped yellow onion
3 large russet potatoes, peeled and cut into ½-inch cubes
3 cans (3.5 ounces each) chopped clams in clam juice
1 can (12 ounces) evaporated milk
Kosher salt and freshly ground black pepper

1 In a large saucepan, melt the butter over medium-high heat. Add the onion and cook, stirring occasionally, until soft, 7 to 10 minutes. Add 2 cups water, the potatoes, and the clams and their juice, bring to a boil, and adjust the heat to maintain a simmer. Cook uncovered, stirring occasionally, until the potatoes are tender, about 10 minutes.

2 Pour in the evaporated milk and bring to a boil. Season with salt and pepper. Ladle into warmed individual bowls.

serves 6

※

IMAGINE A TWENTY-ONE-ROOM VICTORIAN HOUSE on the top of a hill set in the middle of four hundred acres of rolling pastureland in the Berkshire Hills of western Massachusetts. This was the caretaker's home that William Cullen Bryant, the romantic poet and editor-in-chief of the *New York Evening Post*, gave to my great-grandfather. It was also the dairy farm where my mom grew up with her parents (my grandparents), Russell and Dot Sears.

Grampa Sears, besides being a dairy farmer, was also a fantastic cook whose ingredients came from the farm. There was very little he didn't grow, and if he didn't grow it, he'd trade with the farmer next door for it. He made his own sausages, tapped the maple trees for syrup, had a henhouse full of chickens, and kept hundreds of dairy cattle. I don't think I ever heard him use words like *local*, *sustainable*, *heirloom*, *organic*, or *seasonal*, but he lived these principles every single day.

During the summers, Grampa Sears hosted New Yorkers who, in an effort to beat the heat, would come to stay on the farm, where he cooked them breakfast, lunch, and dinner. Even though he was a busy guy, every summer Saturday he somehow found time to entertain me, my mom, my sisters, and my brother with a picnic lunch under a huge maple tree.

Sitting in the shade of the majestic maple tree, we feasted on Grampa Sears's incredible chicken salad sandwiches (see page 18). He made the salad with chicken from his own coop mixed with silky homemade mayonnaise, and served it on warm, flaky baking powder biscuits, with a side of crisp potato chips he'd fried himself. The flavors were so fresh and nuanced that they stick with me to this day. For dessert, he scooped hand-churned maple-walnut ice cream (see page 20). Guess where the maple syrup came from? Yup, the tree above us.

Of course I didn't realize it at the time, and I'm sure I probably even complained about spending the day on the farm, but this simple summer picnic was the epitome of artisanal cooking that helped influence my entire culinary career.

right center:
Grampa Sears made the best biscuits in the world.
top center:
Grampa Sears's handwritten recipe.

⁓

x

Biscuits ___

2 cups general-purpose ___

1/2 teaspoon salt

2 teaspoon sugar

1/2 teaspoon c of tartar

5 teaspoon baking ___

8 tablespoon shorten___

grampa's chicken salad sandwiches

I used to watch, fascinated, as Grampa Sears made his tender, flaky biscuits, lifting the flour mixture with his hands high above the bowl, then sifting it through his fingers to incorporate as much air as possible. It was his secret to light, pillowy biscuits, and now it's mine.

BAKING POWDER BISCUITS

2 cups all-purpose flour

1 teaspoon kosher salt

1 tablespoon baking powder

¼ teaspoon baking soda

6 tablespoons unsalted butter, chilled and diced

¾ cup buttermilk, at room temperature

CHICKEN SALAD

1 chicken, about 3 pounds, quartered

1 carrot, peeled and coarsely chopped

1 small yellow onion, quartered through the stem end

Kosher salt and freshly ground black pepper

½ cup homemade mayonnaise (page 277)

3 stalks celery, diced

6 small butter or red-leaf lettuce leaves

1 To make the biscuits, preheat the oven to 450°F. In a medium bowl, sift together the flour, salt, baking powder, and baking soda. Scatter the butter over the flour mixture, then, using your fingertips, rub the butter into the flour, lifting the mixture far above the bowl and dropping it back into the bowl to incorporate air, until the mixture resembles coarse meal. Pour in the buttermilk a little at a time, mixing with a fork just until the mixture holds together and forms a rough mass. Do not overmix.

2 Turn the dough out onto a well-floured work surface and roll it out into a rough rectangle about ¾ inch thick. Fold the dough in half, roll it out again into a rough rectangle about ¾ inch thick, then fold the dough in half again. Finally, roll it out into a round about ½ inch thick.

3 Flour a 2½-inch round biscuit or cookie cutter and cut out 10 rounds from the dough, cutting straight down and lifting straight up as you work. Transfer the rounds to an ungreased baking sheet. (Press the scraps together and re-roll to create more biscuits if you like.)

4 Bake the biscuits until golden, 10 to 15 minutes. Transfer to a wire rack and let cool. You will have 10 biscuits. You will need only 6 biscuits for the sandwiches; reserve the remainder for another use.

5 While the biscuits are baking, cook the chicken. In a large pot, combine the chicken, carrot, onion, 1 teaspoon salt, and water to cover. Bring to a boil over high heat, reduce the heat to medium-low, and simmer, uncovered, until the juices run clear when the meat is pierced with a fork, 25 to 30 minutes. Remove the pot from the heat and remove the chicken from the broth. Let the chicken cool completely. Strain the broth and reserve for another use.

6 When the chicken is cool, remove and discard the skin and bones. Chop the chicken into ½-inch pieces and place in a bowl. Add the mayonnaise and celery, mix well, and season with salt and pepper.

7 Cut the 6 biscuits in half horizontally and place the bottoms, cut side up, on individual plates. Distribute the chicken salad evenly among the biscuit bottoms. Top each mound of chicken with a lettuce leaf and then close the sandwiches with the biscuit tops.

serves 6

maple and toasted walnut ice cream

Grampa Sears made this memorable ice cream using his own maple syrup, fresh eggs, and rich cream from the farm. Regardless of where you get your ingredients, no store-bought ice cream will ever match one scoop of this deliciousness.

3 cups heavy whipping cream
1 cup whole milk
⅔ cup maple syrup
2 tablespoons sugar
1 vanilla bean
9 large egg yolks
½ teaspoon pure maple extract
1½ cups walnut halves

1   In a medium saucepan, combine the cream, milk, maple syrup, and sugar. Using a sharp knife, split the vanilla bean pod lengthwise, then, using the tip of the knife, scrape the seeds from the pod and add the seeds and pod to the pan. Place over medium heat and heat until small bubbles appear along the edges of the pan. Watch closely to ensure the mixture does not boil.

2   In another medium saucepan, whisk the egg yolks until blended. Slowly drizzle the scalded cream mixture into the yolks while whisking constantly. Place the yolk-cream mixture over medium heat and heat, stirring constantly with a flat-bottom wooden spoon, until the mixture thickens enough to coat the back of the spoon, 2 to 3 minutes. Do not allow the mixture to boil. Remove from the heat immediately, strain through a fine-mesh strainer into a medium bowl, and then whisk gently for 30 seconds. Let cool, whisk in the maple extract, cover, and refrigerate for at least 2 hours or up to overnight to chill.

3   Preheat the oven to 375°F. Spread the walnuts on a rimmed baking sheet and toast until light golden and aromatic, 5 to 7 minutes. Immediately pour onto a cutting board, let cool, and then coarsely chop.

4   Transfer the chilled custard to an ice cream maker and freeze according to the manufacturer's directions. During the last 2 minutes of the cycle, add the walnuts.

5   Store the finished ice cream in an airtight container in the freezer until serving. It tastes best if eaten within 1 week.

makes 1½ quarts

❧

AFTER LUNCH ON MY GRANDPARENTS' FARM, my mom and I would sit on the wrap-around porch—which Nana and Grampa Sears called the piazza—and look out over the Berkshire Hills. We had this funny little game we played where I asked her the same question, knowing full well the answer would be the same every time.

"Mom, what's that hill over there?"

With a twinkle in her eye, she would always say, "It's California!"

Mind you, it was the village of Goshen, population 317, just seven miles away, but I didn't know any differently. I'm not sure she did, either. All I knew was that the hill was California and that I was going to go there one day. It would be years before my feet would follow, but my mind was already wandering the world.

I loved sitting there on the piazza talking to my mom about old times. "Tell me Mom, what was your grandmother Lettie like?"

"She was a great cook," were the first words out of her mouth. "She was also very stern."

Inside my grandparents' farmhouse were pictures of Great-grandma Lettie, and to be honest, she kind of scared me. She was tall and burly and looked like a prizefighter in drag. I couldn't imagine being gathered into her arms and cuddled, the way my Nana Sears hugged me.

"But she was an amazing baker! Wow, could she bake! Homemade bread, cloverleaf rolls, Boston cream pie, baking powder biscuits, blueberry muffins with wild berries we'd pick along the roadside, and her famous lightning cake filled with homemade strawberry jam."

"What do you mean? She made a cake when there was thunder and lightning outside?" I asked.

"No, it was so quick and easy to make, it was fast like lightning."

I still wish I'd met Great-grandma Lettie—despite the fact that she seemed a little scary—and had a chance to bake with her. But I am lucky enough to have the original handwritten recipe for her famous lightning cake. It's over 140 years old, but beyond the stains and smudges, I can still make out her surprisingly delicate script. In recent years, I've made Lettie's lightning cake (see page 22), and as the sweet fragrance of vanilla and strawberries wafts through my kitchen, I think maybe Great-grandma Lettie wouldn't have been so intimidating after all.

lettie's lightning cake with wild strawberry jam

WILD STRAWBERRY JAM
  About 1½ pounds or 1 quart wild or cultivated
  strawberries, hulled, washed and sliced
  1 cup granulated sugar
  1 tablespoon freshly squeezed lemon juice

LIGHTNING CAKE
  6 tablespoons unsalted butter
  ⅓ cup whole milk
  3 large eggs, at room temperature
  1⅓ cups granulated sugar
  1⅔ cups all-purpose flour
  1½ teaspoons baking powder
  ¼ teaspoon kosher salt
  1 teaspoon vanilla extract

  Powdered sugar for dusting

1 To make the jam, in a bowl, using a potato masher or a large fork, crush the strawberries coarsely. In a saucepan, combine the berries, sugar, and lemon juice, place over medium-high heat, and cook, stirring constantly, until the sugar dissolves and the mixture comes to a full rolling boil. Reduce the heat to medium-low and simmer, stirring constantly, until the mixture has thickened slightly, 10 minutes. Remove from the heat and, using a large spoon, skim off any foam from the surface.

2 Ladle the jam into a clean container, let cool, cover tightly, and refrigerate. You should have about 3 cups. You will need 1 cup for the cake. The remainder will keep refrigerated for up to 3 weeks. For longer storage, process jars of jam in a hot-water bath for 10 minutes.

3 To make the cake, preheat the oven to 350°F. Butter an 8-inch round cake pan, then line the pan bottom with parchment paper.

4 In a small saucepan, combine the butter and milk and place over low heat until the butter melts. Remove from the heat. In a mixer fitted with the beater, combine the eggs and granulated sugar and beat on medium speed until ivory colored, fluffy, and smooth, 3 to 4 minutes. Sift together the flour, baking powder, and salt over the top of the butter-sugar mixture, then, using a rubber spatula, fold in the flour mixture just until evenly blended. Add the warm milk mixture and the vanilla and fold just until all of the ingredients are thoroughly mixed. Do not overmix.

5 Pour the batter into the prepared pan. Bake until a wooden toothpick inserted into the center comes out clean, 45 to 50 minutes. Let cool for 30 minutes in the pan on a cooling rack. Run a thin knife blade along the inside edge of the pan to loosen the cake, then invert the cake onto the rack, lift off the pan, and peel off the parchment.

6 Mark the midpoint of the height of the cake with a shallow cut. Then, with the cut as a guide, and using a serrated knife, score the cake ½ inch deep around the entire perimeter of the cake. Slip a string several inches longer than the cake's circumference in the score line, cross the ends of the string, and pull the ends away from each other to cut the cake into 2 even layers. Alternatively, using the serrated knife and a sawing motion, cut the cake horizontally into 2 layers.

7 To assemble the cake, place the bottom layer on a cake plate or stand. Using an offset spatula, spread 1 cup jam evenly over the top of the layer. Top with the second layer. Dust the top of the cake with powdered suger. Cut into wedges to serve.

serves 8

XMAS 1954

TRAVELING FROM MY MATERNAL GRANDPARENTS' idyllic Victorian farmhouse in the Berkshire Hills to my paternal grandparents' farm in the Connecticut River Valley, just twenty-two miles away, was like traveling from night to day. We might as well have arrived in the Old Country of Lithuania, where Mama Anna and Papa Jonas, my father's parents, were born.

Picture a huge tobacco farm that's also home to cows, pigs, chickens, and fields of corn and cucumbers. The house was saturated with the aromas of dill, sauerkraut, vinegar, pickles, and dark rye bread. I'd never been to Lithuania, but believe me, we went there every time my dad pulled our 1956 Chevy into Mama Anna and Papa Jonas's circular dirt driveway. My grandparents had such strong accents that it was a wonder my father spoke English. And Papa Jonas was smart—so smart, my mother always said, that he had Mama Anna's brains too.

Mama Anna wore the same kind of dress every day: a perfectly ironed cotton print dress that looked as if it had been washed a million times. I don't think I ever saw her without one of her many aprons—each with a different print—tied around her plump waist. Her dress and apron were so long that they nearly touched her heavy, chunky-heeled

from left:
Mama Anna on the farm in Whately, Massachusetts, in the 1950s. Mama Anna, Auntie Ruthie, my mom, and Aunt Doris making Christmas dinner in Mama Anna's kitchen in 1954.

⚊⚊⚊

✗

black lace-up shoes. Even with those heels, she was just about as tall as she was wide. Ringed with white hair tied up in a bun, her face, scorched from hard work in the sun, had wrinkles that looked like a crossword puzzle.

My mother didn't think Mama Anna could cook. I could tell by the way her mouth curled at the edges when she put a bite of Mama's food into it. She never said anything, but she didn't have to. It was written all over her face, especially when the wild mushrooms Mama foraged and canned came out of the cold cellar. Behind my grandmother's back, my mother would swipe her finger across her throat and mouth the words, "Don't eat them!" shaking her head back and forth. She didn't trust my grandmother's foraging skills, and mostly, I think she didn't want us to die.

My grandfather Papa Jonas was always out in the fields or in the barn milking the cows. The highlight of summer was when he'd pick an armful of the most tender Butter & Sugar corn and bring it directly from the field into the kitchen. Mama Anna would fill a big blue-and-white enamel pot with water, add a handful of salt, and bring it to a boil. She would drop in the corn and it would be ready in minutes. As she lifted the corn from the pot, you could see a mosaic of yellow and white through the steam. This was the only time we could run our hot ears of corn directly over Mama's ultra-salty chunk of homemade butter, leaving a groove that showed that corn had been there. Just thinking about that corn makes my mouth water!

Running through the cornfields and hiding in the barn where Mama Anna stored big earthenware crocks filled with homemade dill pickles (see page 27) and sauerkraut were among our favorite things to do on the farm. And when we needed a quick snack, we'd lift up the brick and the wooden cover that kept everything sealed up and fermenting in the crocks and steal a vinegary pickle or a good pinch of sauerkraut for a delicious taste, the sharp scent of fermentation stinging our nostrils.

Although we loved those stolen bites of Mama Anna's sauerkraut directly from the crock, it was worlds better after she'd braised it for hours with pork shoulder (see page 27) from a pig that had just been butchered by Papa Jonas, the biting acidity of the sour cabbage mellowed by the rich, meltingly tender strands of pork.

When other kids were eating slices of orange cheese that had been individually wrapped in cellophane, Mama Anna was making her own farmer cheese. I'd watch as she heated fresh cow's milk and let it sit on the back of the stove until it had transformed into white, shiny chunks floating in cloudy water. Then she drained the curds into cheesecloth and tied them up into a bundle that looked like a balloon. Next, she hung the balloon upside down over the sink to drain. At this point my patience usually waned and I'd head out to explore, only to return to find the deflated balloon set on the drain board next to the sink topped with a wooden board and a brick.

Our family loved it when Mama Anna sent us home with a chunk of cheese on Sunday night, along with some dark rye bread that Papa Jonas had bought at the local Polish bakery that morning. My mom would heat up her big cast-iron pan and fry the cheese until it was a melting and oozy mess, which we then slathered onto the dark rye.

My mom may have had her doubts about Mama Anna's kitchen prowess, but I remember eating quite well at her house. The scents and flavors of Mama and Papa's farm, so different from that of Nana and Grampa Sears's, left a unique, indelible impression on my palate.

mama's pickles

3 pounds pickling cucumbers, each 3 inches long
6 dill sprigs
8 garlic cloves, halved lengthwise
3 cups filtered water
2 cups distilled white vinegar
3 tablespoons kosher salt
2 teaspoons mustard seeds

1 Cut a thin slice off of the blossom end of each cucumber. Leave the cucumbers whole. Have ready 2 sterilized 1-quart canning jars with two-part lids. Place 1 dill sprig on the bottom of each jar. Pack half of the cucumbers into each jar, adding 4 halved garlic cloves along the way and another dill sprig at the midway point.

2 In a saucepan, combine the water, vinegar, and salt. Bring to a boil over high heat, stirring to dissolve the salt. Pour over the cucumbers, filling each jar to within ½ inch of the rim. If you run out of vinegar solution, add more vinegar.

3 Tap the jars to remove any trapped air bubbles. Place a dill sprig and 1 teaspoon mustard seeds on top. Wipe the jar rims clean, top with the lids, and screw on the ring bands. Do not screw the bands too tightly. Place the jars, not touching, in a large stockpot. Add hot water to reach three-fourths up the sides of the jars. Over medium-high heat, bring the water to just below a boil. Reduce the heat to low and simmer for 25 minutes.

4 Remove the jars from the pot, place them on a countertop, leave them undisturbed for 2 days, and then put them in the refrigerator. They are ready to eat after 2 days, but are better after 1 week. They'll keep in the refrigerator, sealed, for 1 year; once opened, they keep for 2 weeks.

makes 2 quarts

braised pork with sauerkraut

2 tablespoons unsalted butter
1 boneless pork shoulder roast, about 3 pounds, trimmed of excess fat and cut into 2 chunks
   Kosher salt and freshly ground black pepper
2 slices bacon (about 2 ounces), diced
1 large yellow onion, chopped
4 dried juniper berries, coarsely crushed
¼ teaspoon caraway seeds, coarsely crushed
1 cup dry or semidry Riesling or Gewürztraminer
1 cup chicken stock (page 276)
2 pounds prepared sauerkraut, drained
1 head green cabbage, cored, cut through the stem end into 8 wedges, and thinly sliced crosswise
1 pound kielbasa (Polish) sausage, cut into 2-inch lengths
24 small red or Yukon Gold potatoes
   Assorted mustards for serving

1 In a large, heavy soup pot, melt the butter over medium-high heat. Season the pork all over with salt and pepper, add to the pot, and brown on all sides, about 12 minutes total. Transfer to a plate.

2 Add the bacon, onion, juniper berries, and caraway seeds to the fat in the pot and cook, stirring, until the onion is soft, about 10 minutes. Add the wine, stock, sauerkraut, and cabbage and return the pork to the pot. Reduce the heat to medium-low, cover, and cook, stirring occasionally, for 1½ hours. Add the kielbasa and potatoes and continue to cook until the cabbage, pork, and potatoes are all tender, about 30 minutes longer.

3 Transfer to a warmed serving bowl or serve directly from the pot. Serve with the mustards.

serves 6

GROWING UP WITH ALL OF THAT delicious food meant that my father was as obsessed with food as my mother was. He didn't have the gift for cooking that my mom did, but he had a few specialties. The first time I ever saw him grating fresh horseradish in the blender, I thought it was weird that he was doing it out in the garage. When he wasn't looking, I took the cover off the top of the blender and stuck in my nose to take a whiff. As my eyes filled with tears, I thought my head was going to fall off. No wonder he was in the garage!

Dad couldn't get enough of that sharp, hot flavor. He'd toss the grated horseradish with salt and cover it with vinegar, then put a dab on his kielbasa, mix it with Heinz ketchup to make his "famous" cocktail sauce for poached shrimp, or enjoy it with his other specialty: freshly shucked, raw cherrystone clams.

He'd find any vehicle to use his beloved fresh horseradish, but a small spoonful dabbed on top of a raw cherrystone was perfection in his eyes. Nobody else in the family particularly liked raw cherrystones, but I didn't like seeing my dad eat alone, so one day, starved for his attention, I decided to give eating the clams a try. Instead of chewing, I thought it might be best to just swallow the clam. I was amazed at how much I liked the briny flavor. It tasted like swimming in the ocean—if you had swallowed a little of the seawater! I smiled up at my father, and he grinned ear to ear. After that we became kindred spirits eating our raw cherrystones together. But the truth is that when he added cracker crumbs and gobs of butter to those sweet bivalves and then baked them in the oven, I liked them even better.

dad's baked cherrystone clams

12 cherrystone clams in shells, scrubbed
2½ cups coarsely crushed round butter crackers
1 garlic clove, minced
6 tablespoons unsalted butter, melted
Kosher salt and freshly ground black pepper

1 Preheat the oven to 375°F. Using a clam or similar small, sharp knife, carefully open each clam, capturing all of the liquid in a small bowl. Using the knife, free each clam meat from its shell, leaving the tough foot portion behind. Separate each clam shell at its hinge, cut away and discard the foot, and place all of the shells, hollow side up, on a rimmed baking sheet. Chop the clams coarsely and add them back to the shells.

2 In a bowl, combine the crackers, garlic, butter, and reserved cherrystone liquid and mix well. Season with salt and pepper. Distribute the crumb mixture evenly over the clams. Bake the clams until the crumbs are golden, 18 to 20 minutes.

serves 6

ON FRIDAY NIGHTS, when the rest of the world was eating fish, my mom was making potato pancakes, a dish my father grew up eating. Mom's motive was twofold. If you asked her, she'd tell you she was re-creating one of Dad's favorite meals out of the goodness of her heart. But I secretly think she was trying to prove what a better cook she was than Mama Anna, taking Mama's recipe and improving it.

I'd watch as Mom grated huge baking potatoes, her hand sliding rhythmically up and down the big box grater. She'd drain the slivers of potato, add some flour, salt, and egg, and fry them up into golden pancakes. The beautiful sizzle as mounds of grated potato hit hot oil in the cast iron skillet was music to my ears. The result: crisp-on-the-outside, tender-on-the-inside potato perfection. Topped with a dollop of cottage cheese, my siblings and I ate those pancakes as fast as Mom could make them.

I don't remember ever tasting Mama Anna's potato pancakes, but I can't imagine any version could hold a candle to Mom's. Even Dad agreed. It was a delicious melding of two food worlds and our bellies were the benefactors. And certainly no one in our house was missing the boxed fish sticks our friends were eating.

friday-night potato pancakes

4 russet potatoes
2 large eggs, whisked
⅓ cup beer
¼ yellow onion, finely diced
½ cup all-purpose flour
   Kosher salt and freshly ground black pepper
½ cup canola oil
1½ cups small-curd cottage cheese
2 green onions, thinly sliced

1 Peel the potatoes and coarsely grate them on the large holes of a hand grater into a medium bowl. Let stand for 30 minutes. Drain the potatoes, discarding the liquid, and return them to the bowl. Add the eggs, beer, yellow onion, flour, 1 teaspoon salt, and ¼ teaspoon pepper.

2 Preheat the oven to 200°F. Line a large rimmed baking sheet with paper towels. In a large nonstick frying pan, warm 1 tablespoon of the oil over medium-high heat. In batches, drop ¼-cup mounds of the potato mixture into the hot oil, shape into pancakes, and cook, turning once, until golden, 2 to 3 minutes on each side. Repeat with the remaining potato mixture, adding oil to the pan as needed. Transfer to the towel-lined pan to drain and keep warm in the oven until serving.

3 Divide the pancakes among warmed individual plates and garnish with a dollop of cottage cheese and a scattering of green onion.

serves 6 to 8

the

BAKING SODA CHRONICLES

MY MOM WAS A GREAT COOK, and food was always a central theme in our home. She had mastered many of the American classics. Meat loaf, mashed potatoes, spaghetti and meatballs—she could win a cook-off in these categories without breaking a sweat. Although she was no Julia Child—more like Betty Crocker or Fanny Farmer—my mother emulated Julia and loved watching her on PBS every chance she got. Mom didn't like watching alone, so she'd gather us in front of the television to watch with her as Julia roasted a duck or whisked egg whites in a copper bowl to make a fluffy soufflé. I didn't always like getting dragged away from playing outside, but I knew I could use a few pointers, especially after my oatmeal raisin cookie fiasco (see page 40).

Mom was always in the kitchen. When she was sad, she cooked. When she was happy, she cooked even more. As much as she liked cooking family dinners, baking was her real passion. She was hell-bent on making just about every well-known Americana cake, pie, sweet bread, and cookie. She baked for the PTA, the church fair, baby showers, bake sales, Christmas, Thanksgiving, New Year, and every holiday in between.

Whoopie pies, which straddled the line between the world of the cookie and the cake, were my favorite. I loved the pillowy white frosting that oozed out from between the small, spongy chocolate cakes (see page 37). And I'll never forget her Mississippi mud cake (see page 38). Sure, it was rich, fudgy, and sticky sweet, and sat somewhere between a cake and a pudding on the dessert spectrum, but I especially liked that it was so aptly named. Mom baked nonstop. When it wasn't one of those two recipes, it was peanut butter cookies (see page 38), snickerdoodles, oatmeal lace cookies, brownies, blondies, banana bread, zucchini bread, hot milk sponge cake, chocolate cake, or every kind of pie imaginable.

Our cabinets were chock-full of chocolate chips, raisins, coconut, brown sugar, granulated sugar, powdered sugar, molasses, cinnamon, nuts, flour, baking powder, baking soda, and more. And the refrigerator was the same: pounds of butter, quarts of milk and cream, and dozens of eggs. We joked that in our house we had only "ingredients" and no ready-made "food" to eat. I didn't know how lucky we were. All I knew was that sometimes I didn't want to wait for Mom to whip up a batch of whoopie pies. I wanted an Oreo. I was just a kid and I was beginning to resent the word *homemade*.

right center:
Sitting on the steps with my mom, with baby brother John in her arms, and my older sister, Nancy.

bottom left:
My mom's handwritten note about being a chef that she gave me when I was a kid.

be a cook - you have to love
hard, with enjoy using your hands
and be able to work fast.

It's a profession that demands
visual style, sophistication of
taste, organizational ability,
creativity - in fact it demands
your all if you're to be tops
in the field. But if you
love your work, it is one

mom's whoopie pies

To store these marshmallow-filled, cakey chocolate sandwich cookies so they wouldn't dry out, Mom would wrap them individually in waxed paper—although they never even lasted that long in our house. For us kids, these sweet little packages made the perfect grab-and-go snack! Whoopie!

COOKIES

2 cups all-purpose flour
½ cup unsweetened cocoa powder, sifted
1 teaspoon baking soda
½ teaspoon kosher salt
½ cup unsalted butter, at room temperature
1 cup granulated sugar
1 large egg
1 teaspoon vanilla extract
1 cup buttermilk

FILLING

¾ cup unsalted butter, at room temperature
1 cup powdered sugar, sifted
1½ cups prepared marshmallow creme
2 teaspoons vanilla extract
¼ teaspoon kosher salt

1 To make the cookies, preheat the oven to 375°F. Butter 2 rimmed baking sheets or line them with parchment paper.

2 In a medium bowl, whisk together the flour, cocoa, baking soda, and salt. Set aside. In a mixer fitted with the beater, combine the butter and granulated sugar and beat on medium speed until ivory colored and creamy, about 2 minutes. Add the egg and vanilla and beat until thoroughly mixed. On medium-low speed, beat in the flour mixture in three batches alternately with the buttermilk in two batches, beginning and ending with the flour mixture and mixing thoroughly after each addition.

3 Drop heaping tablespoon-size scoops of the dough onto the prepared baking sheets, spacing them 2 inches apart. You should have 30 scoops.

4 Bake the cookies, rotating the pans from front to back midway through baking, until they puff and spring back when lightly pressed with a fingertip, 7 to 9 minutes. Remove from the oven and, using a spatula, transfer the cookies to cooling racks. Let cool completely.

5 To make the filling, in the mixer fitted with the beater, combine the butter, powdered sugar, marshmallow creme, vanilla, and salt and beat on medium-high speed until smooth and creamy, about 2 minutes.

6 To assemble the whoopie pies, turn half of the cookies flat side up on a work surface. Spread the filling on the upturned cookies, dividing it evenly, then top each cookie with a second cookie, flat side down. Store in an airtight container for up to 2 days.

makes 15 whoopie pies

mississippi mud

Cake, pudding, or pie? In my house it was just "Mississippi Mud" because that's exactly what it looks like. It's the richest, sweetest, gooiest, most chocolaty delicious mess you'll ever encounter. I like to dress it up with vanilla ice cream and raspberries.

  1 cup all-purpose flour
  2 teaspoons baking powder
  ½ teaspoon salt
  1¼ cups granulated sugar
  2 tablespoons plus ¼ cup unsweetened cocoa
     powder, sifted
  ½ cup whole milk
  1 teaspoon vanilla extract
  2 tablespoons unsalted butter, melted
  ¼ cup firmly packed light brown sugar

1 Preheat the oven to 350°F. Butter a 7½- by 12-inch or 1½-quart shallow baking dish.

2 In a medium bowl, sift together the flour, baking powder, salt, ¾ cup granulated sugar, and 2 tablespoons cocoa powder. Add the milk, vanilla, and butter and beat with a whisk until smooth. Pour the batter into the prepared dish.

3 In a small bowl, stir together the brown sugar, the remaining ½ cup granulated sugar, and the ¼ cup cocoa powder. Sprinkle the mixture evenly over the batter, then gently pour 1¾ cups very hot water over the top.

4 Bake until the batter is set around the edges and slightly firm in the center, about 40 minutes. Remove from the oven and let cool for 20 minutes. Scoop into dessert dishes and serve warm.

serves 6 to 8

jean's peanut butter cookies

When I was a kid, my mom packed homemade cookies in my school lunch every day. I was the envy of the lunch table, especially when I brought these rich peanut butter cookies with hash marks carefully crafted by Mom with fork tines.

  1 cup natural chunky peanut butter
  ¾ cup sugar
  1 large egg
  1 teaspoon vanilla extract
  ½ teaspoon kosher salt

1 Preheat the oven to 350°F. Line 2 rimmed baking sheets with parchment paper.

2 In a mixer fitted with the beater, combine the peanut butter, sugar, egg, vanilla, and salt and beat on medium-high speed just until well mixed.

3 Scoop up spoonfuls of the dough, shape into 1-inch balls, and place on the prepared baking sheets, spacing the balls 2 inches apart. Using the back of a fork, make a crisscross pattern in the top of each ball, flattening it slightly.

4 Bake the cookies, rotating the pans from front to back midway through baking, until the bottoms have firmed up but the cookies are still slightly soft, about 10 minutes. Let the cookies cool on the baking sheets on cooling racks for about 1 minute, then transfer the cookies to the racks to cool completely. Store in an airtight container at room temperature for up to 4 days.

makes about 2 dozen cookies

I COULDN'T HAVE BEEN MUCH OLDER THAN NINE when I decided to bake cookies all by myself. I pulled out my mother's wooden recipe box and riffled through it, looking for the perfect recipe. As I flipped through the cards, I came across one with tattered corners and greasy circles from old egg yolk and butter stains. Oatmeal raisin cookies, the loopy cursive announced. I figured they must be good because the card had clearly gotten a lot of use (see page 42 for the recipe).

I put on one of Mom's aprons, circling the long strings twice around my tiny waist before tying them in front. I gathered all of the ingredients, then measured everything and organized the items neatly on the white Formica countertop.

As I poured baking soda into the measuring cup, I yelled out, "Mom, we just ran out of baking soda."

"That's funny," she called back from the living room where she was watching *As the World Turns*. "I bought a new box last week."

Focused on the task at hand, I mixed the dough, meticulously scooped it up, rolled each portion into a one-inch ball, and then placed the spheres exactly two inches apart on a baking sheet as the recipe instructed. They were beautiful. I looked at them admiringly, not knowing if I was more excited about how evenly I'd rolled them all or about tasting a hot cookie the moment they were done.

I popped the baking sheet into the oven and then pulled up a chair to watch the cookies work their magic. As I sat there mesmerized, peering through the clouded window on the oven door, the cookies seemed to melt on the baking sheet into one massive cookie. This can't be right, I thought, as I watched the dough spread across the entire pan and edge up and over the sides.

"Mom, come here! It's not a lot of little cookies. The dough is growing into one big cookie!"

My mother opened the oven door gingerly and peeked inside. By now, my monster cookie was flooding over the sides of the pan, and gobs of dough were baking onto the floor of the oven. It turned out that I had used 1½ cups of baking soda instead of 1½ teaspoons.

Later, as we scraped the cookies off of the baking sheet and into the trash, my mother tasted a small bite, looked over at me, and said with a smile, "They still taste good, honey!"

My mom in her whites at her first professional cooking job.

×

oatmeal raisin cookies

As long as you measure the baking soda in teaspoons, and not in cups like nine-year-old me, you'll be rewarded with crisp yet chewy, perfectly sweet oatmeal cookies. Sometimes you just have to learn the hard way!

  1 cup all-purpose flour
1½ teaspoons baking soda
  1 teaspoon kosher salt
¾ cup unsalted butter
¾ cup firmly packed light brown sugar
¾ cup granulated sugar
  1 large egg, whisked
  1 teaspoon vanilla extract
  3 cups old-fashioned rolled oats
  1 cup raisins

1 Preheat the oven to 350°F. Line 2 large rimmed baking sheets with parchment paper.

2 In a small bowl, sift together the flour, baking soda, and salt. Set aside. In a mixer fitted with the beater, combine the butter and both sugars and beat on medium speed until ivory colored, fluffy, and smooth, 1 to 2 minutes. Add the egg and vanilla and beat until creamy. On medium-low speed, add the flour mixture slowly in two batches and beat until well mixed. With a wooden spoon, stir in the oats and raisins, mixing well.

3 Drop walnut-size scoops of the dough onto the prepared baking sheets, spacing them 2 inches apart. Pat down each mound slightly with a floured hand.

4 Bake the cookies, rotating the pans from front to back midway through baking, until light golden on the edges, 12 to 15 minutes. Let the cookies cool on the baking sheets on cooling racks for 5 minutes, then transfer the cookies to the racks to cool completely. Store in an airtight container at room temperature for up to 5 days.

makes about 5 dozen cookies

WHEN HE WAS IN HIS MIDSIXTIES, my maternal grandfather suffered a massive heart attack while giving a speech at the town hall. I was too young to understand fully what losing my Grampa Sears meant, but I did know that one of my favorite memories in the world, those summer picnics under the maple tree at Nana and Grampa's farm, were over. And I knew I'd never taste a chicken salad sandwich or homemade potato chip anywhere near as good as what he'd made for me. My grandmother was so lonely on the farm that she came to live with us. It was then that I learned where my mother inherited her love of sweets. Every afternoon, rain or shine, Mom and Nana Sears would sit together with steaming cups of Lipton tea with sugar and milk and a plate of desserts. They were both crazy about lemon, so that plate of sweet treats often hosted lemon cookies, lemon squares, or lemon meringue pie. As a child, I wasn't fond of lemon; it stung my tongue and made my face squeeze together when I swallowed. Now anytime I taste a lemony dessert, I picture those two together again and yearn for a cup of tea myself.

lemony lemon squares

¼ cup powdered sugar, plus more for dusting

¾ cup plus 2 tablespoons all-purpose flour

¼ cup almond flour

⅛ teaspoon kosher salt

½ cup cold unsalted butter, cubed

4 large eggs

1 cup granulated sugar

1 tablespoon grated lemon zest

¼ teaspoon baking powder

⅓ cup freshly squeezed lemon juice

1 Preheat the oven to 350°F. Butter the bottom and sides of an 8-inch square pan and line the bottom with parchment.

2 In a bowl, sift together the ¼ cup powdered sugar, ¾ cup flour, almond flour, and salt. Scatter the butter over the flour and, using 2 forks, cut the butter into the flour until the mixture clings together. Sprinkle 1 tablespoon water over the top, then form the dough into a ball. Press the dough evenly onto the bottom and 1 inch up the sides of the pan. Freeze for 10 minutes. Bake the crust until light golden and slightly firm, 20 to 25 minutes.

3 In a mixer, beat the eggs, sugar, lemon zest, 2 tablespoons flour, and the baking powder until smooth. Beat in the lemon juice.

4 Pour the filling into the warm crust. Bake until a knife inserted into the center comes out clean, 20 to 25 minutes. Let cool completely in the pan, then dust the top with powdered sugar.

makes 9 squares

A COUPLE OF YEARS AFTER MOVING IN WITH US, Nana Sears passed away. To this day, I believe that she died of heart problems: a broken heart from missing my grandfather so much.

Soon after her death, Mom and I got into the Impala and drove to my grandparents' farm to clean their belongings out of the house. I wasn't sure what was happening, but I knew it was a big deal because I didn't have to go to school that day. As we drove from our house to the farm where Mom grew up, tears rolled down her cheeks. Every once in a while, she'd take a white cotton hankie out of her pocketbook that sat between us and wipe the tears away. It made me so sad that I turned away and looked out my window.

"Mom, are you okay?" I whispered.

"I'll be okay, honey. I'm happy you're with me."

I was happy to be with her, too. I wanted nothing more than to take a little of the pain she was feeling and put it inside me, so she would hurt less.

Usually when we went to the farm, I'd run off to play with my cousins, but this time I stayed by Mom's side. All day as we walked from room to room, I felt like I had a brick

Nana and Grampa Sears and their Victorian house in the Berkshires in western Massachusetts.

×

on each of my shoulders. Every so often I'd catch Mom staring at an old photograph of my grandparents. Her eyes looked glassy, like she was a world away. Backing out of the driveway that evening, I took one last look at the picnic table under the maple trees and dreamed of the chicken salad sandwiches and freshly churned maple-walnut ice cream Grampa Sears had served us not so long ago. I knew visiting the farm would never be the same.

For a while after that visit to the farm, time stood still, and Mom wasn't her bubbly self. Her sadness seemed to lift slightly when she kneaded bread, ribboned egg yolks and sugar, or folded cake batter. Baking allowed her to escape, to forget her sadness, but only until the kitchen timer trilled, snapping her back to reality.

Then one morning, she got a phone call from the Northampton School for Girls, a local private school, asking her to come to work as the head cook. Finally, her eyes once again sparkled, and it was time for all of us to breathe more easily.

That first day of work she looked very smart in her crisp white dress and spotless shoes. And she had a little skip in her step as she went out the door.

Her boss was Charlotte Turgeon, Julia Child's Smith College roommate and the author of several French cookbooks. Charlotte was a "beautiful cook," Mom told us, a huge compliment coming from my mother. Charlotte was serious about food and loved desserts, which is probably why she and Mom got along so well.

Charlotte was always in the middle of writing a cookbook, and my mother constantly tested recipes for her. My sisters, brother, and I would come home from school to discover the kitchen counters full of desserts—and I do mean full. There were days Mom had ten different sweets for us to try. She'd hover over us, hands on hips, eager to hear which one was our favorite. At first, we loved it, but believe it or not, there's a limit to how much sugar a child can consume. Walnut tortes, coconut macaroons, hermit bars (see page 49)—we couldn't make a dent.

"How do you like the hermits?" she'd ask before we could even swallow our first bite. "What about the coconut macaroons?"

"Delicious, Mom!" I'd reply. But I could see her disappointment as she glanced around at the still-full counter. If we really liked everything so much, she expected the counters to be empty.

My mom was as sweet as her desserts. None of us wanted to hurt her feelings, but our little bellies couldn't handle all that sugar. So we got smart! On recipe-testing days, we'd bring our friends home from school with us. Patty, Susie, Robbie, Cindy, Peggy—all of the neighborhood kids became Mom's testers. Sweets made the kids happy, and an empty counter thrilled my mom. These were kids whose own moms didn't cook, let alone bake. The first time they saw our kitchen filled with Mom's goodies, I thought their eyes might pop out of their heads. They felt they had hit the jackpot. At the end of the day, the counters were empty, and Mom had a huge smile on her face.

hermits

My mom got this recipe at a party years ago. Whenever she discovered a new recipe she was crazy about, she'd make it over and over and over again. I'm not exaggerating when I say I've enjoyed these chewy, spiced hermit cookies hundreds of times. They are aptly named as you can store them for a long time.

½ cup walnut halves
1½ cups all-purpose flour
1½ teaspoons ground cinnamon
½ teaspoon ground cloves
½ teaspoon baking soda
¼ teaspoon kosher salt
½ cup plus 2 tablespoons sugar
6 tablespoons unsalted butter, at room temperature
1 large egg, whisked, with 2 teaspoons reserved for brushing
2 tablespoons blackstrap molasses
½ cup raisins

1 Preheat the oven to 350°F. Line a rimmed baking sheet with parchment paper.

2 Spread the walnut halves in a single layer on a small rimmed baking sheet and toast until light golden and aromatic, 6 to 8 minutes. Pour onto a cutting board, let cool, and chop coarsely. Leave the oven on.

3 In a medium bowl, sift together the flour, cinnamon, cloves, baking soda, and salt. Set aside. In a mixer fitted with the beater, combine the sugar, butter, egg, molasses, and 2 tablespoons water and beat on medium speed until smooth, about 2 minutes. Add the flour mixture to the sugar-butter mixture and beat on low speed until well combined. Using a rubber spatula, fold in the walnuts and raisins.

4 Divide the dough in half. On a lightly floured work surface, roll half of the dough into a log 1 inch in diameter. Transfer the log to the prepared baking sheet and flatten it until it is 1½ to 1¾ inches wide. Repeat with the remaining dough, spacing the logs about 3 inches apart.

5 Brush the top of each log lightly with the reserved whisked egg, then bake until light golden on the edges and slightly soft in the center, about 17 minutes. Let the logs cool on the pan on a cooling rack for about 5 minutes.

6 Transfer the logs to a cutting board, and while still warm, cut each log on the diagonal into slices 1 inch wide. Return the cookies to the rack to cool completely. Store in an airtight container at room temperature for up to 5 days.

makes 20 to 24 cookies

MASTERING THE ART
OF
French Cooking

By JULIA CHILD
LOUISETTE BERTHOLLE
SIMONE BECK

Volume One

in search
of
CILANTRO
AND
SAFFRON

194

SOME CLASSIC COMBINATIONS

The same cream and egg-yolk fish sauce described in the recipe for *filet de poisson gratinés à la parisienne* on page 191 becomes even richer and more velvety if a fairly large quantity of butter is beaten into it just before serving. The more you beat in, the more delicious the sauce becomes. But as in all heavily buttered sauces, it cannot be kept warm once buttered or the butter will liquefy and either thin out the sauce, or rise up and float on top. Here in outline are some traditional combinations of poached fish fillets and various shellfish garnitures to give you an idea of what you can do. You can, of course, make up your own selection. In each case, in the following recipes, the sauce takes on the name of the dish. Serve your finest white Burgundy with any of these, and then should be considered a separate course, accompanied only by hot French bread.

* SOLE À LA DIEPPOISE

[Fish Fillets with Mussels and Shrimps]

This recipe is the model for the variations

For 6 people

WHITE WINE SAUCES

boil, stirring, for 1 minute. Thin out with more cream if necessary, and correct seasoning. Strain. Film top of sauce with a tablespoonful of melted butter if not to be served immediately.

2 to 8 oz. softened butter (3 to 4 oz. is usual)

Just before serving the fish, bring the sauce to simmering point. Then remove it from heat and beat in the butter a little at a time.

Final assembly

6 whole cooked shrimps in their shells

Immediately spoon the sauce over the shrimps and truffles

6 to 12 thin sli...

FAST-FORWARD TO 1975. With a bachelor of fine arts degree from the University of Massachusetts under my belt, long curly hair to my waist, and a suitcase full of hopes and dreams, I said good-bye to my family and my hometown of Northampton, Massachusetts, and drove ninety miles east to Boston and my new home in adjoining Cambridge. My knees were weak and my heart was in my throat as I headed toward my new apartment on Chestnut Street.

Looking through the want ads in the *Boston Globe* was disheartening. I took the first job that would take me, as a sales clerk in the housewares department at the Harvard Coop, located in the center of Harvard Square. My BFA degree had landed me a job selling dish towels, Chemex coffee makers, and instant-read thermometers.

Working in the linen department next door was a woman my age named Charlotte, who had also recently moved to Cambridge and loved food, cooking, and eating as much as I did. We became fast friends, doing everything related to gastronomy together.

It didn't take long to realize that being a clerk in a department store wasn't for me. My feet ached from standing for hours on a concrete floor, product inventory was tedious, and I craved human interaction beyond requests to find the latest oven mitts or what

Enjoying my summer in Truro on Cape Cod.

non-stick pan performed well. Minutes felt like hours. I was bored and almost always hungry. After twenty-one days, I was out the door with an eight-piece set of blue enameled Le Creuset cookware, an electric juicer, and a set of knives—all purchased with my employee discount. I was eager to move on to something other than demonstrating how to use a melon baller.

I returned to the want ads in the *Boston Globe*, but this time I hit the jackpot. Twenty-three years old and I couldn't wait to tell my parents that I'd landed my first "professional" job as a junior high school art teacher working Monday through Friday, no nights, no weekends, and summers off! My new job would give me time to put my Le Creuset cookware and knives to the test. The only problem was that I was finding my repertoire of recipes rather slim.

While paging through the Cambridge School for Adult Education catalog one Saturday morning over coffee with Charlotte, I came across a list of cooking classes. "This is it!" I said to Charlotte. "Do you want to take a cooking class with me? I see one here at Casa Romero in the Back Bay. I love Mexican food and have absolutely no clue how to make it. You up for it?"

"Sure!" was all I needed to hear. I enrolled us in three back-to-back Saturday classes.

"Who's tasted fresh cilantro before?" asked Leo Romero, our new Mexican cooking teacher, that first Saturday. Only one hand went up, and it wasn't mine.

Chef Romero proceeded to introduce the dishes he was about to demonstrate. Everything was so foreign. I had no clue what pico de gallo was or how to make guacamole. I was learning a whole new language.

I watched in amazement as our chef swiftly chopped plum tomatoes and deftly diced red onions. When he slid latex gloves onto his hands to chop the jalapeño, I thought he was being a bit dramatic. Was he preparing for some sort of surgery? But after he gave us a little taste of the raw chile, I understood the precaution.

"If you can find serrano chiles, I prefer those. They add a pleasant sweet heat, but they aren't as easy to find. Jalapeños are the workhorse and more readily available," chef Romero explained as he placed everything in a bowl.

Next, he chopped cilantro leaves and stems and added both to the bowl. The fresh green smell of the herb permeated the room. "There's just as much flavor, if not more, in the stems as the leaves," chef Romero explained.

Interesting, I thought. I had a million questions but the most crucial, if I were ever to make these dishes at home, was where to find the ingredients. I'd certainly never seen them at the Stop & Shop.

Next, chef Romero leaned firmly on a lime as he rolled it back and forth across the counter. "This simple action will give you more juice," he grunted. He cut the lime in half and squeezed its juice into the bowl, then added a good pinch of salt and stirred everything together. As the citrusy scent of the cilantro mixed with the aroma of vibrant lime and sweet tomato wafted across the room, my mouth began to water.

"That's pico de gallo," chef Romero announced. "Let's move on to guacamole!"

I was enthralled.

Chef Romero held an avocado in one hand and a large knife in the other. He sliced into the leathery skin of the avocado and then slowly spun the fruit around the blade, incising

*Making
guacamole in my
San Francisco
kitchen. Choose
ripe avocados
that yield to
gentle pressure
for the best
results.*

~~~~~~~

✕

it lengthwise. Next, he twisted the halves in opposite directions to reveal a giant, perfectly round pit at the center. Tapping the pit with the sharp blade of his knife, he removed it. That's a trick I'll take home, I thought. With a large spoon, he scooped out the creamy flesh into a bowl and mashed it with a fork. He added a handful of diced red onion, minced jalapeño, and chopped cilantro; a squeeze of lime juice; and a hefty pinch of salt and stirred. In just minutes, chef Romero had transformed this unfamiliar fruit with pebbly skin into rich, creamy guacamole studded with robust new flavors. I couldn't wait to try it.

Next, we watched as he fried wedges of corn tortilla, drained them on paper towels, and sprinkled them with salt. The effervescent sizzle that was emitted as soft, white tortillas were transformed into crispy, golden chips was magical. Sitting and watching was beginning to border on painful. We were salivating. At last, when chef Romero scooped the final batch of chips from the oil, it was time to taste.

He passed a small plate of the pico de gallo, guacamole, and warm tortilla chips for each of us to taste. I tried to take in every flavor, every nuance. I loved the way the salt balanced the acid in the pico de gallo (see page 56) and how the cool, silky, rich texture of the guacamole (see page 56) contrasted with the crisp, warm tortilla chips. Feet still firmly planted in Cambridge, my taste buds had just completed their first journey through Mexico, and I couldn't wait to return.

My hand shot up into the air. "Where can I get cilantro, jalapeños, and ripe avocados?" I asked.

Chef Romero smiled. I'm sure he knew my question was coming.

"You can find the cilantro in the Middle Eastern market in the South End, but it's available only on Saturdays. The jalapeños are sold in the Spanish market in Watertown, and the avocados at Quincy Market. When you buy the avocados, they'll be as hard as rocks. Let them sit on your counter for a few days to ripen."

As I scribbled notes in the margins of my recipes, I whispered to Charlotte, "That's a lot of driving, don't you think?"

"It's worth it," she said.

guacamole

My first avocado encounter was lackluster. It was midwinter in New England, and the fruit was as hard as a raw potato and tasted just about as good. This flavorful guacamole—made with creamy, ripe avocados—changed everything, and sparked my lifelong affinity for Mexican cuisine.

3 avocados, halved, pitted, and peeled
⅓ cup minced red onion
½ to 1 serrano chile, seeded and minced, or more to taste
½ cup chopped cilantro
2 tablespoons freshly squeezed lime juice, or more to taste
Kosher salt
Tortilla chips for serving

Put the avocados in a medium bowl and coarsely mash with a fork. Add the onion, chile, cilantro, and lime juice, season with salt, and mix well. Taste and adjust the seasoning with more lime juice and minced chiles if needed. Accompany with the tortilla chips.

serves 6

pico de gallo

I have a little confession to make: a crunchy tortilla chip mounded with this salsa is my secret guilty pleasure. I could eat it all day, every day. An explosion of fresh flavor and heat fills your mouth and keeps you reaching for more.

1½ pounds ripe tomatoes, diced
⅓ cup chopped cilantro
¼ cup diced red onion
½ to 1 serrano chile, seeded and minced
2 to 3 tablespoons freshly squeezed lime juice
Kosher salt

In a medium bowl, combine the tomatoes, cilantro, and onion and stir gently to mix well. Add the chile, lime juice, and salt to taste and mix again.

serves 6

Arroz Con Pollo — STEPHANIE
3 lb chicken cut
1 large onion chopped
⅓ C. oil
1 green p...
1 t. saf...
pinch ...
½ t. c...
1 can to...
2 C. ri...

2 t oregano
salt / pepper
4-5 garlic cloves

TABOOLEY
1 C. med-fine bulghur (cracked wheat)
½ C. olive oil
juice of 4 lemons (about ¾ C.)
1 bunch scallions finely chopped
2 large bunches parsley fine chopped
4 large tomatoes finely chopped
1 small bunch celery "
2 small cucumbers "
vegetable salt to taste
garlic
romaine lettuce leaves or Syrian bread

Layer bulghur and oil and garlic
Layer veges in order listed
and cover loosely refrigerate at
least 24 hrs. longer = better
(up to 2 wks) to serve, mix together
serve on with lettuce leaves or
Syrian bread 6-8 servings

I FOUND A PARKING PLACE on Brattle Street and then ran across two lanes of traffic and into Cardullo's, the only shop in Cambridge that I knew might have saffron. I grabbed a jar of the delicate flame-colored strands from the shelf and turned it over to look at the price: $6.99! Ouch! I thought to myself. As an art teacher, I was bringing home a whopping $156 a week, and this little jar of saffron threads was making a big dent in my food budget.

It took nearly the whole day to shop. Like a scavenger hunt, I drove from Harvard Square to Watertown, stopping along the way at Martignetti Liquors in Brighton for the cheapest bottle of dry white wine I could find. A little Spanish shop in Watertown had the paella rice and the Spanish olives I needed.

I got back into my car and took every shortcut I knew to get home quickly. No sooner had I raced into my kitchen and thrown on my apron than the doorbell rang. In traipsed

Two much used—and much loved—recipes from my old wooden recipe box.

my brilliant Boston crew: Charlotte, my best food friend and roommate; my boyfriend, Gasper; my brother, John, an architecture student; Liz, another budding architect; and Mariann and Claude, friends from Belgium who were teaching at MIT. Among this cast of characters, I was known as the "chef." With only a handful of cooking classes under my belt, I was anything but a chef, but I was about to fool them again.

"Who wants to set the table?" I asked as I poured the rice and green olives into the simmering pot. Tomatoes, onions, sweet red bell peppers, garlic, red chile flakes, and my precious saffron bubbled away beautifully in my blue Le Creuset dutch oven. Conversation swirled as I put the finishing touches on my Spanish-inspired supper.

In no time at all, the seven of us sat down to enjoy what was becoming one of my signature dishes, *arroz con pollo* (see page 60). I spooned the sun-yellow rice onto my sage-green Bennington pottery plates, making sure everyone received an ample serving of meltingly tender chicken. Although the table in our eat-in kitchen didn't accommodate the entire group, no one cared. Some of us perched on countertops and then played musical chairs when anyone popped up from the table for a second or third helping.

⤬ ● ⤬

BOSTON IN THE 1970S WAS A MELTING POT, and I was finding my culinary footing with a diverse group of friends who loved food as much as I did. I cooked with my Belgian friends, Mariann and Claude, who showed me how to make the crispiest french fries; it was all about double-frying those potatoes at just the right temperature. My French friend Adrienne taught me how to make the most delicate crepes that we brushed with homemade orange marmalade and flamed with Grand Marnier.

Once when I went to dinner at my friend Pamela's, who was Lebanese, I was greeted by the scent of garlic, lemon, and roasting lamb before I even stepped foot in the door. Then, with Lebanese music playing in the background, she taught me how to make hummus and baba ghanoush, two of the classic dishes that make up the comforting cuisine of her family's homeland.

That dinner got me started on a Middle Eastern food kick. I stopped in at The Middle East, a little café just a few blocks from my house, almost daily. I was obsessed with its falafel sandwich. For less than five dollars, I could get warm pita stuffed with crisp yet tender, spiced chickpea patties doused in tahini sauce so redolent with garlic and lemon that five minutes later my mouth still stung from the sauce. That didn't stop me, however. The flavor was worth the pain. I went back again and again for the "punishment" of loving food.

On Saturdays, I liked going to a Middle Eastern bakery in Boston's South End to get pita bread just as it came out of the oven, puffy like a football. I'd buy an armful and nibble on it all the way home. If there was any pita left when I got to my kitchen, I would fill it with my friend Liz's homemade tabbouleh (see page 63). The fresh lemony salad was like nothing I had ever tasted. When I was growing up, parsley turned up in dishes primarily as a garnish. To see it take center stage in this refreshing salad was a revelation. Discovering that the world was full of exotic dishes like this that I'd never tasted only served to fuel my passion for food.

arroz con pollo

Whenever I make this Spanish dish, which can be prepared in a single pot, I am taken back to my first "grown-up" apartment in Cambridge. My friends loved eating this golden-hued saffron rice and chicken, which kept me at the stove making it again and again.

1 whole chicken, 3 to 3½ pounds
   Kosher salt and freshly ground black pepper
2½ teaspoons dried oregano
2 tablespoons extra-virgin olive oil
1 yellow onion, diced
1 red bell pepper, seeded and cut lengthwise
   into ½-inch-wide strips
4 garlic cloves, minced
1 teaspoon saffron threads
⅛ teaspoon red chile flakes
   Pinch of freshly grated nutmeg
2½ cups peeled, seeded, and diced tomatoes
   (fresh or canned)
½ cup Sauvignon Blanc or other dry white wine
2 cups Spanish Bomba or other short-grain
   white rice
½ cup pitted Spanish green olives, sliced
1 cup fresh or frozen shelled English peas

1 Cut the chicken into 8 pieces total: cut each breast in half crosswise and then divide each leg into the drumstick and the thigh. Reserve the wings and back for stock or for another use. Rub the chicken pieces all over with 1 teaspoon salt, lots of black pepper, and the oregano. Place in a large bowl, cover, and set aside in the refrigerator for 1 hour.

2 Preheat the oven to 350°F. In an 8-quart dutch oven or other heavy pot, heat the oil over medium-high heat. Working in batches if necessary to avoid crowding, add the chicken pieces in a single layer and cook, turning as needed, until golden on all sides, about 10 minutes. Transfer the chicken to a plate. Pour off all but 2 tablespoons of the fat from the pot.

3 Return the pot to medium-high heat and add the onion, bell pepper, garlic, saffron, chile flakes, nutmeg, and ½ teaspoon salt. Cook, stirring often, until the vegetables have softened, about 10 minutes. Increase the heat to high, add the tomatoes, 2½ cups water, the wine, and the chicken, and bring to a boil. Cover the pot and place in the oven for 30 minutes.

4 Remove the pot from the oven, add the rice, olives, and ½ teaspoon salt, and stir well. Re-cover the pot, return it to the oven, and cook for another 20 minutes. Retrieve the pot again, add the peas, and fluff the rice with a fork. Re-cover the pot and return it to the oven for a final 10 minutes. At this point, the rice and the chicken will be tender and the liquid will be absorbed.

5 Remove from the oven and let stand, covered, for 10 minutes before serving.

serves 6

tabbouleh

When I was in my twenties, my go-to dinner consisted of homemade tabbouleh, warm pita bread, a chunk of feta cheese drizzled with olive oil, and a bowl of Kalamata olives. My obsession with Mediterranean flavors started long ago and continues to this day.

1 cup medium bulgur

⅔ cup extra-virgin olive oil

4 or 5 garlic cloves, minced

1 cup freshly squeezed lemon juice

　Kosher salt

8 green onions, cut into ¼-inch-thick slices

2 large bunches flat-leaf parsley, chopped

⅓ cup chopped fresh mint

5 large ripe tomatoes, cut into ½-inch dice

2 English or 6 Persian cucumbers, peeled, halved, seeded, and cut into ½-inch dice

　Freshly ground black pepper

　Romaine lettuce leaves and/or wedges of warmed pita bread, for serving

1 Put the bulgur in the bottom of a large salad bowl. To make the dressing, in a small bowl, whisk together the oil, garlic, lemon juice, and 1½ teaspoons salt. Drizzle the dressing over the bulgur and stir together.

2 In the order given, layer the green onions, parsley, mint, tomatoes, and cucumbers on top of the bulgur. Season the top layer of cucumbers with 2½ teaspoons salt and ¼ teaspoon pepper and cover the bowl with plastic wrap. Refrigerate for at least 24 hours or up to 48 hours.

3 Bring to room temperature. Toss together all of the salad ingredients, then taste and adjust the seasoning. Serve with the lettuce leaves and/or pita for scooping up the salad.

serves 6 to 8

BOSTON'S NORTH END was the neighborhood I visited when I wanted to escape to Italy. I would often go with Gasper, whose smile made my heart skip a beat, and we would buy almond biscotti from Salumeria Italiana, a bakery and grocery story there. We'd make French press coffee, adding anise-flavored Galliano, and then pour it into tall glasses and top it with sweet cream we'd whipped ourselves. We'd eat the cream with a spoon, then dip the crisp biscotti into the Galliano-infused coffee. Sip, dunk, crunch. I'd close my eyes and we were sitting in a piazza in Milan. It was heaven. Gasper once told me he loved me like he loved apple pie. I didn't know if that was a compliment or not, but after that, I made apple pie every chance I got.

To beat the heat one summer, I rented a little cottage on the edge of the dunes in Truro on Cape Cod. I invited Gasper and his friends, Brett and Brian, to come for the weekend. Brett was in the midst of a yearlong professional cooking course with Madeleine Kamman

left:
An afternoon
in the countryside
outside Boston.

right:
A favorite dish
from my
recipe box.

at Modern Gourmet in Newton, just outside of Boston. I agonized over what to cook. Feeling intimidated has always been a weakness of mine. Instead of seeing Brett's visit as a way to gain knowledge, I felt nervous.

I finally settled on a seafood stew (see page 66). It was summer on Cape Cod, and I decided I'd let the local catch sing. I cooked onions and garlic in a huge pot, adding lots of ripe summer tomatoes, white wine, red chile flakes, thyme, and saffron threads. The feisty live lobsters presented my first challenge. I practically had to chase them around the room. When I finally captured them, it took every bit of nerve I had to dunk them quickly, head first, into boiling water. I simmered them until they were bright reddish orange. My heart was racing with trepidation, but I'd done it. Scrubbing the clams and mussels and preparing the sea scallops was easy after those hellish lobsters.

The broth smelled divine as I added my diced potatoes. While we waited for them to cook, we all sat around the table drinking wine and telling stories.

"I almost forgot the potatoes!" I yelled as I ran to the stove, worried they had overcooked. Phew! They were still as hard as when I added them. Back to my friends!

Thirty minutes later, I checked again. Still not done. "Brett, can you help me?" I cajoled.

Brett poked a fork into the potatoes. The fork didn't make a dent. She looked puzzled. "How long have they been cooking?"

"Probably an hour!"

"Give them another thirty minutes!"

We did that at least two more times. No one minded the delay; wine continued to flow. But Brett and I were confounded. We were learning the hard way that potatoes don't cook as easily when mixed with lots of tomatoes. Exasperated, Brett and I scooped the potatoes out of the stew with a slotted spoon and cooked them in a saucepan of salted water. In the meantime, we added the fresh seafood, finished the stew, and tossed in the cooked potatoes at the end.

At midnight, we finally sat down to eat. The stew was bursting with the sweet, salty flavors of the sea. Everyone ate bowl after bowl, sopping up every last drop of the aromatic broth with crusty bread. I had to laugh, but I was also embarrassed. All night as I tried to sleep, I kept thinking about the hard potatoes simmering in tomato broth. In the morning, I had a hangover I couldn't sleep off.

Cape Cod Fish Stew — capecod

1 lb. fish, cod scallops clams
1 c. chopped onions
1/3 c. oil
1 can tomatoes   peppers
2 c. potatoes   veges(zucchini
1 c. water   summer squash)
1/4 c. ketchup
1/2 t. salt

provincetown seafood stew

This recipe, from the Portuguese fishermen at the Provincetown pier at the tip of Cape Cod, always reminds me of my potatoes-in-tomato broth fiasco. I've never made that mistake again! When fish is fresh, you don't have to do much to bring out its beautiful oceanic flavor. Just be sure to boil your potatoes separately.

3 tablespoons extra-virgin olive oil

1 yellow onion, chopped

1 garlic clove, minced

2½ cups peeled, seeded, and chopped tomatoes (fresh or canned)

3 tablespoons tomato paste

10 cups fish stock (page 276) or water

¾ cup Sauvignon Blanc or other dry white wine

Pinch of red chile flakes

Pinch of dried thyme

1 teaspoon saffron threads

1 bay leaf

Kosher salt and freshly ground black pepper

2 freshly boiled lobsters, 1¼ pounds each

1 pound littleneck clams in shells, scrubbed

1 pound mussels in shells, scrubbed and beards pulled off

1 pound firm white fish fillets, such as cod, sea bass, or halibut

½ pound sea scallops

½ pound extra-large shrimp in shells (20 to 25 per pound), peeled and deveined

1¼ pounds small Yukon Gold or red potatoes, halved, boiled until tender, and drained

1 tablespoon chopped flat-leaf parsley

1 In a large soup pot, heat the oil over medium heat. Add the onion and cook, stirring occasionally, until soft, about 8 minutes. Add the garlic and cook for 1 minute. Add the tomatoes, tomato paste, stock, wine, chile flakes, thyme, saffron, and bay leaf and stir well. Season with salt and pepper and simmer, uncovered, for 30 minutes to blend the flavors.

2 Meanwhile, remove the claws and tail from each lobster. Cut the tails crosswise into 1-inch chunks. Crack the claws. Ready the clams and mussels. Cut the fish into 2-inch pieces and put them in a bowl. Trim away the muscle from the side of each scallop. Add the scallops and shrimp to the fish.

3 When the tomato broth has simmered for 30 minutes, add the clams and cook until they begin to open, about 2 minutes. Add the mussels and cook until they begin to open, about 2 minutes. Add the lobster, fish, scallops, and shrimp and cook until the fish can be easily flaked with a fork, 3 to 4 minutes. Add the potatoes, stir together gently, and simmer until the potatoes are heated through, 2 to 3 minutes.

4 Ladle the stew into warmed individual bowls, discarding any clams or mussels that failed to open and removing the bay leaf. Garnish with the parsley.

serves 6

IN THOSE DAYS, my cookbook collection was slim: *Mastering the Art of French Cooking* by Julia Child, Louisette Bertholle, and Simone Beck and *American Cookery* by James Beard. I was working my way through those two books and finding myself pretty proficient. But I knew there was only so much I could learn alone in my kitchen.

It was time to break out the big guns and take a class from a big-name chef. I enrolled in a series of cooking classes taught by Madeleine Kamman, at the time the greatest female French chef and cooking instructor in America. The course was called Food of the Women of the French Provinces. For six consecutive Thursday nights, I sat entranced as a different French province was explored each week.

Class began promptly at 5:30 p.m. and went on for hours as Madeleine recalled stories from her French upbringing. I hung on every word and every technique she pounded into our brains. Whether she was boning chicken legs and stuffing them with walnuts and blue cheese (see page 70) or gracefully preparing paper-thin crepes, she was an absolute master of her craft.

On our evening in Provence, Madeleine spoke passionately of her friend Magaly Fabre, owner of the Mont-Redon winery in the south of France and brilliant chef in her own right. As she prepared a whole leg of lamb for roasting in the manner Magaly had taught her, Madeleine recalled stories of her annual visits to the paradisiacal winery. Rosemary, thyme, and garlic infused the grassy, sweet lamb with traditional Provençal flavors, the tantalizing aroma teasing us for the duration of the class.

Madeleine was serious about French cuisine and wanted everyone in the room to be just as dedicated. Heaven forbid if you were a doctor's wife or a wealthy blonde with perfectly manicured fingernails in class only for lack of something better to do on Thursday night. Madeleine could spot an imposter, and she wasn't shy about letting that person know what she thought. I sat there amazed at her talent and the depth of her perception. I was young, naïve, and equally in awe and petrified of her.

I almost fell off my chair the day she pointed at me and said, "You!" Then again two seconds later, "You!" Oh my God, I thought to myself, please, not me! I looked around hoping she was talking to the doctor's wife behind me. No such luck. She was looking straight into my eyes. "You have the face of French porcelain!" she remarked.

I realized it was a compliment and counted my blessings, then scooted a little lower in my seat so she wouldn't make mention of my now rosier cheeks. That was the extent of my direct interaction with Madeleine at the time.

I'm not sure if the dishes Madeleine made were complicated or if it was just the way she prepared them. I only know that we would spend hours on a single sauce or technique. Class would finally culminate around 11:00 p.m. with a miniscule tasting. But I savored every morsel, every drop of sauce like it was my last bite. Madeleine's food was rich and sultry, the flavors deep and complex. I didn't know food could be so satisfying. I was hungry for more, both figuratively and literally: I was eager to learn more about the endlessly fascinating culinary world, and I couldn't wait to race home and eat dinner.

leg of lamb on a bed of potatoes

This classic Provençal recipe comes from Magaly Fabre, owner of the renowned Mont-Redon winery, by way of Madeleine Kamman. Whenever I make this dish, I'm transported to the south of France and reminded of those Thursday night classes with Madeleine and how much they influenced me in the kitchen.

2 tablespoons extra-virgin olive oil, plus more for rubbing

3 large yellow onions, sliced into thin rings

6 garlic cloves, 3 minced and 3 thinly sliced lengthwise

½ cup chopped flat-leaf parsley

2 pounds russet or other baking potatoes, peeled and sliced crosswise

Kosher salt and freshly ground black pepper

About 6 cups rich veal stock (page 106) or chicken stock (page 276)

1 bone-in leg of lamb, 4 to 5 pounds

1 teaspoon chopped fresh thyme

1 teaspoon chopped fresh rosemary

1 teaspoon chopped fresh savory (optional)

3 tomatoes, cut into ⅓-inch-thick slices

2 tablespoons unsalted butter, cut into small bits

1   Preheat the oven to 400°F. Oil a large baking dish. In a large frying pan, warm the 2 tablespoons oil over high heat. Add the onions and brown, turning once, until light golden on both sides, about 4 minutes on each side. Using a slotted spoon, transfer to a plate and set aside.

2   Reduce the heat to low, add the minced garlic, and cook, stirring occasionally, until soft, 1 to 2 minutes. Do not let the garlic turn golden. Stir in the parsley and remove from the heat.

3   Arrange half of the potato slices in the bottom of the baking dish and season with salt and pepper. Spoon the onions evenly over the potatoes and then top evenly with the garlic and parsley. Top with the remaining potato slices and season with salt and pepper. Pour enough stock into the baking dish until it reaches almost level with the top of the potatoes. Bake in the oven for 30 minutes.

4   Meanwhile, trim away any excess fat and skin from the lamb. Cut small slits about ½ inch deep all over the surface of the lamb, then insert a garlic slice into each slit. Rub the lamb all over with oil, with half of the thyme, rosemary, and savory, and with salt and pepper.

5   When the potatoes have baked for 30 minutes, remove them from the oven and arrange the tomato slices evenly over the top. Sprinkle the remaining thyme, rosemary, and savory evenly over the tomatoes and season with salt. Dot the tomatoes with the butter. Set the lamb on top of the tomatoes.

6   Roast the lamb until an instant-read thermometer inserted into the thickest part of the leg away from bone registers 125°F to 130°F for medium-rare, 1 to 1¼ hours. If the potatoes dry out before the lamb is ready, add more stock as needed.

7   Remove from the oven, transfer the lamb to a cutting board, and let rest for 10 minutes. If there are any excess juices at the bottom of the baking dish, spoon them into a small saucepan and reduce them over high heat until thickened to a sauce.

8   To serve, carve the lamb into slices. Spoon the potatoes, onions, and tomatoes into a large serving platter. Arrange the sliced lamb on top of the vegetables and spoon the sauce, if any, over the top.

serves 6 to 8

chicken legs stuffed with blue cheese and walnuts

6 large whole chicken legs (thigh and drumstick)
  Kosher salt and freshly ground black pepper
⅓ cup walnuts
2 tablespoons unsalted butter
6 ounces button mushrooms, stem ends trimmed
  and coarsely chopped
¾ cup fresh bread crumbs
2 large egg yolks, whisked
¼ cup crumbled bleu de Bresse or stilton cheese
1 tablespoon walnut oil
3 ounces thick-sliced bacon, cut crosswise into
  ⅓-inch-wide pieces
12 shallots, peeled and left whole
¼ cup Sauvignon Blanc or other dry white wine
½ cup rich veal stock (page 106) or low-sodium
  beef or chicken broth
2 tablespoons heavy whipping cream
  Chopped flat-leaf parsley for garnish

1 First, bone the chicken legs, keeping the skin intact: Lay each leg, skin side down, on a work surface and, with a sharp knife, make shallow slices on top of the leg and thigh bone to expose the bones. Next, cut down along either side of each bone to expose it completely, then slide the knife under the bones to free them from the flesh. Finally, trim away any strips of white cartilage from the flesh. Season the meat generously with salt and pepper. Set the chicken aside.

2 In a small frying pan over medium heat, toast the nuts, shaking the pan occasionally, until fragrant and lightly browned, about 5 minutes. Pour onto a cutting board, let cool, and chop. Set aside.

3 In a large ovenproof frying pan over medium-high heat, melt the butter. Add the mushrooms and cook, stirring occasionally, until they release their moisture and then the moisture evaporates, 8 to 10 minutes. Transfer the mushrooms to a bowl and let cool completely. Set the pan aside.

4 Add the bread crumbs, egg yolks, cheese, and walnuts to the cooled mushrooms, mix well, and season with salt and pepper.

5 Lay the boned legs, flesh side up, on a work surface. Divide the mushroom mixture evenly among the legs, spooning it into the center, then wrap each leg around the stuffing. Using a needle and fine kitchen string or coarse thread, loosely sew each leg closed, giving it the shape of a small ham.

6 Preheat the oven to 375°F. Wipe out the frying pan, place over medium-high heat, and add the oil. When the oil is hot, add the chicken legs and cook, turning once, until golden brown on both sides, about 10 minutes total. Transfer the chicken legs to a plate. Pour off and discard the excess oil.

7 Add the bacon and shallots to the same pan and cook until the bacon is golden, 2 to 3 minutes. Return the chicken, skin side up, to the pan and roast in the oven until an instant-read thermometer inserted into the thickest part of a thigh registers 165°F, about 45 minutes. Transfer the chicken to warmed individual plates, tent with foil, and drain off any excess oil from the pan.

8 Add the wine to the pan and simmer over medium-high heat, scraping up any browned bits on the bottom of the pan, until reduced by half, about 1 minute. Add the stock and cream and simmer gently until the sauce coats the back of a spoon, 1 to 2 minutes. Spoon the sauce over the chicken, dividing the shallots and bacon evenly. Garnish with the parsley.

serves 6

DEJEUNER

FOIE DE CANARD FRAIS AUX POMMES

MAGRET DE CANARD AU POIVRE VERT

LEGUMES DE SAISON

SALADE

FROMAGES

TARTE AUX FRAISES

CHAMPAGNE HENRIOT
MOUTON CADET BLANC
MOUTON BARON PHILIPPE 1964
MOUTON ROTHSCHILD 1944
MOUTON ROTHSCHILD 1918
YQUEM

22 JUILLET 1977

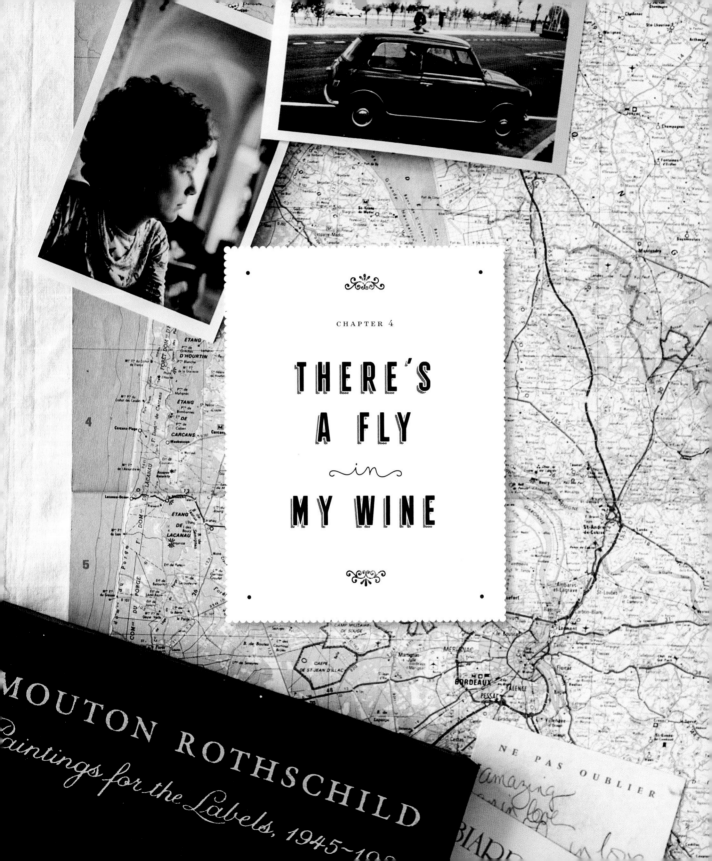

CHAPTER 4

THERE'S A FLY in MY WINE

BINGO! I FOUND THE WINEGLASSES," I said with a smile as I opened a cardboard box with *fragile* scribbled on the side. "Hey Charlotte, have you come across the corkscrew yet? Let's take a break!"

I grabbed the wine that David, our friend and the previous tenant of our new apartment, had given my roommate, Charlotte, and me as a housewarming gift. As David hauled his boxes out of the prewar brick building on Williams Street in Cambridge, we moved our boxes in. He had passed not only the apartment on to us but also a couple of mice and some tiny, very fast cockroaches. Maybe the place wasn't perfect, but I was young and it was home.

Charlotte and I sat down at the table in the corner of our new eat-in kitchen. We had our priorities. That corner was the first space we'd arranged that morning. Now the setting sun beamed through the windows, bathing the slightly weathered secondhand table in soft light. The setup was perfect.

I was glad to see that the wineglasses hadn't broken during the move. Of course, that would have been next to impossible since they were as thick as Coke bottles. When it came to opening wine, I wasn't a pro, but my handy winged corkscrew did the trick. I plucked the cork from David's bottle of Mouton Cadet rouge and poured a hefty dose into each of our glasses. We'd been unpacking boxes all day, so the wine and a toast to our new place were well deserved.

In France, in my Diane von Furstenberg dress after a couple of glasses of wine.

⚬⚬⚬

x

"Mmmmm, tastes good!" was about the best I could come up with, given my limited wine knowledge. All I knew was that it was red and easy to drink. We sat and sipped and talked over our vision for the apartment: new curtains here, new paint on the walls there. We'd be ready to host a dinner party in no time.

It didn't take long to finish the bottle. As I put the last sip of wine to my lips, I spotted something in my glass. "Oh, yuck!" I screeched. "Charlotte, look! This is disgusting!" Clinging to the inside of my glass was a big, black fly that looked like it had been floating in the wine for years.

This happened at a time in my life during which I enjoyed writing customer service departments whenever I encountered a defective product. In other words, I had considerably more free time than I do nowadays. Just a few months before the wine incident, I'd nearly broken a tooth on a small stone I came across in a package of dried apricots. I had written a letter to the company, and as an apology, I received two boxes of dried apricots in the mail.

I scooped the wine-soaked fly out of the glass, wrapped it in aluminum foil, and slid it into an envelope. I enclosed a handwritten letter of complaint and sent the fly back across the ocean. Little did I know that I was sending an insect to what was considered one of the top wineries in the world: Château Mouton Rothschild.

I wasn't sure if I'd get a reply. Weeks passed and I had almost forgotten about that French fly's journey home. Then, one afternoon, I opened my mailbox to find a Telex from France. It read:

> *Attention Ms. Joanne:*
> *We thank you for your letter and sending the fly you found in your bottle of Mouton Cadet rouge. We are sorry for your trouble. This has never happened before. If you are planning a trip to France, we invite you to be our special guest for lunch at Château Mouton Rothschild.*
> *We await your answer.*
> *Regards,*
> *Xavier de Eizaguirre*

My jaw dropped. This was way better than two free boxes of dried apricots. Lunch at a winery in Bordeaux? I'd be a fool to pass up this opportunity. I was going to France!

I wasn't wealthy, of course, but because I was a school teacher, I did have my summers off, and summer vacation had just begun. On my last day of school, I'd been handed a check for all ten weeks of my summer pay—a check that was burning a hole in my pocket. Plus, August 2 would be my twenty-fifth birthday. What better place to celebrate my first quarter century than in France? I was sold; now I just needed someone to travel with me.

"Charlotte, want to go to France this summer?" I had barely gotten the words out of my mouth and she was on the phone making plane reservations.

Then reality hit. I knew nothing about wine beyond the color in the glass: white, red, or rosé. I needed to do some studying.

I made a beeline for the local bookstore and bought the only two wine books I could find: Hugh Johnson's *World Atlas of Wine* and *Alexis Lichine's Encyclopedia of Wines & Spirits*. For the next month, instead of reading novels in bed, I studied these books cover to cover. I memorized the wine regions and the grapes that came from each one. I learned that *appellation d'origine contrôlée*, or AOC, was a system of regulations that was applied to all high-quality wines in France. I knew that Burgundy's white was made from Chardonnay grapes and the red from Pinot Noir. I studied the *crus* of Beaujolais until I could recite all ten. Who knew that Champagne, the bubbly celebratory drink from France, was actually from the region of Champagne? Now I did.

When it came to the chapters on Bordeaux, I memorized every page. Bordeaux was known for a blend of red wines: Cabernet Sauvignon—the workhorse—plus Merlot, Cabernet Franc, Malbec, and Petit Verdot. When it came to whites, I couldn't wait to taste the fresh, herbal Sauvignon Blanc often blended with Sémillon. I read about Sémillon and Sauternes. I had always thought that Sauternes was a sickeningly sweet wine that street people drank. I was fascinated to learn that the name was used for both one of the cheapest wines and one of the most expensive wines in the world. I was hoping to get a chance to taste the latter.

When I got to the section on Château Mouton Rothschild, I was stunned by the immaculate manicured grounds and regal château pictured in the photographs. Only then did I realize that I was about to have lunch at one of the most prestigious wineries in the world.

Just one month later, Charlotte and I were walking across the white stone–covered driveway of Château Mouton Rothschild, with the sound of each step echoing loudly in my ears. We were both wearing our best Diane von Furstenberg wrap dresses and espadrille pumps to match. My ensemble was navy blue, Charlotte's was kelly green. Xavier de Eizaguirre, the thirty-something exporting agent who had sent the invitation and would be our host, walked toward me with his arms outstretched. He wore a slightly wrinkled white linen suit and was so handsome and debonair that I felt short of breath. Was there such a thing as love at first sight?

Xavier and his assistant, Pierre, also in white linen, were consummate guides. After a tour of the breathtaking property, the four of us, with Xavier next to me, sat for lunch in a room that will remain in my memory forever. Our table, set with fine china, highly polished silver cutlery, perfectly pressed white linen napkins, and crystal wineglasses, was the centerpiece of the elegant, cream-colored sandstone room. At each place setting was a menu written in French. Next to the dining table was a smaller table topped with decanters at least eighteen inches tall, all of them filled with red wine. In each corner of the room stood a life-size *mouton* (sheep) sculpted in sandstone. Vases of fragrant pale pink roses were set throughout the room. Huge arched windows overlooked the lush green vineyards. It wasn't just because I was an impressionable twenty-four-year-old: the setting was truly stunning.

A server dressed in a crisp black suit and white gloves entered the room carrying tall, delicate flutes of Champagne on a silver tray. As he gently placed the thin glasses on our table, I thought of our Coke-bottle-thick wineglasses back home, then shook my head and returned to the moment.

The first course was served: on each plate sat a warm butter-drenched slice of fine-textured *pain de mie* that had been cut on the diagonal into two triangles and then topped with lightly caramelized duck livers and thin slices of sweet apple (see page 78). They were luscious pillows of richness that literally dissolved in my mouth. I sipped the Champagne and felt my eyes roll to the back of my head. I had to suppress a moan. When

My dear friend Charlotte Robinson. Me, in the driver's seat of our rented Austin Mini.

〜〜〜

×

I had eaten every last morsel on the Limoges plate, all that remained was the embossed Château Mouton Rothschild crest. "Someone pinch me," I said to myself.

As I finished the duck liver, a splash of chilled Mouton Cadet blanc was poured. I took a taste. "Delicious," I said politely, but it was no match for the Champagne. Xavier laughed, "That's the same label as the wine in which you found the fly! You had the red, and this is the white counterpart." I couldn't believe it. As I lifted my glass for another taste, that was the reason for this lunch after all, I noticed that Xavier had barely taken a sip. Clearly this was their entry-level wine and he was waiting for the wines that were yet to come.

× ● ×

OUR SERVER, WHOSE NAME WAS BERNARD, picked up one of the carafes and poured a 1964 Baron Philippe de Rothschild into our huge balloon glasses. It looked like a splash in the bottom of the glass compared with what I was used to pouring. Xavier picked up his glass and studied the wine. Then he swirled the glass so vigorously that I thought the wine was going to fly out of it. I watched as he put his nose past the rim and inhaled deeply. Finally, he took a sip and then made slurping sounds that made me smile.

I took a sip along with him, a sip that went directly from the glass and straight down my throat. The wine was smooth and elegant.

For the main course, Bernard placed a plump seared duck breast in front of me (see page 81). It was thinly sliced, precisely fanned across the plate to reveal its slightly pink center, and then topped with a silky green peppercorn sauce. Bernard carefully explained in French—and Xavier translated—that the duck breast was from the same duck as the liver we had just eaten.

The plate looked like a work of art, but I couldn't wait to devour everything on it. I took my first bite and chewed slowly, allowing the flavors to play on my palate. The rich, delicate, sweet duck contrasted perfectly with the zippy, pungent peppercorns. I detected a splash of Cognac in the sauce and, from its color, perhaps some red wine. I tried the wine again and this time, after tasting the food, it took on a whole new dimension. It now had peppery notes and complemented the food superbly. I was astounded.

duck liver and apple toasts

Looking over the elegant menu at Château Mouton Rothschild, I knew that foie *meant "liver" in French, and it made me nervous. Thankfully, these tender, sweet duck livers taste nothing like the pungent calf's liver of my childhood. So rich and decadent, they literally melt in your mouth. The Sauternes-infused apple adds a sweet-tart note to the dish and makes a perfect accompaniment.*

6 slices *pain de mie* (French sandwich bread)

4 tablespoons unsalted butter, plus 2 tablespoons, melted

2 small Honeycrisp or other red-skinned apples, halved, cored, and cut into ⅛-inch-thick slices

1 teaspoon sugar

⅓ cup Sauternes

¾ pound duck livers, trimmed of any green spots or connective tissue

Kosher salt and freshly ground black pepper

1 cup torn frisée or watercress

1   Cut the crusts off the bread slices, then toast the bread. Brush one side of each slice with the melted butter. Cut each slice in half on the diagonal and place on individual plates.

2   In a large frying pan, melt 2 tablespoons of the butter over medium-high heat. Add the apples and sugar and cook, turning the apples after about 1 minute, until they begin to soften, about 2 minutes total. Add the Sauternes and cook until it is reduced by half, 1 to 2 minutes. Transfer the apples and liquid to a bowl and set aside.

3   Return the pan to medium-high heat and add the remaining 2 tablespoons butter. When the butter just begins to turn golden brown, add the duck livers and season with salt and pepper. Cook the livers, turning them occasionally, until they are golden and crispy on the outside and are slightly soft and pink in the center, 30 to 45 seconds on each side. Add the apples and their liquid, stir together carefully, and then let warm for 1 minute.

4   Using tongs, arrange the livers and apples on the toast, distributing them evenly. Drizzle the sauce from the pan over the livers. Garnish with the frisée. Serve immediately.

serves 6

seared duck breasts with green peppercorn sauce

The table was silent as we sampled our first bite of crisp-skinned duck breast bathed in a buttery green peppercorn sauce, the quietest we'd been all day. The only discernible sound was silver forks against Limoges china, lips smacking, and the aeration of wine. This dish, served to me at Château Mouton Rothschild with a 1964 Baron Philippe de Rothschild, was my first real exposure to the incredible art of food and wine pairing. No 1964 Rothschild on hand? Try it with a Cabernet with hints of pepper.

6 duck breast halves with skin attached, about ½ pound each
Kosher salt
1 cup Cabernet Sauvignon or dry red wine
2 cups chicken stock (page 276)
2½ tablespoons drained brined green peppercorns
1 tablespoon Cognac, Armagnac, or other brandy
2 tablespoons unsalted butter, at room temperature

1 Preheat the oven to 400°F. Place the duck breasts on a work surface and trim off the excess fat, then place the breasts skin side up. Using a sharp knife, score the skin in a diagonal grid pattern, cutting no deeper than halfway through the skin. Be careful not to cut into the meat. Season the skin well with salt.

2 Heat a large ovenproof frying pan over medium-high heat. Add the duck breasts, skin side down, and cook until the skin is golden and the fat from the skin has rendered, 6 to 8 minutes. Turn the duck breasts over, transfer the pan to the oven, and continue to cook until an instant-read thermometer inserted into the thickest end of a breast registers 118°F to 120°F for medium-rare, 6 to 8 minutes.

3 Remove the pan from the oven and place over high heat. Using tongs, transfer the duck breasts to a platter and tent loosely with foil. Be careful when grasping the handle of the pan as it will be very hot! Pour off and discard all of the fat in the pan.

4 Pour in the wine and deglaze the pan, stirring to dislodge any browned-on bits from the pan bottom, then simmer briskly until reduced by half, 2 to 3 minutes. Add the stock and peppercorns and continue to cook until the liquid is reduced by half, about 5 minutes. Remove the pan from the heat; whisk in the Cognac and butter until the butter melts.

5 Cut each duck breast on the diagonal into slices ½ inch thick, and fan the slices on a warmed individual plate. Spoon the sauce and peppercorns over the duck.

serves 6

"XAVIER, WILL YOU TEACH ME to taste wine?" I asked flirtatiously.

"Of course. Pick up your glass," he instructed. "What do you see?"

"Purple, the color of blackberries and dark cherries."

Next, he taught me to swirl. I discovered the hard way that I was much better at swirling if I kept the base of the glass resting on the table rather than lifting the glass into the air.

"You swirl to give oxygen to the wine, which will bring out the aromas. Okay, now put your nose in the glass. What do you smell?" Xavier's accented English was like music to my ears.

"*Poivre!*" I cried out in French. It smelled just like black pepper to me.

Everyone laughed at my enthusiasm. It seemed our formal lunch was slipping into raucous-party territory.

"You are right. Now let's taste!"

"Oh, I like this part!" I giggled.

More wine was poured. This time, it was a 1944 Baron Philippe de Rothschild.

"As you take a sip of wine, draw some air over your tongue. Make noise!" Xavier directed.

With Pierre and Xavier in the cellars at Château Mouton Rothschild. On the streets of Andorra a few days later.

"Swish the wine around in your mouth almost as if you're gargling with it. It's going to seem strange and feel funny at first."

Charlotte and I did exactly as instructed. The effect amazed me. The wine was even silkier than before and the flavors detonated in my mouth. Even after I swallowed, the taste of the wine lingered on the back and sides of my tongue. I noticed that both Xavier and Pierre were now drinking their whole glasses of wine right along with us. Unlike the Mouton Cadet blanc, they weren't leaving a single drop behind. As a matter of fact, they were pouring us all seconds.

"Wow, this is so much fun!" Xavier exclaimed. "When we got your letter with the fly in aluminum foil, we thought you were going to be old women, maybe in your forties!"

More laughter! More wine.

Bernard announced in French, "1918 Château Mouton Rothschild, Premier Grand Cru Classé, 77 percent Cabernet Sauvignon, 12 percent Merlot, 9 percent Cabernet Franc, *bon millésime, nez légèrement compoté, mi-palais sucré, ce présent bien d'un grand millésime.*"

Suddenly I understood every word of French that Bernard spoke. Even more shockingly, I was responding in French that I'd learned in elementary and junior high school.

Dessert brought another surprise: a 1922 Château d'Yquem. Yquem was one of the wines I'd read so much about during my pre-trip study sessions. I never dreamed I'd get to taste it, let alone one from 1922.

"Don't drink! Put your nose in the glass. Tell me what you get from that," Xavier commanded.

"Honeysuckle?" I said timidly.

"Maybe some apricot?" Charlotte's response lifted into the air like a question.

"Excellent! The nose is subjective. You get one thing and Charlotte gets another. That's fine. Now take a sip and remember to let it roll over your tongue. Give it time. Good things always take time!" he said with a grin.

I did exactly what he told me. Was it his voice with that sexy French accent, or was it the wine that made me feel like I was floating?

The flavors exploded in my mouth and slowly spread across my tongue like honey. The 1922 Château d'Yquem tasted like pure gold.

Bernard presented each of us with a slice of strawberry tart (see page 84). The delicate, buttery crust was topped with a silky smooth kirsch pastry cream and crowned with perfectly glazed, ripe red strawberries. My brain, with its newfound capacity to spout French phrases, came up with the most fitting description: "*Crème de la crème.*"

Just when I didn't think it could get any better, I heard Xavier say, "Bernard, please pour us the 1892 d'Yquem."

I gasped, "This is the nectar of the gods." It truly was.

We stepped away from the table and walked outside into the sunlight and back to reality. Our magical day was coming to an end. As we said our good-byes, Xavier brushed his hand across my cheek. Would I ever see him again, I wondered, as we slipped into our rented Austin Mini.

We drove away, windows wide open, singing old Beatles songs as loudly as we could all the way to Biarritz.

sweet summer strawberry tart

At the age of twenty-four, there's nothing quite like the sweetness of puppy love to set your heart aflutter. Add a slice of fresh strawberry tart and a glass of 1892 Château d'Yquem and life is pretty much perfect. Since I can't re-create the entire experience for you, just the tart will have to do. It's the best part... almost.

SHORTCRUST PASTRY
- 1 cup all-purpose flour
- 1 tablespoon sugar
- ¼ teaspoon kosher salt
- ¼ teaspoon grated lemon zest
- ½ cup unsalted butter, cubed
- ½ teaspoon vanilla extract

PASTRY CREAM
- 2 cups whole milk
- Large pinch of kosher salt
- 3 tablespoons cornstarch
- ½ cup plus 1 tablespoon sugar
- 2 large eggs
- 1 tablespoon kirsch
- 2 tablespoons unsalted butter, at room temperature

- 2 cups medium-size strawberries, hulled
- 1 cup strawberry jam, strained

1 To make the pastry, in a bowl, whisk together the flour, sugar, salt, and lemon zest. Scatter the butter over the flour mixture and, using your fingers, work the butter into the flour mixture until the mixture is the consistency of coarse cornmeal. In a bowl, stir together 1 tablespoon water and the vanilla. Drizzle the mixture over the flour-butter mixture and stir with a fork until evenly moistened. Gather the dough into a ball, wrap in plastic wrap, and let rest for 30 minutes.

2 Press the pastry evenly onto the bottom and up the sides of a 9-inch round tart pan with a removable rim. Line the tart shell with foil and place in the freezer for 30 minutes. Preheat the oven to 375°F.

3 Fill the tart shell with pie weights or dried beans and bake until light golden brown, 15 to 20 minutes. Remove the pie weights and foil and continue to bake until the tart shell is baked all the way through, about 5 minutes longer. Let cool completely on a cooling rack.

4 To make the pastry cream, in a heavy saucepan, combine the milk and salt over medium-high heat and heat until small bubbles appear along the edges of the pan. Meanwhile, in a bowl, whisk together the cornstarch and sugar. Add the eggs and whisk until smooth. Slowly drizzle half of the milk into the egg mixture while whisking constantly. Pour the egg-milk mixture back into the hot milk, return the pan to medium heat, and continue until the custard thickens, about 2 minutes. Remove from the heat and pour through a fine-mesh strainer into a bowl. Stir in the kirsch and let cool for 10 minutes, stirring occasionally. Add the butter and stir until combined. Cover the bowl with plastic wrap, pressing the plastic wrap directly onto the top of the pastry cream, and refrigerate until well chilled, about 2 hours.

5 Spread the pastry cream evenly into the tart shell. Halve the strawberries. Starting at the edge of the shell, arrange the strawberries, cut side down, in tight concentric circles, covering the pastry cream nearly completely.

6 In a saucepan, combine the jam and 1 tablespoon water over medium-low heat and stir until the jam liquefies. Brush the strawberries with the jam. Let set for 20 minutes before serving.

serves 8

Menu · Chez Panisse

P CURTAN

Nocino

16⅔ oz. sugar
30 green walnuts, quartered
1 liter vodka or akvavit
5 cloves
2 sticks cinnamon
1 lemon

Put nuts in container.
Add spices & a piece of lemon
  zest.
Cover w/ alcohol.
Cover tightly & set in sun
4 weeks shaking once per day
Add the sugar, cover
  & leave 2 weeks.
Filter & bottle.

the

LUNCH

that

CHANGED MY
LIFE

MENU
CHEZ PANISSE CAFE

LUNCH · MONDAY · 9 JULY 1991

Ligurian broth with Arborio rice and greens, $
Chino Farm leeks vinaigrette
Three endive sal

AS WE WALKED UP THE STAIRS, I couldn't take my eyes off of the unruly branches of kumquats that overshot the vase meant to contain them. So vividly orange, they looked like they'd been plucked out of my grandfather's orchard that very morning. Seeing them reminded me that it was late winter in California.

"Welcome to the Café at Chez Panisse. Do you have a reservation?" the host inquired, snapping me out of my trance.

My sister Nancy and I followed him past the tall, stately bartender in a crisp white shirt and long black apron to his ankles who was pouring a glass of red wine. My mind flashed back to my trip to France. Was I in Bordeaux?

We continued on past the salad station. A huge case of bright green first-of-the-season fava beans sat on the counter. I stood for a moment and watched as a cook shucked fava beans with deft speed. A busser came by and lent a hand with the task until he was called back to clear a table.

As we journeyed along, I spotted a high wooden counter filled with an array of desserts, both rustic and refined. A ruby-red rhubarb *crostata*, its golden crust dusted with coarse sugar, sat alongside a vintage plate stacked with rich dark chocolate cookies. Behind the counter "the line" of cooks was busy at work. One was pouring freshly drained green *fedelini* into a sauté pan holding peas, asparagus, and crisp pancetta. Another was stoking the wood-fired grill. A stout, mustached *pizzaiolo* in a white cap spun a round of dough high into the air. I was mesmerized. As he caught the dough without even looking, he smiled and winked at me. I laughed out loud. I decided that he must be Italian.

Everything I'd read and heard about Chez Panisse Café, which had opened in 1980, a year prior to my visit, was true. If I had stopped right then and not eaten a single bite of food, I still would have understood what all the buzz was about. I could tell by the smell

I've always loved a good lunch!

of the freshly baked pizza, the crust perfectly blistered and singed, the garlic that perfumed the air, the energy in the room, the patina of burnished copper gleaming from the open kitchen. This place felt special, like it had somehow been here way beyond its years. I took my seat and ordered a drink, and I could feel every beat of my heart.

As I sipped my glass of Navarro sparkling wine, a small plate of grassy green olives and a basket of warm bread appeared in front of me. I couldn't stop myself from eating the olives, almost by the handful, along with the crusty *pain levain* slathered with creamy butter. The butter tasted just like the homemade butter Mama Anna, my paternal grandmother, used to make. My meal had barely begun, but I already knew that this was not just another restaurant. My food world was about to make a seismic shift for the better.

× • ×

I DON'T KNOW WHERE I'D FIRST HEARD about Chez Panisse. It could have been on *All Things Considered* on NPR or in *Gourmet* magazine, but I had promised myself that on my next trip to California, I would eat there. Now here I was.

I was taken aback when I first arrived at the restaurant. For a place with such an esteemed reputation, the brown-shingled bungalow set behind a large monkey puzzle tree on Shattuck Avenue in Berkeley was surprisingly unassuming. Chez Panisse was making waves at a time when the American food scene was still in its infancy, but I could have easily missed the modest entryway, which was exactly what Chez Panisse intended.

The inception of the restaurant was innocent. In a country where fast food reigns supreme, a band of like-minded people was starting a food revolution in North Berkeley, an area known as the "gourmet ghetto." At the forefront of the revolution was Alice Waters. During a student year abroad in France, instead of reading textbooks and going to class, Alice had spent her time drinking coffee in cafés, soaking up the lifestyle, and falling in love with everything French, especially the local attitude toward food. When she returned to Berkeley, she brought home the ideals she lived by every day in France. Then, with a group of friends who shared her belief in fresh, locally sourced, organic ingredients, Alice opened Chez Panisse in 1971, a restaurant committed to revamping the way Americans perceived food.

Chez Panisse never aimed to be a fancy dining experience. First and foremost, it was a place for Alice and her friends to gather and spend time together. In terms of the menu, the restaurant was dedicated to finding the best-tasting organic foods available and preparing them simply, to enhance, not mask, the beauty of their inherent flavors. The offerings changed daily according to what was in the market and only locally sourced ingredients were used, a new concept at the time.

Stories circulated of foragers who delivered chanterelles from the Berkeley Hills and watercress gathered along stream banks that bordered back roads in nearby Marin County. Nasturtium flowers for salads came from neighborhood gardens. Farmers brought in their sweetest carrots, peppery French breakfast radishes, and succulent figs so ripe that they threatened to burst if you touched them. The milk from goats raised in Sonoma County was used to make goat cheese exclusively for the restaurant. Every summer, a neighbor regularly arrived at the back door with a case of flawless raspberries he'd picked himself just minutes before.

In *40 Years of Chez Panisse: The Power of Gathering*, Alice explains that the intent of the restaurant was to offer "the simple good food of Provence, the atmosphere of tolerant camaraderie and great lifelong friendships, and a respect for both the old folks and their pleasures and the young and their passions." It sought "to re-create an ideal reality where life was lived close to the land, where food was produced by people who were sustained by each other and by the earth itself, where life and work were inseparable, and where the daily pace left time for an afternoon anisette or a restorative game of *pétanqué*."

× ● ×

BY THE TIME NANCY AND I finished our olives and bread and were studying the menu, I was aware of Alice's philosophy at work. The food sounded fresh, clean, and just my style. I wanted one of everything.

"Do you have any questions about the menu?" our server inquired.

"Yes, what is mignonette?" I asked shyly. What I really wanted to ask was, "Can I have a job here?" But that didn't seem appropriate at the moment.

"It's a sauce made with Champagne vinegar, Champagne, minced shallots, and freshly cracked black pepper. Any other questions?"

I laughed and shook my head, biting my lip.

"Would you like to order now?" our server asked.

"We're going to share a half dozen oysters, the pizza with parsley salad, and baked goat cheese," the three quintessentially Chez Panisse dishes I'd heard and read so much about.

The oysters arrived on an austere cream-colored plate loaded with shaved ice. Nestled in the ice were six impeccably shucked Tomales Bay oysters circling a white ramekin holding what I guessed was the mignonette (see page 92). I took the tiny demitasse spoon and drizzled a bit of the sauce onto the top of my first ice-cold oyster. I picked up the half shell, being careful not to lose any of the juices it held, put it to my lips, and, with an almost imperceptible slurp, slid the oyster onto my tongue. My mouth was awash with the fresh, clean, briny taste of ocean balanced by the pungent acidity of the mignonette. A faint hint of cracked pepper lingered after I swallowed. It was perfection in a shell.

That first oyster was so satisfying that I wanted to savor its flavor forever. I sipped my sparkling wine, the tiny bubbles dancing on my tongue. The briny flavor returned and was alive in my mouth again. At that moment, I knew that there was nowhere in the world I'd rather be.

"Remember the raw cherrystones I used to eat with Dad when I was little?" I asked my sister.

We both laughed.

Ever since my very first visit to Chez Panisse, I've saved every single menu. I have quite a large collection.

×

oysters on the half shell with mignonette

My sister Nancy always refused raw seafood, even Dad's special cherrystones. That's why I was so surprised when she picked up an oyster at Chez Panisse, spooned sauce over the top, and slurped it down. She smiled and said, "I like raw seafood now!" I've always been proud of my older sister and never more so than at that moment.

¼ cup dry white wine, such as Sauvignon Blanc, or sparkling wine

1½ to 2 tablespoons white wine or Champagne vinegar

1 shallot, minced

Coarsely cracked black pepper

36 oysters in shells, scrubbed

Flat-leaf parsley sprigs for garnish

Lemon wedges for serving

1 To make the mignonette sauce, in a small bowl, stir together the wine, 1½ tablespoons of the vinegar, the shallot, and the pepper. Taste and adjust with more vinegar if needed.

2 Place the bowl of mignonette sauce on a large platter or tray and surround it with a bed of crushed or shaved ice.

3 Grasp an oyster in one hand, with the top shell (the flatter of the two) facing up and the rounded end (the hinge end) pointing toward you. Using an oyster knife, insert the tip in the hinge and twist the knife to snap the hinge. Carefully slide the knife along the top shell to free the oyster meat, then lift off and discard the top shell. Now, run the knife under the oyster to free it from the bottom shell. As you work, be careful not to spill the liquor in the bottom shell. Nest the oyster on its bottom shell in the ice. Repeat with the remaining oysters, adding them to the ice.

4 Garnish the platter with the parsley and accompany with the lemon wedges.

serves 6

꩜

"CAN I GET YOU SOMETHING ELSE TO DRINK?" our server asked as she whisked away our now-empty wineglasses.

"Sure, what do you suggest?" I responded.

"With the goat cheese salad, a chilled glass of Domaine Tempier Bandol rosé would be a perfect marriage. The wine has notes of peach, alpine strawberries, and blood orange. It's rich and full bodied with bright minerality and can stand up to the creamy fresh goat cheese." She sounded like she knew the wine intimately.

After that description, how could I say no? When I tasted the wine, the fresh, crisp flavors rolling over my taste buds, I was happy I'd agreed. This Boston girl may not have known what an alpine strawberry was or how a blood orange should taste, but I knew this wine was spectacular.

Our salad arrived: a disk of warm goat cheese dusted with crisp, golden brown bread crumbs surrounded by the most gorgeous selection of greens I'd ever seen (see page 96). They looked more like herbs than the iceberg and romaine lettuce I was used to getting at my local Stop & Shop in Cambridge. Tiny jet-black olives were scattered throughout the greens and colorful flower petals were strewn over the top.

I lifted my fork and took my first bite of the goat cheese and the salad. I tasted the creamy, tart warm cheese; the crunchy, subtly salty bread crumbs with hints of fruity olive oil; the cool, herbaceous greens. Each of these flavors on its own would have been palate pleasing, but in juxtaposition, they made the dish transcendent. Its perfection was not only because of the flavors, however. It was also the temperatures and textures: hot, cold; creamy, crunchy; tart, sweet. Although a seemingly simple dish, it was so much more than just a salad.

After the goat cheese salad, I could barely wait for the pizza to arrive. I'd long said that pizza would be my last meal on earth. Now that I knew Chez Panisse could create such a memorable salad, I wondered how the kitchen would do with my beloved pizza.

I could smell the pizza even before it arrived at our table. As our server set it down, I was speechless. In my experience, pizza was doughy crust topped with tomato sauce and gloppy cheese. Sitting in front of us now was a crisp flatbread topped with a heaping mound of tiny, pristine flat-leaf parsley leaves glistening with a garlicky vinaigrette and punctuated with shards of shaved parmigiano-reggiano (see page 99). The golden brown crust, charred in all the right places by the wood-fired oven, was brushed with fruity olive oil. I took a bite and almost squealed with delight. If this had been my last meal on earth, I would be dying happy.

The dessert menu was placed in front of us. I had just eaten one of the best meals in my life; I was completely sated and happy. Maybe we could just skip dessert. Then I remembered the tall counter of temptations that I'd spied on our way in. These weren't sticky sweet, overly rich offerings. I'd be a fool not to try one of the seasonal fruit-forward desserts.

"Let's try the rhubarb *crostata* with chestnut honey ice cream," I suggested.

Chez Panisse is all about sharing, and that's exactly what we did. Passing the *crostata* back and forth, Nancy and I savored every inch of the flaky crust topped with sweet-tart rhubarb (see page 100). As the chestnut honey ice cream, with its complex, almost mysterious dark, spicy flavor melted into the tart, we began to melt into our seats. Through the windows I could see the sun setting in the west.

Our server returned with a little taste of Sauternes. "It's your gift from us."

I smiled up at her and finally managed to ask, "Can I have a job here?"

Everyone laughed, but I was serious.

As we headed out the door and into the setting sun, I made a big life decision. I was leaving Boston and moving west! It was time to get serious about pursuing a life in food.

The unassuming entry to Chez Panisse.

~~~~~

✕

baked goat cheese salad with mesclun and flowers

This is the salad that changed my life. That may sound farfetched, but it's true. Seemingly simple, yet so full of nuanced flavor and texture, one bite set my life on a new course. It officially inspired me to pursue my passion for food.

¾ cup extra-virgin olive oil

6 large thyme sprigs

4 large oregano sprigs

1 large rosemary sprig

¾ pound fresh goat cheese log, 1½ inches in diameter

1 teaspoon Dijon mustard

1 garlic clove, minced

2 tablespoons red wine vinegar
Kosher salt and freshly ground black pepper

1½ cups fine dried bread crumbs, preferably homemade

5 large handfuls of mesclun (mixed baby greens) or torn mixed salad greens

½ cup mixed pesticide-free edible flowers, such as marigolds, nasturtiums, rose petals, and borage, in any combination
Coarsely cracked black pepper

1　In a small saucepan, heat the oil over medium heat until warm. Meanwhile, using the back of a chef's knife, tap the thyme, oregano, and rosemary sprigs to bruise the stems, releasing their flavor. Add the sprigs to the warmed oil and remove from the heat. Let the oil cool to room temperature.

2　Cut the cheese log crosswise into 6 rounds each about ¾ inch thick. Place the cheese rounds in a single layer in a baking dish and pour two-thirds of the oil over them. Strain the remaining oil and reserve it to use as the dressing. Cover the dish and refrigerate for at least 2 hours or up to 3 days.

3　When you are ready to serve, preheat the oven to 400°F.

4　In a small bowl, whisk together the mustard, garlic, and vinegar. Whisk in the reserved oil and season with salt and ground pepper. Set aside.

5　Spread the bread crumbs in a shallow bowl and season with salt and pepper. Remove the goat cheese from the oil and coat each round on all sides with the bread crumbs. Place in a single layer on a rimmed baking sheet and bake until the cheese is bubbling slightly around the edges, 4 to 5 minutes.

6　Just before the cheese rounds are ready, in a medium bowl, toss the mesclun with the reserved dressing. Divide the greens evenly among individual salad plates.

7　Carefully transfer each cheese round to a plate, placing it in the center. Sprinkle the flowers over the mesclun and top the cheese with coarsely cracked pepper.

serves 6

pizzetta with parsley salad and shaved parmigiano-reggiano

Who doesn't love salad and pizza together? Only Chez Panisse could come up with something so novel and execute it so flawlessly.

Pizza dough (page 279)
2 garlic cloves, minced
4 tablespoons extra-virgin olive oil
1 tablespoon freshly squeezed lemon juice
Kosher salt and freshly ground black pepper
⅔ cup coarsely shredded Italian fontina
(about 3 ounces)
⅔ cup coarsely shredded mozzarella
(about 3 ounces)
1 large bunch tender, young flat-leaf parsley
3-ounce chunk parmigiano-reggiano cheese

1 Prepare the pizza dough. Then, 30 minutes before you are ready to bake, place a pizza stone on the lowest rack in the oven and preheat the oven to 500°F or to the highest temperature possible.

2 In a small bowl, combine the garlic and 2 tablespoons of the oil and let stand for 30 minutes.

3 In another bowl, whisk together the remaining 2 tablespoons oil and the lemon juice and season with salt and pepper to make a vinaigrette. Set aside. In a medium bowl, combine the fontina and mozzarella, toss lightly to mix well, and set aside.

4 Lightly flour a work surface. Punch down the dough and transfer it to the floured surface. Divide the dough in half and form each half into a ball, but do not work the dough at all. Roll out 1 dough ball into a 10- to 11-inch circle about ¼ inch thick. (Alternatively, press and stretch the dough on the floured surface into a 10- to 11-inch circle.)

5 Lightly flour a pizza peel (or a rimless cookie sheet) and transfer the dough circle to the peel. Brush the dough circle to within ½ inch of the edge with half of the garlic-infused oil. Sprinkle half of the fontina-mozzarella mixture evenly over the oil-brushed dough.

6 Slide the pizza onto the pizza stone and bake until golden and crisp, 8 to 12 minutes.

7 Meanwhile, in a bowl, toss the parsley leaves with the vinaigrette.

8 When the pizza is ready, using the peel, remove it from the oven and slide it onto a cutting board. Top it with half of the parsley salad. Using a vegetable peeler, shave 10 to 12 paper-thin pieces of parmigiano-reggiano evenly over the top of the pizza, then cut the pizza into wedges and serve. Repeat with the remaining dough and topping ingredients to make a second pizza.

makes two 10- to 11-inch pizzas

rhubarb crostata with chestnut honey ice cream

My mother loves rhubarb, so I've eaten many a bowl of stewed rhubarb in my life. This Chez Panisse dessert—a rustic, free-form tart—was unlike any rhubarb dessert I'd ever tasted. Rather than screaming with sugary sweetness, it made fresh rhubarb the star and had a depth of flavor I didn't realize could exist in a dessert. Tucked into a simple, buttery crust, the finished crostata is paired with delicately flavored honey ice cream for a truly exceptional end to a meal.

PASTRY

1½ cups all-purpose flour
¼ teaspoon kosher salt
¾ cup unsalted butter, ice-cold, cut into 12 equal pieces
4 to 5 tablespoons ice-cold water

RHUBARB FILLING

1¼ pounds rhubarb, trimmed and cut into ½-inch pieces
⅔ cup sugar
2 teaspoons cornstarch
½ teaspoon grated orange zest
¼ teaspoon ground cinnamon
⅛ teaspoon freshly grated nutmeg

Chestnut Honey Ice Cream (page 278)

1 To make the pastry, in a bowl, whisk together the flour and salt. Scatter the butter over the flour mixture and, using a pastry blender or 2 forks, cut in the butter until it is the size of peas. Sprinkle 1 tablespoon of the ice water evenly over the top and mix gently with a fork. Add more ice water, 1 tablespoon at a time, mixing gently after each addition, just until the dough is evenly moist and holds together. Gather the dough gently into a ball and flatten into a thick disk. Wrap the disk in plastic wrap and chill for at least 2 hours or up to overnight.

2 Preheat the oven to 400°F. Lightly flour a work surface and a rolling pin. Unwrap the dough, place on the floured surface, and roll out into a circle 13 inches in diameter and about ¼ inch thick. Using scissors or a knife, trim the edges of the circle so they are even. Roll the dough around the rolling pin, position the pin over a rimmed baking sheet, and unroll the dough onto the baking sheet. Chill for 15 minutes.

3 Meanwhile, make the filling. In a small bowl, combine the rhubarb, sugar, cornstarch, orange zest, cinnamon, and nutmeg and stir to mix well.

4 Remove the dough from the refrigerator and spoon the rhubarb onto the center of the circle. Spread the rhubarb to within about 1½ inches of the edge. Fold the border up and over the filling, forming loose pleats as you go.

5 Bake the crostata until the fruit is soft when pierced and the crust is golden brown, 40 to 45 minutes. Let cool completely on the pan on a cooling rack.

6 To serve, using 1 or 2 wide metal spatulas, carefully transfer the crostata to a serving plate. Cut into wedges and serve each slice with a scoop of the ice cream.

serves 8

CHAPTER 6

THREE
GRAINS
of
SALT

Madeleine Kamman Inc.
A Professional Cooking School
P. O. Box 184, Glen, New Hampshire 03838

PROGRAMS 1984-1985

Course Calendar

1984 Ending March 17, 1984 Basic Chef's
Training Program
July 2-13 – In Annecy, France
Modern French Cuisine Dissected
July 16-27 – in Annecy, France
A Gastronomic Tour of France in the Ka...
November 5-30 – in Glen, New H...
Four-week seminar for...
1985, January...
1986

AS I UNLOADED MY CAR, my eyes welled with tears and my face stung from the icy-cold wind. I was wearing a tweed wool coat I'd bought for sixty bucks in a vintage store back in San Francisco. The wind was howling right through it, and I realized this coat was never going to get me through the winter. Mid-January, the start of a blizzard, and I couldn't work fast enough to haul my belongings from the trunk of my rental car into my new home in the White Mountains of New Hampshire. All the while, I was thinking about how crazy I was to have left San Francisco and returned to the East Coast.

I'd spent the last couple of years living in San Francisco saving every penny I could, and then I'd applied to study with Madeleine Kamman in Glen, New Hampshire. Madeleine was a brilliant teacher with encyclopedic knowledge, an award-winning cookbook author, a historian, linguist, and restaurateur. She was also surrounded by controversy. On one hand, she was known to be generous, warmhearted, loving, and gifted; on the other, she was a merciless perfectionist, brutally frank, demanding, abrasive, and volatile. Still, the waiting list for her ten-month Master Chef Training and Apprenticeship Program was lengthy and as tough to get into as Stanford or Harvard.

I was heartbroken when Madeleine's letter arrived explaining that she had a three-year waiting list and no space for me in the course. I was also determined and promptly wrote back:

> *Dear Madeleine,*
> *I cannot tell you how disappointed I am to receive your letter telling me that your course is full and you have no room for me. I cannot wait three years. I'm thirty-two years old and getting older by the minute, and I'm afraid this is my only chance.*
> *If you can see any way to include me in your course or if you have a cancellation, please let me know. I will be waiting to hear from you.*
> *Sincerely,*
> *Joanne*

A few weeks passed and one day the phone rang. A sweet, soft voice with a melodic French accent on the other end of the line said, "Joanne? Joanne? Is that you? This is Madeleine, Madeleine Kamman."

With my mentor and teacher Madeleine Kamman and with Kim (right), a fellow student.

I nearly fell over.

"I've moved some things around and made space for you in the program. We will begin on January 11. Can you come?" she continued.

I couldn't believe it. And in an instant I knew that of course I would come.

As I unpacked the car and looked at the shingled A-frame house in which I would be living with seven other students, I wanted to get back in the car and drive away. Fear took hold of me. I continued to choke back tears as I unpacked my suitcase and set up my tiny, green bedroom just off the kitchen. That first night I tacked a calendar to my wall and checked off the first day by putting a big black *X* through it.

After I met my fellow residents, I went to bed. I was tired but my mind wouldn't rest. The wall phone, which was right next to my room, rang at least ten different times throughout the night. Thoughts of the snowy drive from Boston, the freezing-cold temperatures, my thin wool coat, the telephone, and my first day of cooking school starting at eight o'clock the next morning swirled in my head. I tossed and turned and never slept a wink. There was a roaring wind outside and an anxious voice that I couldn't quiet inside.

That next morning, the temperatures were so bitter cold that the radio carried warnings not to stay outside for more than five minutes at a time. The temperature, with the wind chill, was 28 degrees below zero. School was only a couple of miles away, but it was impossible to walk. Thankfully, Holly, one of my new housemates, offered me a ride.

The schedule for the master chef and apprenticeship program was grueling. Each morning, Madeleine lectured for four hours. I knew she was brilliant, but I had no idea that her wisdom transcended food. In one breath, she talked about Cro-Magnons cooking food in skin-lined vessels over heated stones; in the next, she taught us about Apicius, the first-century Roman gourmand. You'd have thought we were in an advanced organic chemistry class when we got to hydrolysis, syneresis, emulsification, retrogradation, sanitation, denaturation, and oxidation. She even tackled geology, one of her favorite subjects, describing in detail volcanoes and their effect on the food supply, earthquakes, climate change, glaciers, and various earth materials. Each lecture always returned to food, and from classical cooking to the newest techniques, Madeleine covered it all. To say she was an engaging speaker would be an understatement. Madeleine was captivating.

Toward the end of each lecture, Madeleine would spout recipes, and we'd scribble them down as fast as our fingers could write. In the afternoon, we'd move into the kitchen and try to decipher our scrawl so we could cook the recipes. Once a week, Madeleine would rattle off a list of ingredients she called her "creative list," and we would improvise dishes rather than use recipes. At the beginning of the course, this was challenging and terrifying, but once we became accustomed to it, we found it an excellent way to get us to think creatively so we could begin developing our own cooking style.

Madeleine taught us how to make a thirty-second omelet and stood next to each of us until everyone had mastered the technique. She spent hours over the stove showing us the necessary steps for making an "essence," her transcendent sauce made from rich homemade veal stock (see page 106), bits of meat, and hours of patience and know-how. The first time I sampled its velvety texture and intensely robust flavor, I understood it was worth the time and effort. This woman knew what she was talking about.

rich veal stock

No veal stock is as rich and luxurious as Madeleine Kamman's. Make a big batch on the weekend and store it in the freezer. It's guaranteed to take a special dinner to the next level.

5 pounds veal breast
1 large yellow onion, coarsely chopped
1 large carrot, peeled and coarsely chopped
2 bay leaves
3 thyme sprigs, or ¼ teaspoon dried thyme
12 flat-leaf parsley sprigs

1 Preheat the oven to 400°F. Cut between the ribs of the veal breast, separating the breast into 6 to 8 pieces. Put the pieces in a single layer in a roasting pan, leaving space between the pieces. Roast the veal until russet brown on all sides, about 2 hours.

2 Transfer the veal to a large stockpot. Pour off and discard any fat in the pan, then place the pan over high heat on the stove top. Add about 1½ cups water, bring to a simmer, and deglaze the pan, stirring to dislodge any browned bits on the pan bottom. Pour the deglazing liquid into the stockpot. Add the onion, carrot, bay, thyme, parsley sprigs, and water to cover by 2 inches.

3 Bring to a boil over high heat and immediately reduce the heat to low, skimming off any foam that rises to the surface. Simmer gently, skimming as needed, until the meat is falling off the bone and the stock tastes very rich, about 6 hours. As the level of the liquid decreases in the pot, replenish it with water to maintain the original level.

4 To ease straining, scoop out and discard the larger pieces with a slotted spoon, then strain the stock through a fine-mesh strainer into a large bowl. If using immediately, use a large metal spoon to skim off as much of the fat from the surface as possible. If not using immediately, let cool at room temperature and then refrigerate overnight to solidify the fat. The next day, using a spoon, lift off and discard the fat that solidifies on the surface. Transfer the stock to airtight containers and refrigerate for up to 4 days or freeze for up to 2 months.

makes about 4 quarts

*Working the
room at L'Auberge
Madeleine in
Glen, New
Hampshire. With
the other students
in my class.*

OCCASIONALLY, MADELEINE WOULD LOOK AROUND the room and see that we were tired and that our minds were exhausted from trying to absorb all this new information. At that point, she'd make each of us a cup of hot cocoa loaded with bittersweet chocolate, heavy cream, and just a pinch of sugar. She called herself our "cooking mother," and it was beginning to feel that way.

As the class progressed, it was obvious that each student had his or her own agenda, some more serious than others. Sarah Beth was there for lack of something better to do with her trust fund. Deborah, a nurse who liked baking chocolate-chip cookies, came because she wanted to escape her boring New Jersey life. Justin, an ex–flight attendant and drama queen from the West Village, was looking to improve his Manhattan dinner parties. And Jenny seemed to be there just to gossip and get the group riled up; it didn't take long to realize her knife skills were limited to stabbing fellow classmates in the back. The rest were serious, dedicated students like me: Kim from Juneau, Alaska; Kendra from Miami; and Holly, my generous driver, all became trusted friends.

"Joanne, what does this need?" Madeleine asked one day as she tasted the shrimp and roasted red pepper mousseline I was making.

I sampled my rich, creamy sauce and guessed, "Maybe a little bit of salt?"

Madeleine nodded. I watched in awe as she added one, two, three granules of kosher salt to my bowl. *Three* granules. As I stirred, I wondered, how could that possibly make a difference? But when I put the mousseline to my lips again, it was altered. Flavors that were muddled before now came through brilliantly. The sweetness of both the shrimp and the red pepper was accented by the subtle tang of lemon juice from my hollandaise base. My sauce had been good before, but now it was great. This is precisely why I'm here,

I smiled to myself. *This woman is a genius.* I kept my head down and continued stirring the contents of the bowl.

As we cooked each afternoon, Madeleine moved with eagle eyes and determined steps from person to person, tasting food, correcting, admonishing, praising, and comparing one student to another. She had no filter; thoughts went directly from her mind to her mouth.

One minute she was full of warmth and love. But the next moment she would snap because Sarah Beth wasn't stirring the crème anglaise with a flat-bottom wooden spoon in the correct direction.

"I just showed you how to make a crème anglaise! Why don't you ever listen?" Madeleine demanded as she grabbed the proper wooden spoon, stepped in front of Sarah Beth briskly, and began stirring the pot herself.

On another occasion, Jenny roasted veal breast for stock at 425°F instead of 400°F. When the veal bones came out of the oven, they were dark brown and charred. I immediately knew there would be trouble. Veal stock was Madeleine's pride and joy, and no one made a stock better than she did.

"Do you want a bitter sauce, Jenny? Do you know how much those veal bones cost? Are you sure this is a career for you, or are you just passing time here?" Madeleine spewed.

Madeleine had an insatiable desire for perfection. She also had the uncanny ability to read people's minds. She could tell who was serious about the program and who wasn't. She also played favorites. These characteristics would prove to be her enemy.

A few of us, Kim, Kendra, Holly, and me, escaped Madeleine's scrutiny for good reason. We were there to learn and we respected Madeleine, and Madeleine, who recognized that, was good to us because of it. The less serious students didn't get the same treatment and took offense. Madeleine was hard on them. Usually someone went home crying. I could feel trouble brewing.

Every night, I stayed in my room with the door closed, writing notes and studying material from the day's lecture. Just beyond my threshold, my not-so-serious housemates sat around the kitchen table drinking and talking about the horrible things Madeleine had done that day. Most nights I wore ear plugs to bed.

On Saturday nights, we ran a fifty-seat restaurant called L'Auberge Madeleine. We spent the day cooking Madeleine's elaborate menus, and in the evening we were each assigned a role by Madeleine on a rotating basis: one of us acted as host, a couple of us were servers, another made appetizers, two were on the hot line, one served desserts and made coffee, and one unlucky soul got to do the dishes. We rotated through all of the roles so we could learn all of the tasks. Despite our different personalities and varying levels of dedication, we ran the restaurant successfully and got rave reviews, but not without many snafus and lots of laughs. The coffee system consisted of a Mr. Coffee machine, and because we didn't have a true line for cooking, we plated dinners on the oven door to keep the plates warm. One memorable night, the rod holding several fur coats collapsed and tumbled into the dining room. We thought it was a bear coming out of the closet.

We worked for days prepping Madeleine's elaborate and refined recipes for the weekend restaurant for the first couple months. A few stand-out recipes follow, including a beef tenderloin roulade (see page 110), a creamy corn and jalapeño pasta (see page 113), and a gorgeous Genoa cake (see page 114).

One of Madeleine Kamman's signature dishes, beef roulade with mushrooms.

beef roulade with mushrooms

1 ounce dried porcini mushrooms (about 1 cup)

1 cup boiling water

1 whole beef tenderloin, 6 pounds, trimmed
   Kosher salt and freshly ground black pepper

2 tablespoons extra-virgin olive oil

1 garlic clove, crushed

2 pounds fresh button mushrooms, stem ends
   trimmed and coarsely chopped

1 tablespoon unsalted butter

10 cups rich veal stock (page 106)

1   In a heatproof bowl, combine the porcini and boiling water. When cool, drain, capturing the liquid in a bowl and leaving behind any sediment. Finally chop the porcini and reserve the mushrooms and liquid separately.

2   Cut off the tapered end ("tail," about 1½ inches) and then the long "chain" (side muscle) that runs along the side of the tenderloin. Cut the trimmings into ½-inch pieces and reserve for the sauce.

3   Starting halfway up from the bottom, make a horizontal cut about ½ inch deep the entire length of the tenderloin. Then, follow the cut in a spiral pattern to create a single piece of meat that will open flat. Using a meat pounder, pound the tenderloin lightly to create an even thickness overall. Season with salt and pepper.

4   In a large frying pan, heat 1 tablespoon of the oil over medium-high heat. Add the garlic and cook until golden, about 1 minute. Remove and discard the garlic. Add the fresh mushrooms and cook, stirring occasionally, until they give off their liquid, 5 to 8 minutes. Add the porcini and continue to cook until the liquid has evaporated, 3 to 4 minutes. Season with salt and pepper, let cool, then spread the mushrooms evenly over the tenderloin, leaving a ½-inch border on all sides. Starting from a long side, roll up the tenderloin tightly and tie at 1-inch intervals with kitchen string. Season the rolled beef with salt and pepper. Cut the rolled beef in half crosswise. Preheat the oven to 400°F.

5   To make the sauce, in a heavy frying pan, melt the butter over medium heat. Add the reserved beef pieces and cook, stirring occasionally, until russet brown on all sides, 30 to 40 minutes. Watch carefully to ensure the pieces do not burn. Pour off and discard any fat from the pan. Return the pan to medium-low heat, add the mushroom liquid, and simmer until the liquid is reduced by half. Add 3 cups of the stock, bring to a simmer, and deglaze the pan, stirring to dislodge any browned-on bits from the pan bottom. Continue to cook the stock and beef cubes until the stock has reduced and is a bubbling glaze. Add 3 more cups stock and reduce until 1 cup remains. Add the remaining 4 cups stock and simmer until the sauce has reduced and coats the back of a spoon. Remove from the heat, pour through a fine-mesh strainer into a saucepan, and keep warm over low heat.

6   Meanwhile, in a large ovenproof frying pan, heat the remaining 1 tablespoon oil over high heat. Add the beef rolls and brown all over, turning them as needed, 6 to 8 minutes. Transfer the pan to the oven and cook until an instant-read thermometer inserted into the center of a roll registers 130°F, 25 to 35 minutes. Remove the pan from the oven, transfer the beef rolls to a cutting board, tent loosely with foil, and let rest for 10 minutes.

7   To serve, slice the beef rolls, removing the strings, and place the slices on warmed individual plates. Spoon the sauce around the edges.

serves 8 to 10

jalapeño pasta
with creamed corn

PASTA

    1 tablespoon olive oil
    1 jalapeño chile, seeded and minced
    2 shallots, minced
    ¼ cup chopped cilantro
    3 large eggs
    2 large egg yolks
    2 cups all-purpose flour
    ½ cup fine-grind white or yellow cornmeal
    ½ cup semolina flour
    ¾ teaspoon kosher salt
      Pinch of cayenne

SAUCE

    3 cups heavy whipping cream
    1½ cups fresh corn kernels
      Kosher salt and freshly ground black pepper
    2 red onions, thinly sliced
    2 tablespoons unsalted butter
    1 teaspoon white wine vinegar
    ½ cup chopped cilantro
      Grated pecorino cheese for serving

1 To make the pasta, heat the oil over low heat in a frying pan. Add the jalapeño and shallots and cook, stirring occasionally, until soft, about 3 minutes. Transfer to a bowl, add the cilantro, stir, and let cool completely. Add the whole eggs and egg yolks and whisk until well blended.

2 In a food processor, combine the flour, cornmeal, semolina, salt, and cayenne and pulse to mix well. With the food processor running, add enough of the jalapeño-egg mixture to moisten the flour mixture evenly (you may not need all of it) and process just until the mixture looks crumbly and almost holds together. Pinch a little of the dough between your fingers; it should feel moist

but not sticky. If it seems dry, add a little egg mixture or water, 1 teaspoon at a time. Gather the dough into a ball, wrap in plastic wrap, and let stand at room temperature for 1 hour.

3 Set up a pasta machine with the rollers on the widest setting and dust them with flour. Divide the dough into 4 portions; keep covered with plastic wrap until ready to use. Flatten 1 portion ½ inch thick and pass it through the rollers. Fold the dough into thirds and pass it through again; repeat this 3 or 4 times. Continue to pass the dough through progressively narrower settings, until it is $\frac{1}{16}$ inch thick. Cut the pasta sheet into 10- to 12-inch lengths. Switch to the fettuccine cutting attachment, and pass the pasta sheets, one at a time, through the cutter. Toss the strands with flour. Line a baking sheet with a kitchen towel, dust the towel with flour, and transfer the fettuccine to the towel. Repeat with the remaining dough portions.

4 To make the sauce, in a heavy saucepan, bring the cream to a boil over medium-high heat, reduce the heat to medium-low, and simmer until reduced to 2 cups. Remove from the heat, add the corn, season with salt and pepper, and keep warm.

5 Sprinkle the red onions with salt and let stand for 30 minutes. Rinse under cold water and pat dry. In a frying pan, melt the butter over medium-high heat. Add the onions and cook, stirring, until they are slightly crunchy, 3 to 4 minutes. Add the vinegar and season with salt and pepper.

6 Bring a pot of salted water to a boil. Add the pasta, stir well, and cook until al dente, 2 to 3 minutes. Drain the pasta and return it to the pot. Reheat the corn mixture, then add it and half of the cilantro to the pasta and toss to mix. Serve the pasta topped with the onions, the remaining cilantro, and the pecorino.

serves 6 to 8

genoa cake with pistachio crème anglaise

PISTACHIO CRÈME ANGLAISE
- ¾ cup pistachios
- 2 cups whole milk
- ½ cup granulated sugar
- 8 large egg yolks
- Large pinch of kosher salt
- 2 tablespoons kirsch

CAKE
- 1¼ cups granulated sugar
- ¾ cup blanched almonds, coarsely chopped
- ¾ cup pistachios
- Pinch of kosher salt
- 4 large eggs
- ½ cup unsalted butter, at room temperature
- 2 tablespoons kirsch
- ¼ cup cornstarch, sifted
- ¼ cup all-purpose flour, sifted
- ½ teaspoon baking powder

Powdered sugar for dusting

1   To make the crème anglaise, combine the pistachios and milk in a blender and process until smooth. Transfer to a bowl, cover with plastic wrap, and refrigerate overnight.

2   The next day, line a fine-mesh strainer with cheesecloth, set it over a heavy saucepan, and strain the pistachio mixture into the pan. Discard the contents of the strainer. Add the granulated sugar to the pistachio milk, place over medium heat, and heat until small bubbles appear along the edges of the pan. Meanwhile, in a bowl, whisk the egg yolks. Do not allow any foam to form.

3   When the milk is ready, remove from the heat. Slowly drizzle the scalded milk into the egg yolks while whisking. Pour the mixture back into the saucepan, place over medium heat, and heat, stirring, until the mixture thickens and coats the back of a spoon, 2 to 3 minutes. Do not allow the mixture to boil. It is ready when your finger leaves a trail on the back of a spoon that does not flow back together. Remove from the heat and pour through a fine-mesh strainer into a bowl. Add the salt and kirsch and whisk to cool slightly. Let cool for 10 minutes, then cover with plastic wrap, pressing it directly onto the surface. Let cool to room temperature, then chill before using.

4   To make the cake, preheat the oven to 325°F. Lightly butter a 9-inch round cake pan, then line the bottom with parchment paper.

5   In a food processor, combine the granulated sugar, almonds, pistachios, and salt and process until the nuts are finely ground. Add the eggs, butter, and kirsch and pulse until well combined. Transfer to a bowl. In a small bowl, sift together the cornstarch, flour, and baking powder. Using a rubber spatula, fold the cornstarch mixture into the butter mixture just until evenly combined.

6   Transfer the batter to the prepared pan. Bake the cake until golden and a wooden toothpick inserted into the center comes out clean, 35 to 40 minutes. Let cool in the pan on a cooling rack for 10 minutes. Run a thin knife blade along the inside edge of the pan to loosen the cake, then invert the cake onto the rack, lift off the pan, peel off the parchment, and let the cake cool completely.

7   Using parchment paper, cut out a decorative stencil for the top of the cake. Place the cake on a cake plate, place the stencil on top, dust with powdered sugar, and remove the stencil. Slice and serve with the crème anglaise.

serves 8

I DIDN'T THINK SPRING WOULD EVER COME. We'd spent January through April enduring the worst that a New Hampshire winter had to offer, and I'd drawn a lot of black *X*s on my calendar, counting down the days. The trees were finally beginning to bud, and the vibrant green heads of daffodils were poking out of the brown earth. I could smell spring in the air, and I was thrilled. But not everyone felt as happy as I did.

Four of the students, Sarah Beth, Deborah, Justin, and Jenny, gathered the rest of us in the kitchen of our A-frame and begged us to revolt against Madeleine's behavior. They were planning to quit the program and wanted us to join them.

"We're being treated unfairly. She hates us. She's nice to the four of you and jumps on the four of us all the time. We can't do anything right. We're paying for this abuse."

Their timing was terrible. For weeks, the rest of us had been studying for our written exam, which was to take place the next morning. We were committed to Madeleine's program and we weren't willing to join their rebellion.

That night, the disgruntled students called a meeting with Madeleine and told her they'd decided not to take the exam. They weren't willing to put up with her any longer and were quitting. Immediately after the meeting, they packed their bags and left.

Close to midnight, the telephone rang. I ran to the kitchen to find Madeleine on the other end of the line speaking as if someone had just punched her in the gut. She told me the news and then said that her heart was racing so madly that she was on the way to the hospital.

On a visit to Mr. Meyer's Mussel Farm in Maine with Madeleine and my classmates.

⤫

That night, the four of us who remained talked until we were talked out. The next morning, we arrived at school ready to take our exam. Madeleine met us at the door wearing a heart monitor. Her face was pale and drawn, and her hair and clothes were rumpled. She appeared defeated. It was heartbreaking to see how personally she had taken the whole ordeal. She shared with us a quote from Einstein by which she lived: "Great spirits have always encountered violent opposition from mediocre minds." With a deep, cleansing breath, she guided us into the classroom where she would administer the exam. We were moving on.

The next four hours were intense. My fingers grew numb as I answered question after question: How do you make a proper génoise? What are the proportions for a classic puff pastry? What are the basic measurements for brioche? When it was over, I was exhausted, and I was relieved to have it behind me. It was a tough exam but my studying had paid off. I knew I'd nailed it.

My reward? The portion of Madeleine's course we'd all been waiting for. Early the next morning, the four remaining students boarded an Air France flight with Madeleine and flew to Paris. We would spend the next two months teaching with Madeleine in Annecy in the Haute-Savoie region of southeastern France.

I fell hopelessly in love with Annecy. The town was made up of medieval turreted castles, meandering canals, the Pont des Amours (Lovers' Bridge), turquoise Lake Annecy with its elegant white swans, and the picturesque, snow-capped Alps as an ever-present backdrop. It was charming. It was romantic. It was everything I needed it to be at the time.

We spent our days at Madeleine's side doing prep, washing dishes, and shopping for her cooking classes. After class, she took us for walks along the winding canals and down idyllic streets lined with pastel houses decorated with rainbows of geraniums cascading from window boxes. She showed us her favorite spots for ice cream, copper pots, and the local handmade pottery. She was more relaxed in her own country, eating the food she loved and speaking her native tongue. It made me sad to think that half of our classmates were missing Madeleine in her element. They were crazy to have passed up this once-in-a-lifetime experience.

Sometimes at night we'd go out for dinner. *Raclette* was one of Madeleine's favorite local dishes. I'll never forget the first time the enormous wheel of cheese on a metal stand appeared beside our table. As a candle melted the cheese, Madeleine showed us how to scrape the soft, oozing cheese onto our plates. As we ate our molten portions with boiled potatoes, cornichons, pickled onions, and lots of Riesling, we felt like locals in this land of culinary riches. One particular night, while enjoying *raclette*, talking, laughing, and carrying on, our candle somehow set the nearby lace curtains on fire. Fortunately, we managed to douse the flames quickly. Madeleine offered to pay for the damage, but the owner said it wasn't necessary. We laughed all the way home.

Each day, class culminated with a substantial lunch that finished around five in the afternoon. One evening, Madeleine invited Holly and me to go for a drive in the country.

"Kids, do you want to go for a ride?" She loved calling us kids.

"Sure!" I said. "Do you want me to drive?"

We weren't in the car fifteen minutes when Madeleine recognized a familiar little roadside restaurant and screeched, "Stop!" As I parked the car, she excitedly announced, "I love this place. I used to come here with my sons. Let's go in and have a coffee."

With Madeleine, you didn't say no. It was best to go along with whatever she suggested because you were bound to have an adventure.

"May I help you?" inquired the maître d'.

"Yes, we'd love to have coffee and dessert."

Dessert? We'd just eaten a late multicourse lunch not more than an hour ago and we were stuffed.

"Oh, the menu looks so good. Before we get dessert, I'd love to order the small fried freshwater fish from Lake Annecy. It's the specialty here. And let's get a bottle of local Pinot Gris. Okay with you?"

Even though it felt like my arteries were starting to block, I had to admit those little golden fried fish were awfully tasty. We ate the entire plate.

"Excusez-moi monsieur, avez-vous la tartiflette ce soir?"

"Mais bien sûr Madame. C'est notre spécialité."

"Excellent! Alors nous prendrons une tartiflette et une autre bouteille de vin s'il vous plait?"

I could hardly believe my ears. She was asking for the local specialty, *tartiflette*, a cross between potato gratin and *raclette*, made of waxy potatoes, heavy cream, smoked bacon, *reblochon* cheese, garlic, and onions. There may not be another dish on earth with more calories.

That night taught me that you can definitely have too much cheese, bacon, and potatoes. As I forced the last couple of bites into my mouth, I thought I might have a heart attack right there on the spot.

Driving home with Madeleine in the passenger seat, I could sense her nodding off. It was late, and the three of us we were beyond full and tired. Her head finally gave way and fell onto my shoulder. She snored during the entire trip back to Annecy. Holly and I laughed until we cried; Madeleine didn't even stir.

No one wanted to leave Annecy, but after two months, it was time to head back to New Hampshire. Before we left, Madeleine informed us she had a little treat in mind.

"What do you say, kids? We have two days before our flight leaves from Paris. On our way, let's drive to Geneva, have lunch with Frédy, spend the night, and then the next day head to Dijon for lunch with Paul. I'll call Frédy and Paul right now and make reservations. Yes?"

We were giddy. Madeleine was offering to take us to lunch at Frédy Giradet's three-star Michelin restaurant in Geneva, followed by lunch the next day at Paul Bocuse's three-star Michelin restaurant in Dijon. These two friends were world-class rock star chefs. The mere thought of meeting and dining with Frédy and Paul was thrilling to us novices. The experience did not disappoint. Frédy's restaurant, in the center of Geneva, was elegant and the food superb. When he entered the dining room, everyone in it stopped for a moment and took note of this legendary chef. I thought I might fall off my chair when he walked toward our table.

Reunited with Madeleine in New York in 1998 when she received the James Beard Foundation Lifetime Achievement Award.

smoked quail with grapes, hazelnuts, and sherry dressing

The first time I tested this recipe at school, I nearly smoked out the other students and the kitchen smelled like Earl Grey tea for a week. It turns out quail takes on a delicate smoky flavor quite quickly. Try other varieties of tea leaves for equally interesting results.

QUAIL

- 6 semiboneless quail, 4 ounces each (bone-in wings and drumsticks)
- 2 tablespoons extra-virgin olive oil
  Kosher salt
- ¼ cup loose Earl Grey tea leaves

SALAD

- ¾ cup hazelnuts
- 1½ tablespoons sherry vinegar
- 4 tablespoons extra-virgin olive oil
  Kosher salt and freshly ground black pepper
- 1 large head escarole, leaves torn into 2-inch pieces
- 1½ cups green or Muscat grapes, halved and seeded
- 3 ripe red plums, halved, pitted, and cut into ½-inch-wide wedges

1 Rub the quail with 1 tablespoon of the oil, then sprinkle all over with salt. Put the tea in the bottom of a dry wok or large, heavy-bottomed soup pot. Place a cooling rack over the tea, making sure it is not touching the tea. Arrange the quail in a single layer on the rack. Place the wok on the stove top and turn on the heat to high. When the tea begins to smoke, cover the pan tightly and set your timer for 4 minutes. After 4 minutes, turn off the heat and leave the quail in the covered pan for 20 minutes. After 20 minutes, uncover the pan and transfer the quail to a plate.

2 While the quail are resting in the wok, ready the salad ingredients. In a small frying pan, toast the hazelnuts over medium heat, shaking the pan occasionally, until they are very fragrant and have darkened, about 5 minutes. Transfer the warm nuts to a coarse-textured kitchen towel and rub vigorously to remove the skins. Do not worry if tiny bits of skin remain. Coarsely chop the nuts and set aside.

3 To make the dressing, in a small bowl, whisk together the vinegar and oil. Season with salt and pepper. Ready the escarole, grapes, and plums.

4 Heat a large frying pan over medium-high heat and add the remaining 1 tablespoon oil. Add the quail, breast side down, and cook, turning once, until golden, 3 to 4 minutes on each side. Transfer to a plate and let cool while you finish the salad.

5 In a large bowl, combine the escarole, grapes, plums, and hazelnuts and toss to mix. Drizzle with the dressing and toss gently to coat evenly.

6 Divide the salad evenly among salad plates. Top each serving with a warm quail.

serves 6

In contrast, Paul Bocuse was warmer and clearly a closer friend of Madeleine's. It was obvious when they kissed on both cheeks. Later, when we finished lunch, Paul invited us to come and dance with him in this cavernous room filled with circus rides and magical music. He asked me to dance and I couldn't say no. I was dancing with Paul Bocuse. At the end, he kissed me on both cheeks. I didn't wash my face for a week.

It was the perfect way to end our two memorable months in France.

Our return to New Hampshire was at the height of summer, just in time for the abundance of fresh local produce. After overindulging in heavy cream, butter, farm cheeses, foie gras, puff pastry, and daily croissants in France, I'd put on a few pounds. Beautiful farm-fresh fruits and vegetables were just what I needed to ease my bursting buttons.

The first thing we did was stock the restaurant to get it back up and running. It was soon humming along. I tacked my calendar onto the wall and once again started crossing off the days. Although I was busy and happy, I was longing for home. It was the middle of August, and we had just sixty-two days to go until our program was complete on October 15.

We ran L'Auberge Madeleine under Madeleine's supervision for the final two months. For a two-week period on a rotating basis, one of us acted as executive chef, which meant planning the menus, doing the purchasing, managing the inventory, and overseeing the prep and service. Our final exam was a restaurant review written by Madeleine, a restaurant critic, two customers, and a previous graduate.

Just the words *executive chef* sent shivers up my spine. My trip to France and the "creative list" exercises we'd done for months had given me inspiration. But I was still a nervous wreck when my turn came to serve as executive chef. I worked hard to develop the best menu possible, and when I presented my dishes to Madeleine, she was as ecstatic as a proud mom.

"You've got some great stuff here, kiddo! There are just a couple of minor adjustments I'd make, but you're onto something. With the carrot soup, you're adding some sambuca to pump up the anise flavor, right? Maybe we can even find some anise seeds in Boston and add those. What do you think?"

"I love it!" I said. Diners were going to fall for this soup before it ever crossed their lips. Its vibrant orange color and the sweet smell of fresh carrot mingling with heady notes of licorice would pave the way for their first satiny sip (see page 122).

"And for your lardon salad, how about putting a poached egg on top? That way, when the guest breaks into the egg, it will run all over the greens and bring some richness?"

I loved the idea of a bacon-and-egg salad (see page 122).

"I'm very impressed with how you smoked the quail for the salad made with grapes and plums. Brilliant! And I love that you added hazelnuts. What's in the vinaigrette?"

"I was thinking sherry vinegar and extra-virgin olive oil. The nutty-flavored sherry vinegar will work well with the hazelnuts and lightly smoked quail. Don't you think?"

"Absolutely! Now, my only issue is the salmon. We can't get especially fresh salmon up here in the mountains. How about if we take a drive to Boston on Monday to pick up some Nova Scotia salmon. You up for that?"

Tying a
medallion
for the salmon
with cucumber
and mint
fettuccine recipe
on page 124.

〜〜〜

×

"Of course!"

The next Monday, the start of my stint as executive chef, Madeleine and I tucked a cooler into the trunk of her VW and headed to Boston to do some shopping. We zipped around the city and found everything we needed: fresh Nova Scotia salmon, a really good bottle of sherry vinegar for the smoked quail salad (see page 119), anise seeds for my soup, and fresh ginger to make a green apple tarte tatin (see page 127) I had planned for dessert. When our shopping was done, we headed toward the car.

"Hey kiddo, you hungry? How about we stop in the North End and have a plate of pasta?" Madeleine asked.

I couldn't say no. As we sat over a plate of pasta carbonara and a glass of Chianti riserva, I realized that Madeleine was more than my brilliant teacher and mentor. At some point during these long months together, she had also become my cherished friend.

"Would you like me to drive home?" I offered. I could see Madeleine was exhausted.

We weren't even to Route 93, just ten minutes outside of Boston, when Madeleine started to doze. As her head once again fell onto my shoulder, I knew she was comfortable with me. It was just the two of us—a sweet moment I have always remembered.

My two-week turn as executive chef went off without a hitch, except that the dishwasher broke and the Mr. Coffee machine went kaput in the middle of service, giving me a real glimpse into the challenges of the restaurant business. Despite those mishaps, my reviews were stellar.

I packed my suitcase and the last of my belongings and then put the final *X* on my calendar, drawing it through October 15. At the beginning of the year, I couldn't wait for this day to come. Now that it was here, I had mixed emotions. I was eager to get back to my home, my life, my friends in San Francisco, but I knew I would miss Madeleine and the camaraderie that I'd found in her kitchen. I'd learned a lot about food and cooking that year, but I'd also learned a lot about people and life. I was ready to go back home and begin the next chapter in my life, this time as a bona fide chef.

carrot soup with anise

2 teaspoons anise seeds
2 tablespoons unsalted butter
1 large yellow onion, chopped
2 pounds carrots, peeled and cut into pieces
6 cups vegetable stock (page 276), chicken stock (page 276), or water
    Kosher salt and freshly ground black pepper
1 cup heavy whipping cream
5 tablespoons anise-flavored liqueur, such as sambuca, ouzo, or Pernod
¼ cup crème fraîche
2 tablespoons chopped chives

1 Toast the anise seeds in a small frying pan over medium heat until fragrant, about 2 minutes. Transfer to a spice grinder and coarsely grind.

2 In a soup pot, melt the butter over medium heat. Add the onion and anise seeds and cook, stirring occasionally, until the onion is soft, 7 to 10 minutes. Add the carrots and cook, stirring occasionally, for 10 minutes. Pour in the stock, bring to a simmer, and cook until the carrots are tender, about 15 minutes. Remove from the heat.

3 In batches, purée the soup in a blender until very smooth, 2 to 3 minutes for each batch. Strain the purée through a fine-mesh strainer into a pot and season with salt and pepper. Place over medium heat, stir in the cream, and heat until hot. Stir in 4 tablespoons of the anise-flavored liqueur and season with salt and pepper.

4 In a bowl, stir together the crème fraîche and remaining liqueur and season with salt. Ladle the soup into warmed bowls. Drizzle with the crème fraîche and sprinkle with the chives.

serves 6

lardon salad, beaujolais style

2 shallots, minced
½ pound thick-sliced bacon, cut crosswise into ⅜-inch-wide pieces, and cooked until crisp, with fat reserved separately
¼ cup extra-virgin olive oil
¼ cup sherry vinegar
    Kosher salt and freshly ground black pepper
½ baguette, cut into ¼-inch-thick slices
3 heads frisée, leaves separated
1 head escarole, leaves torn into 2-inch pieces
2 cups cherry tomatoes, halved crosswise
6 large eggs, poached (page 277)

1 Preheat the oven to 400°F. In a large frying pan over medium-low heat, cook the shallots in 2 tablespoons of the bacon fat, stirring, until soft, about 3 minutes. Stir in the bacon and oil, and remove from the heat. Stir in the vinegar and season with salt and pepper.

2 Lightly brush the baguette slices on one side with bacon fat and place in a single layer on a rimmed baking sheet. Sprinkle the slices lightly with salt. Place in the oven and toast until light golden, about 10 minutes. Set aside.

3 In a large bowl, combine the frisée, escarole, and tomatoes and toss to mix. If the dressing has cooled, warm over medium heat for 1 minute. Drizzle the dressing over the vegetables and toss gently to coat evenly. Divide among salad plates. Garnish the plates with the baguette slices.

4 Place a poached egg on top of each salad. Sprinkle each egg with salt and pepper and serve.

serves 6

salmon with cucumber and mint fettuccine

One of the things that made Madeleine such a wonderful teacher was her ability to inspire creativity in her students. She was the driving force behind the cucumber "fettuccine" and salmon medallions in this elegant dish.

6 center-cut salmon steaks, 8 to 9 ounces each
1 cup fish stock (page 276) or bottled clam juice
1 cup heavy whipping cream
2 shallots, minced
1 cup Sauvignon Blanc or other dry white wine

LEMON DRESSING
1 tablespoon freshly squeezed lemon juice
2 tablespoons extra-virgin olive oil
   Kosher salt and freshly ground black pepper

2 English cucumbers, halved crosswise
3 tablespoons chopped fresh mint, plus small
   leaves from 6 sprigs for garnish
12 thin lemon slices for garnish

1   Working as closely as possible to the large bone in the center of a salmon steak, cut around the bone and remove and discard the bone and attached ribs. Remove any skin or pin bones. You will end up with 2 pieces of fish, each one with a wide end and a narrower end. Repeat with the remaining steaks. Position the pieces from each steak together in a yin-and-yang pattern, forming a medallion. Secure by tying kitchen string around the exterior or with toothpicks (see page 121).

2   In a saucepan over medium-high heat, simmer the stock until reduced by half. In another saucepan, simmer the cream over medium-high heat until reduced by one-fourth, then add the cream to the stock and set aside. In a third saucepan, combine the shallots and wine over medium-high heat and simmer until 3 tablespoons remain when the solids are pressed. Add the wine reduction to the stock and cream reduction and set aside.

3   To make the dressing, in a small bowl, whisk together the lemon juice and oil. Season with salt and pepper and set aside.

4   Using a vegetable peeler or mandoline, slice a cucumber half lengthwise into long, paper-thin ribbons until you reach the core with the seeds, then rotate the cucumber and repeat to cut more ribbons. Continue until only the core with the seeds remains. Discard the core and repeat with the remaining cucumber halves. Place the ribbons in a bowl and add the chopped mint.

5   Brush a large nonstick frying pan lightly with olive oil and place over medium heat. Add the salmon and cover with a lid slightly smaller than the circumference of the pan, resting it directly on the salmon. Reduce the heat to low and cook until the salmon is opaque, about 3 minutes. Turn the salmon, re-cover, and cook until each medallion reveals a thick line of pink in the center, 2 to 3 minutes longer. Season with salt and pepper.

6   While the salmon is cooking, reheat the cream sauce over low heat. Drizzle all but 1 tablespoon of the lemon dressing over the cucumber and mint and toss to coat evenly.

7   To serve, divide the cream sauce among individual plates. Top with the cucumber mixture, place a salmon medallion on each, then brush the top of the salmon with the reserved lemon dressing and finish with 2 lemon slices. Garnish with the mint leaves.

serves 6

golden apple ginger tarte tatin

I'll never forget watching my classmate Jenny flip a tarte tatin and lose half of it on the floor. Don't be a Jenny. The trick is not to hesitate: flip the upside-down tart in one fell swoop. This fresh ginger–laced version was the featured dessert during my executive chef weeks at L'Auberge Madeleine. I'm pleased to report we inverted all tarts without any blunders.

6 tablespoons unsalted butter, at room temperature
¾ cup sugar
⅛ teaspoon kosher salt
5 medium-size Golden Delicious apples, peeled, quartered, and cored
1 tablespoon peeled and minced fresh ginger
1 sheet all-butter puff pastry, thawed if frozen
Lightly whipped crème fraîche or vanilla ice cream for serving

1 Preheat the oven to 375°F. Smear the butter over the bottom and sides of a 9-inch ovenproof frying pan to coat evenly, then sprinkle the sugar and salt over the bottom, distributing them evenly.

2 Starting at the outside edge of the pan, make a ring of apple quarters, placing them rounded side down with the narrower end facing the center of the pan and packing them as closely together as possible. Continue to fill the pan in the same manner with as many apple quarters as will fit snugly. Sprinkle the ginger over the apples.

3 Roll out the puff pastry to ⅛ inch thick. Cut out a 10-inch circle from the pastry. Lay the pastry circle on top of the apples, pressing it down over the apples and tucking the edges down along the inside rim of the pan.

4 Place the frying pan over medium heat and cook until the juices from the apples begin to bubble around the edges, 3 to 4 minutes. Continue to cook until the juices turn deep golden brown and thicken slightly, 8 to 10 minutes longer.

5 Transfer the pan to the oven and bake until the apples are tender and the pastry is golden brown and puffed, 45 to 50 minutes. Remove from the oven and let sit for 5 minutes.

6 If you are serving the tart right away, invert a serving plate over the top of the pan, and holding the pan and plate together as tightly as possible, turn them over together, being careful not to get spattered by the hot liquid, then lift off the pan. If some of the fruit pieces have stuck to the pan, use a metal spatula or fork to dislodge them and replace them on the tart.

7 If you are not serving the tart immediately, leave it in the pan. It will keep well at room temperature for 3 hours. When you are ready to serve the tart, place the pan in a 375°F oven for 15 minutes to melt the caramel before unmolding. It is always a good idea to shake the pan back and forth a few times to loosen the apples after 15 minutes of rewarming time.

8 Serve the tart warm or at room temperature with the crème fraîche.

serves 6 to 8

G
IS FOR GARLIC

Garlic pickles, almonds, and olives

Garlicky salad with green beans, tomatoes,
and a warm goat cheese crouton

Catalan noodles with shellfish essence
and aioli

Grilled duck breast with whole baked garlic,

CHAPTER 7

my

CHEZ PANISSE YEARS

'D BEEN DRIVING AROUND for twenty-five minutes and still hadn't found a parking place. I was starting to get frazzled. I was going to be late. When I finally spotted the backup lights of a car that was leaving, I breathed a sigh of relief. I pulled up and waited for what felt like an eternity and then zipped into the space.

Please don't let me be late. Please don't let me be late. Please don't let me be late. The refrain echoed in my head as I grabbed my résumé and purse from the passenger's seat and raced out of the car. I glanced at my watch: 3:10 p.m. Ten minutes late. My stomach lurched. I bolted up five steps and grabbed the door handle of Chez Panisse. I had returned to the West Coast bound and determined to join the food revolution happening within the humble walls of this acclaimed restaurant.

*Alice Waters
in the early years.*

✕

With the strength that would change my life forever, I heaved open the front door. This was my Mecca, the epicenter of California cuisine, and I was about to meet the mother of it all, Alice Waters.

As I walked through the door, the smell of garlic, lemons, and herbs permeated the air. Cases of perfectly ripe purple Mission figs, golden beets with bright green tops, and bright orange persimmons were stacked near the door. Cooks in pristine white jackets rushed around in the downstairs kitchen, all of them intent on their respective tasks.

I timidly approached the first person I encountered and said, "I have a meeting with Alice Waters." My voice came out as a whisper. My face was flushed. Of course there was only one Alice.

It was November 1985, and I'd just finished a year of study with Madeleine Kamman in New Hampshire and France, earning my master chef diploma. Clutching my résumé in one clammy hand, I was hoping my experience with Madeleine was enough to convince Alice to give me a chance.

I peered into the open kitchen and saw Alice heading toward me, her dark, flowing clothes trailing elegantly behind her as she glided my way. Barbara Neyers, Alice's assistant, followed. My kneecaps were shaking so much that I feared I might tip over. I was about to meet my culinary hero.

"Would you like some fresh mint tea?" Alice asked, and in the same breath, "Tell me a little about your time with Madeleine. We've been friends for years. How's she doing?"

I reached for a little white lie, "She's great. What a rewarding year."

"Why Chez Panisse?" she inquired.

"These last several months with Madeleine, I ate my weight in butter and cream. When we studied the food from the different provinces of France, the food I loved most was the food of Provence." I continued, "I like anything fresh. When I was a kid, my mother would have ten vegetables on the table at dinnertime. And I love food made with olive oil. I could drink it."

Alice smiled. Barbara excused herself, saying, "I think you two can take it from here."

"Have you been to Provence?" Alice was curious.

"Yes, I traveled through Provence during my first trip to France when I was twenty-four years old, and I loved it. I loved the simplicity of the food and the freshness. It reminded me of the first time I ate at Chez Panisse."

"And what was it like the first time you ate here?"

My mind flitted back to that magical meal. "It was lunch about four years ago right after the Café opened. That meal changed my life. The produce was the best I'd ever eaten, aside from that of my grandfathers' farms."

"Is that plural? Grandfathers?"

"Yes, both sets of grandparents had farms," I explained. This piqued her interest, and she proceeded to pepper me with questions. Our meeting was starting to feel more like a pleasant conversation than a formal interview. My heart finally stopped pounding in my ears.

"What do you like to cook for your friends?" Alice wanted to know.

"The other night I made ravioli filled with roasted butternut squash and dressed with brown butter and hazelnuts. Or I'll make a simple roasted chicken with a few sprigs of rosemary and slices of lemon under the skin. Then a butter lettuce salad dressed with tangy lemon, extra-virgin olive oil, and a hint of garlic."

"Oh, I want to eat at your house. And how did you fall in love with cooking?"

I couldn't believe my ears. Alice Waters wanted to eat my food. I felt faint, but I kept it together and smiled. "My mom is a professional cook, and so was her father. My mom grew up on a dairy farm in the Berkshires of western Massachusetts and everything the family ate came from the farm. Growing up in New England, we cooked with the season!"

I saw a gentle flicker of excitement in her eyes, egging me on. "You keep talking about your grandfather. Tell me about him."

I dove into the story about picnic lunches under the maple tree. Alice's interest was palpable. She leaned toward me, fist under her chin, genuinely engrossed in my tales of Grampa Sears, his farm, and his food. I knew I had her. No longer was I stumbling over my words and worrying about my résumé. We were talking about food and life and speaking the same language. It was clear to me that there was no turning back. I had found my culinary home.

"Can you come in tomorrow for a tryout? Be here at 6:00 a.m. You can work with David Tanis and the crew downstairs doing prep for the Café to see how you like it."

Ecstatic didn't even begin to describe my reaction. I felt like I was flying as I returned to my car and crumpled up my résumé. I had a tryout at Chez Panisse. Chez Panisse! The restaurant at the center of a food revolution.

The concept of California cuisine was beginning to take shape, although Alice wasn't necessarily using that term yet. Chez Panisse was committed to serving seasonal, local, organic, and sustainable food. It was all about letting California's abundant ingredients speak for themselves—about allowing natural flavors to shine. Because the staff worked hand in hand with local farmers, customers received the freshest produce available. Carrots tasted bright, sweet, and vibrant, and salads tasted of the earth, like the best lettuce does. Only in-season fruits, plucked at the peak of their flavor intensity, were served. Cooking was brief, to highlight innate flavor.

Although the food was of the highest quality, the restaurant itself had an aura of rustic simplicity. It did not feel formal, pretentious, or stuffy like the fine-dining restaurants I was used to. This more casual atmosphere also meant that rigid hierarchies had no place in the Chez Panisse kitchen. That egalitarian approach encouraged cooks to innovate and experiment with flavor, ingredient, and technique combinations across traditional cultural boundaries.

At Chez Panisse, I wouldn't be beholden to classic culinary traditions. I wouldn't have to douse dishes with heavy sauces, cream, and butter. I was dizzy just thinking about the

I met many great chefs while I worked with Alice at Chez Panisse: (from left) me, Nancy Oakes, Traci Des Jardins, Roland Passot, unidentified chef, Jacques Pepín, Alice, and Jacques's daughter, Claudine.

opportunity to learn and create in this fertile environment. I couldn't wait to take my place in the iconic kitchen. But first, I would have to prove myself. I wondered, what would tomorrow's "tryout" entail?

The next morning, with my knife roll clenched under my arm, I arrived promptly at 6:00 a.m. to meet David Tanis, the chef. It was dark outside, but the kitchen was already buzzing with activity. I was given a chef's jacket with the words *Chez Panisse* embroidered on the pocket. My heart skipped a beat.

Along with the other cooks, I spent the first hour peeling cases of onions and bulbs of garlic. With that task complete, I was swiftly assigned to Richard Seibert, who would train me in the art of making pizza and calzone dough. We measured three cups of dry yeast, a few pounds of rye flour, and equal amounts of warm water into a huge commercial Hobart stand mixer. I watched mesmerized as the enormous paddle blended the ingredients into the yeast starter, or sponge, for our dough, its heady aroma a preview of the flavorful crust it would soon become.

While the sponge sat bubbling and frothing, we shifted our focus to salad greens. Richard taught me to pick through the most delicate young leaves of mizuna, red and green Oak Leaf lettuce, feathery frisée, and peppery arugula. As we gently washed the leaves in ice-cold water, we treated the tender lettuces with such love and care that you'd have thought that, except for the frigid temperature, we were washing a newborn baby.

We dried the greens, a few handfuls at a time, in a small Zyliss salad spinner, the same model I had at home. I must have pulled the string on that salad spinner over a thousand times to get through all seven cases of greens for the day. By the time we were finished, my arm felt like it was going to fall off. But there was no time to rest. The pizza dough was now waiting.

We followed the ripe, yeasty smell back to the Hobart and added ingredients to our foamy sponge: unbleached flour, more warm water, a couple of glugs of olive oil, and some kosher salt. We changed to the dough hook and let the powerful machine slowly and gently knead the dough for ten minutes, until it was soft and supple.

"Now, let's knead the dough," Richard said.

"Knead the dough? Didn't the machine just take care of that?" I questioned.

"No, we finish it up by kneading it for a few minutes on the marble counter."

I stared at the enormous mound of dough threatening to spill out of the top of the mixer. "How do you even get it out of the bowl?" I wondered out loud.

Together, the two of us hoisted all forty pounds of dough up and onto a marble butcher block on the counter. Richard divided the dough in half and set half in front of me. As I started kneading the amorphous blob in front of me, I felt self-conscious. It was practically as big as I was.

Each time I pushed the heel of my hand into the dough, my feet lifted off the ground. But I soon found my rhythm and worked that glob into the silky, smooth, perfectly round sphere it was meant to be. I felt fully accomplished as we loaded our dough into big white buckets and set them just inside the walk-in refrigerator. I also felt sore. Every muscle in my body ached. I thought to myself, phew, thank goodness that's over—at least for today.

pizza with gorgonzola and tomatoes

I love Gorgonzola, I love tomatoes, and I love bread. Put them all together and you have one of my favorite pizzas from the wood-fired oven of Chez Panisse Café.

Pizza dough (page 279)
2 garlic cloves, minced
3 tablespoons extra-virgin olive oil
2/3 cup coarsely shredded Italian fontina
(about 3 ounces)
2/3 cup coarsely shredded mozzarella
(about 3 ounces)
Scant 1 cup crumbled Gorgonzola
(about 1/4 pound)
12 plum tomatoes, peeled, halved, seeded,
and chopped
Kosher salt and freshly ground black pepper

1 Prepare the pizza dough. Then, 30 minutes before you are ready to bake, place a pizza stone on the lowest rack in the oven and preheat the oven to 500°F or to the highest temperature possible.

2 In a small bowl, combine the garlic and 2 tablespoons of the oil and let stand for 30 minutes. In a medium bowl, combine the fontina, mozzarella, and Gorgonzola cheeses, toss lightly to mix well, and set aside.

3 In a medium saucepan, heat the remaining 1 tablespoon oil over high heat. Add the tomatoes and bring to a boil, being careful they do not scorch. Reduce the heat to low and simmer uncovered, stirring occasionally, until the tomatoes are very dry and 1/2 cup remains, 15 to 20 minutes. Season with salt and pepper. Let cool.

4 Lightly flour a work surface. Punch down the dough and transfer it to the floured surface. Divide the dough in half and form each half into a ball, but do not work the dough at all. Roll out 1 dough ball into a 10- to 11-inch circle. (Alternatively, press and stretch the dough by hand on the floured surface into a 10- to 11-inch circle.)

5 Generously flour a pizza peel (or a rimless cookie sheet) and transfer the dough circle to the peel. Brush the dough circle to within 1/2 inch of the edge with half of the garlic-infused oil. Spread half of the tomato sauce evenly over the oil-brushed dough, then sprinkle half of the cheese mixture evenly over the tomato sauce.

6 Slide the pizza onto the pizza stone and bake until golden and crisp, 8 to 12 minutes. When the pizza is ready, using the peel, remove it from the oven and slide it onto a cutting board. Cut into wedges and serve immediately. Repeat with the remaining dough and topping ingredients to make a second pizza.

makes two 10- to 11-inch pizzas

calzone with sausage, greens, and ricotta

I've always said pizza would be my last meal on earth. Then I tasted this Chez Panisse calzone: a pillowy puff of golden dough oozing with melted cheese, spicy homemade sausage, and wilted greens. Delivered hot and steamy on a rustic wooden board, it wins last-meal status. Or can I have both?

Calzone dough (page 279)
1 cup ricotta cheese
¾ pound hot Italian sausage (bulk or removed from casing)
2 tablespoons extra-virgin olive oil
1 garlic clove, minced
6 cups young, tender greens, such as beet greens, Swiss chard, escarole, or radicchio, cut into 1-inch-wide strips
Large pinch of red chile flakes
1 tablespoon balsamic vinegar
½ cup grated parmigiano-reggiano cheese
Kosher salt

1 Prepare the calzone dough. Line a strainer with paper towels and place over a bowl. Spoon the ricotta into the prepared strainer and let drain for at least 1 hour or up to overnight in the refrigerator.

2 Heat a large frying pan over medium-high heat. Add the sausage and cook, stirring occasionally and breaking up the sausage with a wooden spoon, until cooked, 8 to 10 minutes. Using a slotted spoon, transfer the sausage to a large bowl and set aside. Pour off and discard the fat from the pan.

3 Return the pan to medium-high heat and add the oil. Add the garlic and cook for 5 seconds to soften. Add the greens and chile flakes and cook, tossing occasionally, until the greens begin to wilt. Add the vinegar and toss together to mix well. Cover and cook until the greens are wilted and tender, 4 to 5 minutes. Transfer to a baking sheet lined with paper towels and let drain and cool completely.

4 Add the greens, ricotta, and parmigiano-reggiano to the sausage and mix well. Season with salt and reserve.

5 Thirty minutes before you are ready to bake, place a pizza stone on the lowest rack in the oven and preheat the oven to 500°F or to the highest temperature possible.

6 Lightly flour a work surface. Punch down the dough and transfer it to the floured surface. Divide the dough into 4 pieces and form each piece into a ball, but do not work the dough at all. Roll out 1 dough ball into a circle about ¼ inch thick.

7 Generously flour a pizza peel (or a rimless cookie sheet) and transfer the dough circle to the peel. Spread one-quarter of the sausage-ricotta mixture on half of the dough circle, leaving a 1-inch border along the edge. Using a pastry brush, lightly moisten the border with water, then fold the uncovered half of the dough over the filling and firmly press the edges together. Roll the sealed edges inward and press again to ensure a tight seal. Repeat with the remaining dough and filling.

8 Slide the calzone onto the pizza stone and bake until golden and crisp, 10 to 12 minutes (you may need to do this in batches). Using the peel, remove the calzone from the oven and slide it onto a cutting board. Let rest for 10 minutes.

makes 4 medium calzone

"OKAY, NOW WE MAKE PASTA DOUGH, a much firmer, drier dough than the pizza dough. It's basically two ingredients, flour and eggs, with the addition of water. It's more about the technique than about the exact quantities. If it's too wet, we can add more flour; if it's too dry, we can add more liquid. Today, we're making red pepper pasta, adding cayenne, crushed red pepper, and lots of freshly cracked black pepper. We'll serve it in the Café with our fennel sausage, some red peppers, and crisp bread crumbs that we'll toast in the wood oven with lots of olive oil," Richard instructed.

I was salivating, "You're making me hungry. When is lunch?" I laughed, only half joking.

Forty pounds of red pepper pasta dough later, it was 11:00 a.m. and time to break for the staff meal, endearingly called the family meal. Our dough needed to rest for thirty minutes anyway. Although I was physically exhausted, I was still as excited as a kid on Christmas morning. I was cooking, really contributing to the kitchen at Chez Panisse. I was so excited to get back to my pasta dough that I hardly remember the details of that first family meal.

We clamped a hand-crank, commercial-grade Imperia pasta machine onto the counter and proceeded to roll sheet after sheet of soft, supple, delicate rose-colored pasta. It didn't take nearly as long as I expected. We dusted the fettuccine with rice flour and laid it out onto baking sheets lined with kitchen towels. As I slid each pan of pink pasta dough into the speed rack in the walk-in, I smiled with pride.

Working on the line in the Café at Chez Panisse.

pepper fettuccine with sausage, sweet peppers, and bread crumbs

FRESH PEPPER FETTUCCINE

- 2 cups 00 flour
- ¼ teaspoon kosher salt
- ¼ teaspoon cayenne
- ½ teaspoon red chile flakes
- 1 teaspoon freshly ground black pepper
- 2 teaspoons sweet paprika
- 2 large eggs, whisked

- 1½ cups fresh coarse bread crumbs
- 5 tablespoons extra-virgin olive oil
- 3 garlic cloves, thinly sliced
- 1¼ pounds hot Italian sausage (bulk or removed from casing)
- 4 red bell peppers, seeded and thinly sliced
- 1 red onion, cut into thin strips
- 1 cup chicken stock (page 276)
- 3 tablespoons chopped flat-leaf parsley
- Kosher salt and freshly ground black pepper

1 To make the pasta, combine the flour, salt, cayenne, chile flakes, black pepper, and paprika in a food processor and pulse to mix. With the food processor running, add the eggs and 1 table-spoon water and process just until the mixture looks crumbly and almost holds together. Pinch a little of the dough between your fingers; it should feel moist but not sticky. If the dough is sticky, add more flour, 1 tablespoon at a time; if it seems dry, add a little water, 1 teaspoon at a time. Gather the dough into a ball, wrap in plastic wrap, and let stand at room temperature for 30 minutes.

2 Set up a pasta machine with the rollers on the widest setting and dust them with flour. Divide the dough into 4 portions; keep covered with plastic wrap until ready to use. Flatten 1 portion ½ inch thick and pass it through the rollers. Fold the dough into thirds and pass it through again;

repeat this 3 or 4 times. Continue to pass the dough through progressively narrower settings, until it is ⅟₁₆ inch thick. Cut the pasta sheet into 10- to 12-inch lengths. Switch to the fettuccine cutting attachment, and pass the pasta sheets, one at a time, through the cutter. Toss the strands with flour and transfer them to a baking sheet lined with a flour-dusted kitchen towel. Repeat with the remaining dough portions.

3 Preheat the oven to 375°F. Put the bread crumbs on a rimmed baking sheet, drizzle with 2 tablespoons of the oil, and toss to coat. Spread the crumbs in a thin layer on the baking sheet, transfer to the oven, and toast, tossing and stirring occasionally, until light golden and crisp, 10 to 15 minutes. Pour into a bowl and set aside to cool.

4 In a large frying pan, heat the remaining 3 tablespoons oil and the garlic over medium-high heat. Cook, stirring, until the garlic is soft but doesn't take on any color, about 30 seconds. Add the sausage and cook, stirring and breaking up the sausage, until half cooked, 4 to 5 minutes. Add the bell peppers and onion and continue to cook, stirring, until the sausage is fully cooked and the peppers and onion begin to soften, about 5 minutes. Add the stock and stir for 2 minutes to reduce the stock slightly.

5 Meanwhile, bring a large pot of salted water to a boil. Add the pasta, stir well, and cook until al dente, 2 to 3 minutes. Drain the pasta, add it to the frying pan, and toss with the sausage mix-ture. Add the parsley, mix well, and season with salt and pepper. Transfer to a warmed serving dish and top with the bread crumbs.

serves 6

buckwheat linguine with chanterelles, peas, and asparagus

Back in my Chez Panisse days, I often made over forty pounds of fresh pasta daily, more than many an Italian nonna rolls in a year. This buckwheat linguine is one of my favorites, especially when topped with delicate chanterelles and spring vegetables.

BUCKWHEAT LINGUINE

1⅔ cups 00 flour
⅓ cup buckwheat flour
¼ teaspoon kosher salt
2 large eggs, whisked

½ pound fresh chanterelles or other wild
    or common mushrooms
3 tablespoons unsalted butter
2 shallots, minced
½ pound asparagus, tough ends removed and
    cut on the diagonal into 1-inch lengths
1½ cups chicken stock (page 276)
1 cup shelled fresh English peas
¾ cup crème fraîche
½ teaspoon fresh thyme leaves
    Kosher salt and freshly ground black pepper
2 tablespoons chopped flat-leaf parsley

1   To make the linguine, combine both flours and the salt in a food processor and pulse a few times to mix well. With the food processor running, add the eggs and ¼ cup water and process just until the mixture looks crumbly and almost holds together. Pinch a little of the dough between your fingers; it should feel moist but not sticky. If the dough is sticky, add more flour, 1 tablespoon at a time; if it seems dry, add a little water, 1 teaspoon at a time. Gather the dough into a ball, wrap in plastic wrap, and let stand at room temperature for 30 minutes.

2   Set up a pasta machine with the rollers on the widest setting and dust them with flour. Divide the dough into 4 portions; keep covered with plastic wrap until ready to use. Flatten 1 portion ½ inch thick and pass it through the rollers. Fold the dough into thirds and pass it through again; repeat this 3 or 4 times. Continue to pass the dough through progressively narrower settings, until it is ¹⁄₁₆ inch thick. Cut the pasta sheet into 10- to 12-inch lengths. Switch to the fettuccine cutting attachment, and pass the pasta sheets, one at a time, through the cutter. Toss the strands with flour and transfer them to a baking sheet lined with a flour-dusted kitchen towel. Repeat with the remaining dough portions.

3   To make the sauce, trim off the stem ends of the mushrooms, then cut the mushrooms in half. In a large frying pan, melt the butter over high heat. Add the mushrooms and shallots and cook, stirring occasionally, until the mushrooms and shallots begin to soften, 2 to 3 minutes. Add the asparagus and stock and simmer until the asparagus is almost tender and the stock has reduced by half, 3 to 4 minutes. Add the peas and cook, stirring occasionally, just until tender, 2 to 3 minutes. Add the crème fraîche and thyme, stir well, and heat for 1 minute. Season with salt and pepper.

4   Meanwhile, bring a large pot of salted water to a boil. Add the pasta, stir well, and cook until al dente, 2 to 3 minutes. Drain the pasta, add it to the frying pan, and toss and stir with the sauce, mixing well. Transfer to a warmed serving dish and top with the parsley.

serves 4 to 6

Wearing my favorite hat, purchased in Italy, during my Chez Panisse days.

I GLANCED AT THE CLOCK and was surprised to see that lunch service was over and it was nearly 2:00 p.m. My first shift at Chez Panisse had ended, and I had done more than survive. I felt like I had truly thrived. I grabbed a broom and helped the other cooks sweep the floors and clean the butcher-block counters, in preparation for the next round of cooks who were arriving for the dinner shift.

David pulled me aside, "Hey, can we talk for a few minutes?" We stood in the kitchen picking the leaves off sprigs of young parsley. "How'd it go today? Did you have fun?" he asked.

"I loved it," I said in earnest, hoping my enthusiasm came across.

"Want to come back tomorrow for another tryout?"

"Absolutely!"

For a full week, that's how each shift ended. After seven days, I still didn't know if I had a job or not, but I kept showing up, eager to prove myself a valuable member of the team. I finally understood what "tryout" meant. Alice, David, and the rest of the group were thoroughly testing me to ensure I shared their core values and had a great palate and an honest passion for food. In short, did I belong in the Chez Panisse family? When the week ended without an official job offer, I was exasperated. I went home crying, at my wit's end. Surely this was where I belonged. I resolved to keep showing up and working my heart out.

The next afternoon, when I met with David at the end of my shift, he finally uttered the words I'd been dying to hear, "Would you like to come back tomorrow? You're hired! I know it took a while but we didn't have a position open and created one for you."

I wanted to jump up and down screaming, but instead I gave David a huge hug. My smile stretched from ear to ear.

"Are you happy starting out doing prep, making pasta and pizza dough, and washing greens?" David asked, though it wasn't really a question.

"Absolutely. I want to learn everything."

When I got into my car to drive home, I kept my windows closed and let out the scream of excitement I'd been stifling. I was bursting with joy. This was the opportunity of a lifetime.

The next morning, I was hoarse from screaming the entire drive home, but I was also confident as I peeled buckets of onions and garlic as quickly as possible. It felt incredible to be an official part of this family of passionate and talented cooks.

I had told David Tanis I wanted to learn everything, and that's exactly what I did. For the first three months I rolled more pounds of pasta in a day than I could have ever thought possible. One especially humid day, as I struggled with pasta dough that kept sticking to itself no matter how much flour I added, David approached me to say, "I think it's time for you to start working upstairs on the line, making salads, assembling first courses, and opening oysters." His timing could not have been better. I was ready for a change.

My role on the line presented a whole new set of challenges. My very first order was for two dozen oysters. That meant opening oysters rapidly, because, while I was busy shucking, orders for salads and soups kept coming in. Speed and focus were key. Whether

green garlic and mustard blossom soup

I didn't even know green garlic or mustard blossoms existed until I was tasked with making this pleasantly pungent, silky soup. I was just about as green as the garlic.

3 tablespoons unsalted butter
3 leeks, white and 1 inch of the green, diced
¾ pound green garlic heads, outer leaves discarded
¾ pound Yukon Gold potatoes, peeled and diced
8 cups chicken stock (page 276)
1 small bunch mustard greens, coarsely chopped
½ cup heavy whipping cream
1 teaspoon white wine vinegar
   Kosher salt and freshly ground black pepper
¼ cup mustard blossoms

1   In a soup pot, melt the butter over medium heat. Add the leeks and cook, stirring occasionally, until soft, about 15 minutes. Add the garlic and potatoes and cook, stirring, for 5 minutes. Pour in the stock, bring to a simmer, and simmer, uncovered, until the potatoes are tender, 10 to 15 minutes. Add the mustard greens and cook just until tender, 4 to 5 minutes. Remove the pot from the heat and let cool for 15 minutes.

2   In batches, purée the soup in a blender until very smooth, about 2 minutes per batch. Strain the purée through a fine-mesh strainer into a soup pot. Stir in the cream and vinegar, season with salt, and heat over medium, stirring, until hot. If the soup is too thick, add stock or water to thin. Taste and adjust the seasoning with salt.

3   To serve, ladle the soup into warmed individual bowls and grind pepper over each serving. Garnish with the mustard blossoms.

serves 6

I was shelling a case of cranberry beans, whipping up sixteen cups of Meyer lemon mayonnaise or green goddess dressing, pickling countless cucumbers, or shucking two dozen oysters, with five hundred guests a day, everyone had to work efficiently.

The first time I prepared the iconic Sonoma goat cheese salad, a flood of memories came rushing back. I recalled my initial visit to Chez Panisse four years earlier, where a single bite of this brilliantly composed salad set my life on a new course. As I carefully placed flower petals onto the salad, I remembered my instructions: the petals need to look as if they have fallen from the garden. Purposeful randomness was new to me but a signature of the Chez Panisse style.

Alice came into the kitchen every day at 11:00 a.m., before service began, to taste the lunch items we'd be serving that day. Although she didn't spend her days in the kitchen with us, Alice was the driving force and visionary behind Chez Panisse. Every single dish on the changing daily menu had to be approved by Alice's impeccable palate. If something

little gem and pickled cucumber salad with green goddess dressing

GREEN GODDESS DRESSING

- ¼ cup snipped chives
- ¼ cup packed flat-leaf parsley leaves
- 2 anchovy fillets
- 2 tablespoons white wine vinegar
- 3 tablespoons extra-virgin olive oil
- ½ cup crème fraîche
  Kosher salt and freshly ground black pepper

PICKLED CUCUMBERS

- ¾ cup cider vinegar
- 2 teaspoons kosher salt
- 3 pickling cucumbers, thinly sliced

- 6 heads Little Gem lettuce, leaves separated
- 2 cups mixed cherry tomatoes, halved

1 To make the dressing, in a food processor, combine the chives, parsley, anchovy fillets, and vinegar and pulse a few times to combine. With the food processor running, add the oil in a fine, steady stream and process until smooth, stopping to scrape down the sides of the processor bowl as needed. Add the crème fraîche and process until smooth. Season with salt and pepper. Set the dressing aside while you prepare the remaining components, or transfer to an airtight container and refrigerate for up to 3 days.

2 To make the cucumbers, stir together the vinegar, ¼ cup water, and the salt in a bowl until the salt dissolves. Add the cucumbers, stir gently to coat evenly, and let sit for 5 minutes. Drain and pat dry with paper towels.

3 To assemble the salad, put the lettuce in a large bowl, drizzle with the dressing, and toss until the lettuce is evenly coated. Add the cucumbers and tomatoes and toss gently. Divide evenly among salad plates.

serves 6

she tasted didn't meet her standards, it was removed from the menu, even if the menu for the day had already been printed.

Alice's commitment to and fervor for the ideals of California cuisine inspired everyone in the kitchen. Just hearing her brisk footsteps approaching brought a new energy into the room. When Alice sampled our food, we paid attention. Her keen sense of balance in flavor was second to none. Her soft voice belied her strong will, incredible influence, and powerful dynamism. We wholeheartedly supported Alice's crusade to promote local ingredients and artisanal production. Her voice in our heads influenced every move we made in the kitchen.

One day, Alice brought Fanny, her four-year-old daughter, to taste with her. Alice sat Fanny on the counter at the salad station where I was working and waited to taste my endive salad with lemon crème fraîche dressing and salmon roe. When I finished the dressing, Alice dipped a spear of endive into the dressing, topped it with a few bright orange eggs of salmon roe, and handed it to Fanny. Fanny took a taste and looked at her mom with puckered lips, "Too acid!" she proclaimed.

A proud-mom smile spread across Alice's face, "Yes, you're right, Fanny, too acidic."

I added a touch of crème fraiche to temper the acidity and whisked the dressing together again. This time Fanny approved. It brought back memories of my mom's tomato sandwich. "Don't forget to salt the tomatoes," I could hear my mom reminding me. Fanny and I had something in common: when your mom is a cook, you learn how to taste at a young age.

endive salad with lemon crème fraîche and salmon roe

8 heads Belgian endive
1 cup crème fraîche, at room temperature
½ teaspoon grated lemon zest
2 teaspoons freshly squeezed lemon juice
    Kosher salt and freshly ground black pepper
2 ounces salmon roe
2 tablespoons very thinly sliced chives
1 bunch chervil, or leaves of 1 small head frisée

1 Trim off the base of an endive head and discard. Remove any leaves that are loose and place in a large bowl. Cut off another roughly ¼ inch of the endive base and continue to separate the whole leaves until the entire head is reduced to leaves.

As you work, add the leaves to the bowl with the others. Repeat with the remaining endive heads.

2 In a small bowl, stir together the crème fraîche and lemon zest and juice, mixing well. Season with salt and pepper.

3 To serve, toss the endive leaves with the crème fraîche mixture. Transfer the dressed leaves to a platter. Spoon the salmon roe evenly over the endive. Garnish with the chives and chervil sprigs.

serves 6

red onion soup with garlic-gruyère toasts

You cannot cook delicious food without tasting it as you cook. This soup especially is all about the proper balance of balsamic vinegar and fruity red wine, so you'll need to taste it again and again. When neither ingredient outshines the other, you'll know you've got it right.

3 tablespoons extra-virgin olive oil

4 large red onions, halved through the stem end and thinly sliced

4 leeks, white and 1 inch of the green, cut into ½-inch dice

3 ounces pancetta, cut into ¼-inch dice

4 cups chicken stock (page 276)

2 garlic cloves, peeled and left whole

12 to 18 slices baguette or other coarse-textured bread, about ¾ inch thick, toasted

¼ pound gruyère cheese, coarsely grated

1 cup fruity red wine, such as Zinfandel or Amarone

6 tablespoons balsamic vinegar

Kosher salt and freshly ground black pepper

2 tablespoons coarsely chopped flat-leaf parsley

1 In a large, heavy-bottomed soup pot, heat the oil over medium heat. Add the onions, leeks, and pancetta and cook, stirring occasionally, until the onions are soft and the pancetta is light golden, about 20 minutes. Add the stock and 2 cups water, bring to a simmer, and simmer uncovered, stirring occasionally, for about 30 minutes to blend the flavors.

2 Preheat the broiler.

3 Just before the soup has finished simmering, rub each bread slice on one side with the whole garlic cloves, coating it lightly. Place the bread slices, garlic side up, on a baking sheet and top with the cheese, dividing it evenly. Place the baking sheet under the broiler about 4 inches from the heat source and broil until the cheese has melted, 20 to 40 seconds. Watch closely to avoid burning. Remove from the broiler.

4 Add the wine and vinegar to the soup, return the soup to a simmer, and season with salt and pepper. Taste and season with additional wine or vinegar as needed. Ladle the soup into warmed individual bowls and top each serving with 2 or 3 cheese-topped toasts. Garnish evenly with the parsley.

serves 6

MY NEXT KITCHEN ROTATION was just ten feet away working the mesquite-fired grill. For hours, I stoked the 450°F fire, grilling fish, chicken, steaks, and lamb chops. Toward the end of my first shift, I noticed I was almost to the bottom of the bag of mesquite. I placed three loin lamb chops on the grill and looked around for some assistance.

"Hey Michele, where do I get more mesquite?" I inquired as I grabbed the last few chunks of jet-black mesquite from the bag.

"Downstairs!"

I had six orders on the board, but that didn't matter. There was no one who could go and get the mesquite for me, as everyone was just as busy as I was. I took the steps two at a time and then tried to heave the forty-pound bag onto my shoulder. That wasn't going to happen. Instead, I methodically dragged the enormous bag up the stairs, one step at a time, as fast as I could. I learned a valuable lesson that day about self-reliance. I felt strong, I felt capable, and I was proving myself a valuable contributor to the team. I fed the fire and tended to the lamb chops that were charring beautifully on the grates, the air swirling with smoky mesquite and sweet lavender.

lamb chops with lavender salt

1 tablespoon dried unsprayed culinary lavender
  Kosher salt and freshly ground black pepper
2 racks of lamb, 8 ribs each and 3 to 4 pounds
  total, trimmed of excess fat
2 tablespoons extra-virgin olive oil

1 In a spice grinder, combine the lavender and 2 teaspoons salt and pulse until until the lavender is coarsely ground. Transfer to a small bowl.

2 Cut the racks into individual chops. Brush the chops on both sides with the oil, then sprinkle them on both sides with one-third of the lavender salt. Save the remaining lavender salt for use at the table. Set the lamb aside at room temperature for 30 minutes.

3 Heat an outdoor grill to medium-high (about 450°F), or preheat a ridged cast-iron stove-top grill pan over medium-high heat.

4 If using an outdoor grill, position the grill rack 4 inches from the heat source and arrange the chops directly over the fire. If using a stove-top pan, arrange the chops on the pan. Grill the chops, turning once, for 3 to 5 minutes for medium-rare (cut to test). Transfer the chops to a platter and let rest for 5 minutes. Serve with the remaining lavender salt in a small bowl on the side.

serves 4

DINNER

LEEK & POTATO SOUP

PORK & CHICKEN TERRINE
  WITH PICKLED VEGETABLE

FENNEL, PARSLEY AND
  RADISHES WITH PARM

BUTTER LETTUCE WITH
  GREEN GODDESS

GOAT CHEESE WITH ROCK

OYSTERS   anchovis

PIZZETTA WITH ONION
  CONFIT & WALNUTS

PIZZA WITH SUN-DRIED

left center:

My nieces, Liz and Niki, visiting me during my time at Chez Panisse.

bottom center:

A Chez Panisse menu being worked on for that day's service.

WORKING THE SAUTÉ STATION ONE DAY, I was making crispy fried shellfish fritters for serving with Meyer lemon mayonnaise (see page 154). I put sixteen egg yolks and a few tablespoons of Dijon mustard and extra-virgin olive oil in a big bowl to make a silky emulsion. Time-wise, I was a little behind. I began whisking in, by hand, the remaining sixteen cups of oil in a slow, steady stream.

Hoping to make up some time, I poured the oil too quickly. Suddenly, after thirteen cups of oil, my creamy mayonnaise looked like egg yolks floating in oil. I had flooded the emulsion. Panicked, I started again by putting a new egg yolk into another bowl and whisking the broken emulsion into it drop by drop. When I got to cup number ten, I stopped to wipe the sweat from my brow and give my arm a rest. I looked up. A few of the cooks in the kitchen were looking at me and smiling. They had obviously once been where I was now.

One of my fellow cooks came to whisk in the remaining six cups of oil for me. I then added freshly grated Meyer lemon zest, lemon juice, and a touch of mashed garlic and salt. My arm still ached, but less so thanks to the help of my friend. Another day, another kitchen lesson learned. Sure, I had climbed twenty stairs while dragging a forty-pound bag of charcoal, but when I was really struggling, it was nice to know I had a strong, supportive team behind me. The camaraderie of the Chez Panisse kitchen gave me confidence and inspiration on a daily basis. To this day, every time I make mayonnaise, I think of that long-ago batch.

shellfish fritters with meyer lemon mayonnaise

Rules to follow when making mayonnaise: one egg yolk per cup of oil, use room temperature ingredients, and take your time! This bright, creamy sauce is a lovely complement to the crisp and briny fried shellfish.

1 cup all-purpose flour
   Kosher salt and freshly ground black pepper
2 large eggs, separated
2 tablespoons extra-virgin olive oil
¾ cup beer, at room temperature
1 pound clams in shells, scrubbed
1 pound mussels in shells, scrubbed and beards removed
¼ pound sea scallops, trimmed
¼ pound medium shrimp, peeled and deveined
½ pound calamari, cleaned and cut into
   ¼-inch-wide rings
   Rice bran or peanut oil for deep-frying
2 tablespoons chopped flat-leaf parsley
   Maldon sea salt
   Lemon wedges
   Meyer Lemon Mayonnaise (page 277)

1 To prepare the batter for the shellfish, in a bowl, sift together the flour and ½ teaspoon salt. In a small bowl, whisk together the egg yolks, olive oil, and beer until well blended. Pour the egg yolk mixture into the flour mixture and, using a whisk, stir them together just until mixed. Let rest for 1 hour at room temperature.

2 In a large frying pan, bring ¼ cup water to a boil over high heat. Add the clams, cover, and cook just until they open, 4 to 6 minutes. Remove the pan from the heat, then remove the clams from their shells, placing them in a bowl and discarding the shells. Discard any clams that failed to open. Return the pan to high heat and cook the mussels the same way just until they open, 3 to 6 minutes. Add the mussels to the bowl with the clams, discard the shells, and discard any mussels that failed to open. Return the pan to the stove top, reduce the heat to medium, and add the scallops and a little more water if needed. Cover and cook for 1 minute. Using a slotted spoon, transfer to a cutting board, cut into ¼-inch slices, and add to the clams and mussels. Add the shrimp to the pan over medium heat, cover, and cook for 1 minute. Using the slotted spoon, transfer them to a cutting board, cut in half crosswise, and add to the shellfish in the bowl along with the calamari. Season with salt and pepper, cover, and refrigerate until using.

3 Pour the rice bran oil to a depth of 2½ inches into a deep, heavy-bottomed saucepan and heat to about 375°F on a deep-fry thermometer. Line a large baking sheet with paper towels and place near the stove. Preheat the oven to 200°F.

4 While the oil is heating, in a clean bowl, using a whisk or a handheld mixer, beat the egg whites until stiff peaks form. Using a rubber spatula, fold the beaten whites into the batter just until combined, then fold the batter into the shellfish.

5 Drop the battered shellfish by the heaping tablespoon into the hot oil, being careful not to crowd the pan, and deep-fry until golden brown, 3 to 4 minutes. Using a slotted spoon, transfer to the towel-lined pan and place in the oven to keep warm. Repeat with the remaining shellfish.

6 Transfer the fritters to a platter. Garnish with parsley and Maldon salt and accompany with the lemon wedges and mayonnaise.

serves 8

❧

THESE WERE EXCITING TIMES for all of us at Chez Panisse. Every Wednesday afternoon, a jet landed at Oakland International Airport and several cases of precious, rare, priceless cargo were unloaded and transported to the restaurant. We anxious cooks tore open the boxes to see what they held. This delivery from Chino Farms outside of San Diego, which brought the best, most flavorful vegetables and fruits to our door, inspired our menu every week.

Don Chino raised fifteen different kinds of beans, twenty types of melon, and one hundred varieties of the most luscious heirloom tomatoes, as well as other high-quality organic produce. To highlight the farm-to-table mentality and the personal connection Alice fostered with the restaurant's producers, the Chez Panisse menu identified its valued suppliers. Garlic soufflé wasn't simply garlic soufflé. It was Green String Farm Roasted Spanish Roja Garlic Soufflé with Gruyère (see page 158). Good, honest, reputable farmers were getting well-deserved recognition and becoming celebrities in their own right. It was all part of the thrilling California food revolution, and I was participating in it daily.

× ● ×

IN TERMS OF INGREDIENTS AND TECHNIQUES, there were a lot of "firsts" for me at Chez Panisse. One of the most perplexing kitchen deliveries was a case of bright green fig leaves. I couldn't imagine what we would do with these lobed leaves with texture akin to soft sandpaper. And then I saw one of the cooks oiling a fig leaf with a pastry brush, placing a piece of fish on it, and then folding the leaf around the fish to make a little package. Later, we roasted the bundles in the pizza oven.

I was amazed when the slightly charred fig-leaf bundles emerged from the oven. We placed them on serving plates and opened the leaves just slightly to reveal the white, flaky fish. The aroma was intoxicating. The leaves scented the fish, giving it a delicate "green" perfume unlike anything I'd experienced before. We served the fish with a tart *salsa verde*. Even now, whenever I'm in Napa or Sonoma and see a fig tree during the summer, I grab some leaves and take them back to my kitchen.

sea bass roasted in fig leaves with salsa verde

Anytime I see a fig tree in late summer, I snag some leaves for this dish. Can't find fig leaves? No problem. Simply brush the sea bass with olive oil and roast as instructed. The incredibly addictive salsa verde *spooned over the fish more than makes up for the missing leaves.*

2 pounds small red or Yukon Gold potatoes, halved crosswise
5 tablespoons extra-virgin olive oil
  Kosher salt and freshly ground black pepper
1¾ pounds skinned sea bass or halibut fillets
12 fresh fig leaves, stems removed

SALSA VERDE
¾ cup chopped flat-leaf parsley
2 tablespoons chopped chives
1 teaspoon chopped fresh oregano
3 tablespoons capers, chopped
1 teaspoon grated lemon zest
1 garlic clove, minced
3 tablespoons freshly squeezed lemon juice
½ cup extra-virgin olive oil
  Kosher salt and freshly ground black pepper

6 lemon wedges

1 Preheat the oven to 400°F. One hour before serving, put the potatoes in a baking pan, drizzle with 2 tablespoons of the oil, sprinkle with salt and pepper, and toss to coat evenly. Place the potatoes cut side down, cover with foil, and bake until easily pierced with a knife, 45 to 50 minutes. Remove from the oven. Leave the oven on.

2 In the meantime, cut the fish fillets into 12 equal pieces. Place a fig leaf, smooth side down and vein side up, on a work surface. Brush each leaf with a little of the remaining 3 tablespoons olive oil. Place a piece of fish fillet near the stem end and season with salt and pepper. Fold over the stem end, fold in the sides toward the center, and then fold down the top of the leaf, enclosing the fish completely. Repeat with the remaining leaves and fish pieces, then brush the bundles lightly with the remaining oil. Set the bundles aside in the refrigerator.

3 To make the salsa verde, in a bowl, stir together the parsley, chives, oregano, capers, lemon zest, garlic, lemon juice, and oil. Season with salt and pepper. You should have about 2 cups.

4 Place the fish bundles on a rimmed baking sheet and roast until the fish is ready, 8 to 10 minutes. To check on doneness, open a bundle and, using the tip of a knife, pierce the fish. If it is opaque at the center and flakes easily, it is done. Remove the bundles from the oven.

5 To serve, put 2 bundles on each warmed individual plate, partially open each packet, and place a dollop of the salsa verde on the fish. Place the potatoes alongside and garnish with lemon wedges.

serves 6

roasted garlic and gruyère soufflé

Baked in an ovenproof platter, rather than a soufflé dish, this decadent classic cooks in a quarter of the time and is positively show-stopping. I got the idea from the downstairs restaurant at Chez Panisse and use it for ease and the wow factor to this day.

½ cup extra-virgin olive oil
3 large garlic heads, separated into cloves and peeled
1½ cups half-and-half
1 cup heavy whipping cream
5 tablespoons unsalted butter
5 tablespoons all-purpose flour
Kosher salt and freshly ground black pepper
6 large eggs, separated, at room temperature
1 cup finely grated gruyère cheese
1 cup grated parmigiano-reggiano cheese
1 teaspoon fresh thyme leaves
Large pinch of cayenne

1 In a small saucepan, combine the oil and garlic over medium-low heat and cook until the garlic is soft and light golden, 15 to 20 minutes. Remove the pan from the heat and, using a slotted spoon, transfer the garlic to a cutting board. Let cool, then mash with the side of a large chef's knife until reduced to a paste. Set aside. Reserve the garlic-infused oil for another use.

2 In a heavy-bottomed small saucepan, combine the half-and-half and cream, place over medium heat, and heat until small bubbles appear along the edges of the pan. Meanwhile, in a heavy-bottomed medium saucepan, melt the butter over medium heat. Add the flour and whisk for 2 to 3 minutes. Do not allow to color. When the cream mixture is ready, remove from the heat. Slowly drizzle the scalded cream into the butter-flour mixture while whisking rapidly. Cook, whisking often, until the sauce is smooth and thick, 2 to 3 minutes. Season with salt, add the garlic paste, and mix well. Remove from the heat and let cool for 15 minutes.

3 While the sauce is cooling, position a rack in the upper third of the oven and preheat the oven to 450°F. Generously butter a 12-inch oval or rectangular stainless-steel or porcelain ovenproof platter.

4 Add the egg yolks, one at a time, to the cooled sauce, stirring well after each addition. Add the gruyère, ½ cup of the parmigiano-reggiano, ½ teaspoon of the thyme, and the cayenne and season with salt and black pepper, mixing well.

5 Place the egg whites in a clean heatproof bowl. Set the bowl over the heat of the stove and swirl just until the egg whites feel warm to the touch. Do not let them begin to turn opaque. Using a whisk or a handheld mixer, beat the egg whites until stiff peaks form. Using a rubber spatula, fold half of the whites into the cheese mixture with as few strokes as possible. Fold in the remaining whites just until no white streaks remain.

6 Pour the mixture onto the prepared platter. Sprinkle the top with the remaining ½ cup parmigiano-reggiano and the remaining ½ teaspoon thyme. Bake until well puffed, slightly firm to the touch in the middle, and golden brown, 12 to 16 minutes. Serve immediately.

serves 8

TWO YEARS PASSED and I'd made all the rounds in the restaurant except for pastry. I was now training potential newcomers during their tryout, a role I was surprised to find suited me quite well. One morning, as I was teaching a new cook to roll pasta, co-owner and pastry chef Lindsey Shere was spreading batter into cake pans for her transcendent almond cake at the neighboring pastry station.

"That almond cake is my favorite. Lindsey, how many times have you made that?" I wondered aloud.

"Thousands," she said with a smile. "Why don't you give pastry a try?"

I glanced at the perfectly golden cakes being pulled from the oven and quickly responded, "I'd love to."

A few weeks later, as I thumbed through Carol Field's newly released *The Italian Baker*, a recipe for a polenta tart with poached pears (see page 162) caught my eye. It was a perfect dessert for Chez Panisse, and I decided to introduce it to the pastry team.

Standing in the pastry area, I carefully measured out the ingredients for the polenta crust and then quickly assembled it. I let the dough rest and started on the pears. I peeled and sliced an entire case of Sonoma French Butter pears and tossed the slices into a pan with red wine, cinnamon, whole cloves, and sugar, where they simmered until tender and were then left to cool.

With the pears ready, I checked on my pastry. It was firm, perfect for rolling. I grabbed a rolling pin and dusted my work surface with flour. White flecks of flour floated through the air like snowflakes in a blizzard. I rolled a piece of the dough into a thin, smooth circle. Just as the pastry team had taught me, I curled the dough circle around the rolling pin to transfer it to the tart pan. When my crust ripped in half midway to the pan, my heart tore right along with it. But the clock was ticking, and I had to get these tarts ready for service.

I grabbed what I could salvage of the dough and pressed it into the pan. I'd seen Lindsey do this, and I was relieved to find it worked. I lined the remaining tart pans, filled the tart shells with the cooled pears, and then turned my attention to the top crust. I couldn't risk messing it up, too. As I quickly rolled out the dough, I had an idea. I took a heart-shaped cookie cutter and started cutting out hearts. Then, starting at the edge of a tart, I placed the hearts, slightly overlapping them, in concentric circles, working my way to the center. With a huge sigh, I popped the assembled tarts into the oven and said a little cooking prayer.

Forty minutes later, I retrieved the gorgeous golden brown tarts from the oven. They were perfect! I cut a warm slice and the pastry team tasted it. As we savored the crunchy polenta crust, the sweet spiced pears, and the softly whipped cream that melted over the top, I thanked Chez Panisse for letting me introduce Carol Field's slice of perfection.

café almond cake

It takes just three minutes in a food processor to mix the batter for this classic Chez Panisse cake. You'll go nuts for this simple, sweet, moist dessert infused with the taste of marzipan, especially if you're an almond lover like me.

- 1 cup all-purpose flour
- 1½ teaspoons baking powder
- ¼ teaspoon kosher salt
- 1¼ cups granulated sugar
- 7 ounces almond paste
- 1¼ cups unsalted butter, at room temperature
- 6 large eggs, at room temperature
- Powdered sugar for dusting

1 Preheat the oven to 325°F. Butter a 9-inch-round springform pan, then dust the pan with flour, tapping out the excess.

2 In a bowl, sift together the flour, baking powder, and salt. Set aside.

3 In a food processor, combine the granulated sugar and the almond paste and process until well mixed. Add the butter and process until light and fluffy. With the food processor running, add the eggs, one at a time, processing after each addition until fully incorporated. Add the flour mixture and process just until thoroughly blended.

4 Pour the batter into the prepared pan. Bake the cake until a wooden toothpick inserted into the center comes out clean and the center feels springy when gently pressed with a fingertip, 1 to 1¼ hours. Let cool in the pan on a cooling rack for 20 minutes. Run a thin knife blade along the inside edge of the pan to loosen the cake, then unclasp the latch and lift off the rim. Using a wide metal spatula, carefully slide the cake onto the rack and let cool completely.

5 Transfer the cake to a cake plate or stand and dust the top with powdered sugar.

serves 8 to 10

poached pear and polenta tart

FILLING

2 cups hearty dry red wine
¼ cup sugar
12 whole cloves
3 long strips lemon zest
¾ teaspoon ground cinnamon
2½ pounds Bosc pears, peeled, halved, cored, and cut into ¼-inch-thick slices

POLENTA PASTRY

½ cup plus 2 tablespoons unsalted butter, at room temperature
¾ cup plus 1 tablespoon sugar
3 large egg yolks
1½ cups all-purpose flour, sifted
½ cup plus 2 tablespoons fine-grind polenta
¼ teaspoon kosher salt

1 cup heavy whipping cream
3 or 4 drops vanilla extract

1   To make the filling, combine the wine, sugar, cloves, lemon zest, and cinnamon in a saucepan and bring to a boil over medium-high heat, stirring. Adjust the heat to medium and cook until reduced to 1½ cups, about 15 minutes. Add the pears and cook, uncovered, until tender, about 15 minutes.

2   Transfer the pears to a baking sheet lined with paper towels to cool. Strain the cooking liquid through a fine-mesh strainer, return to the saucepan, place over medium-high heat, and boil until reduced by half. Set aside.

3   To make the pastry, in a mixer fitted with the beater, combine the butter and ¾ cup of the sugar and beat on medium-high speed until blended, 1 to 2 minutes. Add the egg yolks, one at a time, beating well after each addition. Add the flour, ½ cup plus 1 tablespoon of the polenta, and the salt to the butter mixture, then mix on low speed just until the dough comes together.

4   On a lightly floured surface, knead the dough lightly, then wrap in plastic wrap and let rest in the refrigerator for 20 minutes.

5   Preheat the oven to 375°F. Divide the dough in half and return half to the refrigerator. On a floured work surface, roll out the first half into a circle about 10 inches in diameter and ¼ inch thick. Transfer to an 8½-inch round tart pan with a removable rim, easing it into the bottom and up the sides of the pan and pressing it in place. Trim off any overhanging dough. In a bowl, stir together the remaining 1 tablespoon each sugar and polenta and sprinkle the mixture over the bottom of the tart shell. Spoon the pear slices into an even layer in the shell.

6   Place the second half of the dough on a floured work surface, and roll it out ¼ inch thick. With a heart-shaped cookie cutter, cut out as many hearts as possible from the dough. Starting near the rim of the pan, arrange the cutouts on top of the pears, overlapping them slightly and covering the top of the tart completely.

7   Bake the tart until the top is golden, about 40 minutes. Let cool on a wire rack.

8   To serve, whisk the cream and vanilla until soft peaks form. Remove the outer ring from the tart pan and cut the tart into wedges. Top each serving with a dollop of the cream and a drizzle of the poaching liquid.

serves 8

"YOU STUDIED WITH MADELEINE KAMMAN a few years ago, right?" David Lebovitz, one of the pastry cooks, asked me one morning. David had been at Chez Panisse for a couple of years before I arrived. "By any chance, do you have her recipe for Chartreuse ice cream?" he begged.

I scoured through the thousands of recipes from my year with Madeleine and took the coveted recipe to David the next morning.

"What do you say we try it out today but fold in some tiny handmade chocolate truffles, the size of peas, at the end? As the ice cream melts in your mouth, so will the truffles," David dreamed.

What a great idea! I'd never thought of adding truffles to ice cream. The result was magnificent: velvety ice cream with an herbal whisper and green shadow of Chartreuse liquor, studded with chocolate truffles that melted in my mouth, exactly as promised (see page 167).

Alice loved ice cream desserts and fresh fruit sorbets, so variations of these two types of sweets appeared on the Chez Panisse menu all the time. My favorite was the fresh raspberry and Zinfandel sorbet (see page 168). The raspberries packed a punch of summery sweetness, and the wine lent a festive feel to every bite. The dessert was not only a simple way to showcase the beauty of the berry but also the epitome of the Chez Panisse philosophy.

Not all of the desserts at Chez Panisse were as straightforward as fresh fruit sorbet, though one of my favorites had the same ethos of simplicity and full flavors. There was something therapeutic about making a chocolate *pavé*, a dense, smooth flourless cake. I had enjoyed the dessert many times in the Café, so I was thrilled when I finally got a chance to learn the secrets behind it from one of the pastry cooks, Mary Jo Thoresen. As she and I melted chunks of bittersweet Valrhona chocolate with butter in a double boiler, they were transformed into a silky pool of decadence right before my eyes. We mixed half of the sugar and eggs into ribbons of pale yellow sunshine and combined them with the chocolate mixture. We whipped egg whites in a giant copper bowl until they stood in soft peaks and then added sugar and continued whipping until we had a stiff meringue. As we folded the two elements together and began to pour the result into a pan, I was tempted to stop and eat the whole bowl of batter. Instead Mary Jo and I baked it, cut it into squares, and treated customers to the most deceptively delicious brownie of all time.

Working on the line at Chez Panisse with Barry Monath. Lots of laughs with David Lebovitz.

chocolate pavé with mint crème anglaise

Neither laden with sugar nor overly rich, this delectable pavé *showcases the beautiful assertive flavors of dark chocolate. It may look like just a brownie, but in typical Chez Panisse fashion, the taste is transcendent.*

¾ cup plus 3 tablespoons unsalted butter
7½ ounces bittersweet chocolate, chopped
7½ ounces semisweet chocolate, chopped
6 large eggs, separated
1 cup plus 2 tablespoons granulated sugar
Powdered sugar for dusting
Mint Crème Anglaise (page 277)
Fresh mint sprigs for garnish

1 Preheat the oven to 350°F. Butter the bottom and sides of a 9- by 13-inch baking pan. Line the bottom with parchment paper, then dust the pan with flour, tapping out the excess.

2 In a large, heavy-bottomed saucepan, melt the butter over medium-low heat. Reduce the heat to low, add both types of chocolate, and stir constantly until just melted and smooth. Be careful not to overheat the chocolate or it will turn grainy. It should register no more than 115°F on an instant-read thermometer. Remove the pan from the heat.

3 In a bowl, using a whisk or a handheld mixer, beat together the egg yolks and ½ cup plus 1 tablespoon of the granulated sugar until when you lift some of the mixture into the air with the whisk, the mixture falls back into the bowl in a ribbon that then slowly disappears. This should take 3 to 4 minutes by hand or 1 to 2 minutes with a mixer. Add the chocolate-butter mixture and beat until combined.

4 Place the egg whites in a clean heatproof bowl and warm them slightly by swirling them above the flame of a gas burner or above an electric burner. Do not let them begin to turn opaque. Using a clean whisk or a handheld mixer fitted with clean beaters, beat the egg whites until stiff peaks form. Add the remaining ½ cup plus 1 tablespoon sugar and continue to beat until the sugar is completely incorporated, about 3 minutes by hand or 1 minute with a mixer. Spread the egg whites over the chocolate mixture and, using a rubber spatula, fold them together quickly without deflating the whites, just until no white streaks are visible.

5 Pour the batter into the prepared pan. Bake the cake until the edges have risen and cracked slightly, 30 to 35 minutes. Let cool in the pan on a cooling rack for 10 minutes.

6 To unmold, run a thin knife blade along the inside edge of the pan to loosen the cake. Invert a cooling rack on top of the cake, and then invert the rack and pan together. While the cake is still warm, lift off the pan and peel off the parchment. Let cool for 15 minutes.

7 Place on a flat serving plate and trim the edges with a serrated knife as needed to even them out. Cut the cake into 12 squares. Let cool completely.

8 Dust the top of each square with powdered sugar. Serve with the crème anglaise spooned around the cake, garnished with a sprig of mint.

serves 12

chartreuse ice cream with chocolate truffles

As the first Madeleine Kamman alum to join Chez Panisse, I was excited to share her teachings with my new restaurant family. With David Lebovitz's addition of pea-size dark chocolate truffles to Madeleine's vivid Chartreuse ice cream, an irresistible new flavor was born.

CHARTREUSE ICE CREAM
9 large egg yolks
⅔ cup sugar
2 cups heavy whipping cream
2 cups whole milk
3 or 4 drops vanilla extract
¼ cup Chartreuse liqueur

CHOCOLATE TRUFFLES
4 ounces semisweet chocolate
1 ounce unsweetened chocolate
5 tablespoons unsalted butter
½ cup plus 2 tablespoons heavy whipping cream
1 to 2 tablespoons Chartreuse liqueur

1   To make the ice cream, whisk together the egg yolks and sugar in a large saucepan just until the sugar dissolves. In a medium saucepan, combine the cream and milk, place over medium heat, and heat until small bubbles appear along the edges of the pan. Remove from the heat and slowly drizzle the scalded cream mixture, a few tablespoons at a time, into the egg yolk mixture while whisking constantly.

2   Place the combined mixtures over medium heat and heat, stirring constantly, just until the mixture begins to thicken enough to coat the back of the spoon, 2 to 3 minutes. Do not allow the mixture to boil. Test the custard with an instant-read thermometer; it should register 160°F. Immediately remove from the heat and pour through a fine-mesh strainer into a clean bowl. Whisk vigorously for about 2 minutes to cool slightly. Add the vanilla to taste and the Chartreuse and let cool completely. Cover and refrigerate until well chilled.

3   To make the truffles, combine both chocolates, the butter, and the cream in a small saucepan, place over low heat, and heat, stirring constantly, until melted and smooth. (Alternatively, combine the ingredients in a heatproof bowl, place over barely simmering water in a saucepan, and heat, stirring constantly, until melted and smooth.) Add the Chartreuse to taste. Pour the mixture into a shallow container, making sure that the mixture is at least ¾ inch deep. Cover and refrigerate until cold but still malleable, about 2 hours.

4   To shape the truffles, have ready a baking sheet. Dip a ½-teaspoon measuring spoon or a small melon baller into hot water, quickly scoop up some of the chocolate mixture, and gently drop it onto the baking sheet. Repeat until you have used up all of the chocolate mixture, arranging the truffles in a single layer and making sure they do not touch one another. Refrigerate the truffles until well chilled.

5   Transfer the chilled custard to an ice cream maker and freeze according to the manufacturer's directions. Fold the chilled truffles into the finished ice cream, then transfer the ice cream to an airtight container and store in the freezer until serving. The ice cream tastes best if eaten within 5 days.

makes 1 generous quart

red wine–raspberry sherbet with berry compote

Alice insists on having a fresh fruit sorbet or granita on the Chez Panisse menu at all times. It's a light and refreshing palate cleanser. Paired with a cookie, it's my definition of the perfect dessert.

SHERBET

- 6 cups raspberries
- 3 cups fruity, rich red wine, such as Zinfandel or Merlot
- 1 cup plus 2 tablespoons sugar

COMPOTE

- 2 cups raspberries
- ⅓ cup sugar
- 1 strip lemon zest, 2 inches long
- ¾ cup blueberries
- ¾ cup *fraises des bois* (wild strawberries), optional
- 1 tablespoon crème de cassis
- 1 teaspoon freshly squeezed lemon juice

1 To make the sherbet, put the raspberries in a large heatproof bowl. In a heavy-bottomed saucepan, combine the wine, sugar, and ⅓ cup water over medium-high heat and bring to a boil, stirring to dissolve the sugar. As soon as the mixture boils, remove it from the heat and pour it over the raspberries. Let steep for 30 minutes.

2 Meanwhile, make the compote. In a food processor or blender, process 1 cup of the raspberries until a smooth purée forms. Strain through a fine-mesh strainer into a small bowl and set aside.

3 In a heavy-bottomed medium saucepan, combine the sugar, lemon zest, and ½ cup water over medium-high heat and bring to a boil, stirring to dissolve the sugar. Reduce the heat to medium and add the blueberries. Cook just until the blueberries begin to crack, about 1 minute. Add the fraises des bois, if using, then remove the pan from the heat. Remove and discard the lemon zest. Add the raspberry purée, crème de cassis, and the remaining 1 cup raspberries and stir to combine. You should have about 2 cups compote. Cover and refrigerate until serving.

4 Transfer the steeped sherbet mixture to a blender and process until a smooth purée forms. Strain through a fine-mesh strainer into a bowl, cover, and refrigerate until well chilled.

5 Transfer the chilled purée to an ice cream maker and freeze according to the manufacturer's directions. Store the finished sherbet in an airtight container in the freezer until serving. It tastes best if eaten within 5 days.

6 To serve, scoop the sherbet into dessert bowls and spoon the compote over the top.

serves 6 to 8

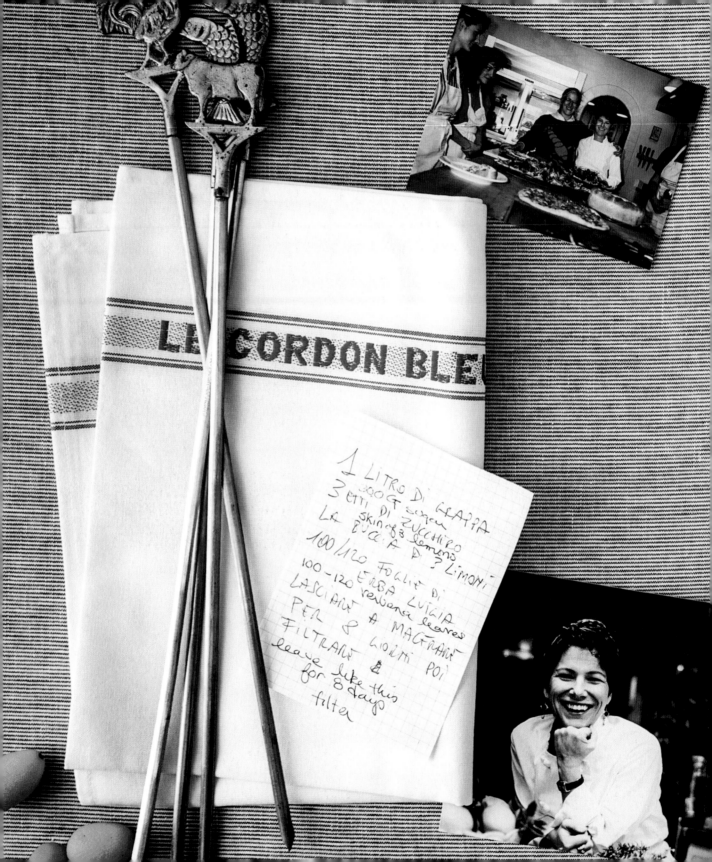

CHAPTER 8

INSPIRED
by
INGREDIENTS

My first few days teaching cooking.

H

OW MANY DAYS A WEEK do I have to work to qualify for my free birthday dinner?" I asked David Tanis half jokingly as we stood shucking fava beans.

"What do you mean?" he replied.

"A few months ago, I reduced my schedule to three days. If I go to two, do I still earn my dinner?"

"Are you leaving us, Joanne?" David retorted with a pout.

Every year, Chez Panisse gave each staff member a celebration dinner in the downstairs restaurant as a birthday gift. Asking about my birthday dinner was just a way of skirting the real issue: I was thinking about leaving Chez Panisse. After five years, it was time for me to make a change, but I was agonizing over the decision.

"Well...I want to teach and travel," I explained. "I was an art teacher in Boston right out of college and also taught some cooking classes with Madeleine Kamman. One of my favorite things I do here at Chez Panisse is train new cooks. I think teaching might be calling my name again. And traveling, it's in my blood. I guess I've made my decision."

On my last day at Chez Panisse, I went into the changing room and removed my chef's jacket. But instead of clearing out my locker, I left my black kitchen clogs in their usual place and my padlock on the door. I still wasn't sure I was making the right decision. I knew what an honor and privilege it was to work within that modest shingled house on Shattuck Avenue. To work with Alice and brilliant cooks who shared the same philosophy that cooking should be based on the finest, freshest seasonal ingredients, sourced locally and prepared simply to enhance natural flavors, and who lived, breathed, and thought about food with the same unbridled passion. Was I crazy to be leaving? I walked out the door that day with a heavy, hesitant heart.

Thankfully, I fell into a great teaching job almost immediately. Mary Risley, owner of Tante Marie's Cooking School in the North Beach neighborhood of San Francisco, was looking for someone to teach a weekly class to her professional students. I had been teaching evening classes at the small cooking school for a few months and liked the idea of training budding chefs.

The class was Improvisational Cooking, which called for me to fill a basket with miscellaneous ingredients with which the students would have to create original dishes. It was just like the "creative list" exercises that Madeleine had used in her classes. This type of teaching, in which young chefs are encouraged to innovate and gain confidence working without recipes, was something I was well suited for. My experience at Chez Panisse, where I was regularly exposed to many new and interesting ingredients, guaranteed that I had a lot to offer. I couldn't wait to see what my students would do with my carefully curated basket.

In preparation for my first class, I drove to Monterey Market in Berkeley, a produce store with a wide variety of high-quality fruits, vegetables, and ingredients, both conventional and unusual. As I was driving out of the parking lot, I glanced across the street at the Berkeley Horticultural Nursery and decided to find an edible garden plant to include in my basket. I was excited to find a couple of small pots of rose geraniums. At Chez Panisse we used the leaves to flavor ice cream. What would my students do with them?

For the class, I packed a big French market basket with some common vegetables and herbs, such as sugar snap peas, new red potatoes, carrots, young zucchini, and mint. Then I added the more obscure ingredients to the mix: green garlic, stinging nettles, first-of-the-season squash blossoms, and the rose geranium plants.

I felt like a kid on the first day of school, anxious, excited, and not quite sure what to expect. I stepped into Tante Marie's Cooking School toting my overflowing basket. The students, all of them in their seats, mirrored my wide-eyed expression.

"Get ready for some fun! Today we're going to do an improvisation class. Anybody know what I mean by improvisational cooking?" I asked.

My question was met with blank stares until the class clown chuckled and said, "Must be an acting class. I'm great at improv!"

"Very funny. In this case, improvisation means that I'll give you a list of ingredients and for twenty minutes you'll jot down menu ideas that use those ingredients. You're all with me so far? Sounds fun, right?" I explained enthusiastically.

"You mean we cook without recipes?" one of the fledglings whispered nervously.

"That's right! You'll love it. Just wait and see," I encouraged. "After you've written down your menu, we'll come back together and discuss your ideas. Then we'll break up into groups of two and cook the dishes we decide on. Got it?"

"We've never cooked without recipes," someone stated.

"Wow, this absence of recipes keeps coming up. Don't look so worried. Cooking without recipes frees you. Here's a hint: Take the basic recipe for a soufflé. Come on, you know how to make a soufflé. Who can tell me?"

"You make a roux. No, you make a béchamel, add egg yolks one at a time, and then add flavorings. Next, you whip egg whites and fold them in," a confident student at the front of the room recited proudly.

"Exactly. Think of it this way: You can make a soufflé any time of the year. All you have to do is vary the ingredients according to the season. You can take that one basic recipe and come up with hundreds of recipes. The only limit is your creativity. I have faith in you. Now, get your pencils ready. These are the ingredients you have to work with: for proteins, you have a leg of lamb, fresh goat cheese, and large eggs. For vegetables and herbs, you have sugar snap peas, yellow onions, carrots, new red potatoes, and green garlic."

I could hear stirring. When I looked up, I saw some very perplexed faces in the room. I continued with my list: "And a half pound of stinging nettles."

"Ouch!" someone yelled so loudly that it startled me.

"Hey, I was also scared the first time I put on latex gloves and cleaned a case of nettles. Who has worked with nettles before?" I asked.

More blank stares. "Don't worry," I quickly said. "I'll show you. Let's continue. One bunch French breakfast radishes."

"Who eats radishes for breakfast?" a voice called from the back of the room.

"You'll love them," I explained. "They're a French heirloom variety, long and thin, crisp and spicy, with red tops and white bottoms. If you keep the greens on, they make a bright, lively garnish."

"I keep hearing the word *heirloom*. What does it mean exactly?" asked the same voice.

"It refers to older varieties of fruits and vegetables that are making a comeback. Have you seen the wide array of colorful tomatoes in the grocery store? Those are heirloom tomatoes. Okay, let's get back to the list. You'll also have two pounds young zucchini, two bunches young spinach, and one-third pound mizuna."

"Who's Ms. Zuna?" the class clown joked.

Despite the fact that this was starting to feel like an improv comedy class, I continued with my basket list. "First-of-the-season squash blossoms, two rose geranium plants…"

"What the heck, we're going to eat a geranium?" It was the class clown again.

"No, you can use the leaves to scent something. They're very aromatic," I stifled a snicker and then went on. "Six fresh roses."

"Geez, we're eating the whole flower garden."

Now I was laughing out loud. This was my first improvisation class; I hoped it wasn't my last. I proceeded to finish off the herbs—"a bunch each of flat-leaf parsley, spearmint, and Italian oregano"—and continued on to the fruits and nuts—"four blood oranges, one cup whole almonds"—to the sugars, flour, and starches—"a loaf of rustic bread, any flour and any sugar you like, baking soda, and baking powder"—to the fats and oils—"one pound unsalted butter, one cup extra-virgin olive oil"—and then to the dairy ingredients—"two cups heavy cream, two cups milk, and some grana padano."

I had made it through those last four categories but not without having to pause for several clarifications. I sliced a blood orange in half to reveal its vivid crimson center. As soon as the class glimpsed the almost blood-red flesh, the name made perfect sense. I recited the spelling of grana padano and then explained that it was a hard grating cheese from northern Italy.

I was beginning to realize how much I'd learned at Chez Panisse. If I could just hang in and make it through this list, I'd be relieved. I hoped that I had not bitten off more than I could chew—no pun intended. I finished up the recitation of my list with a handful of staples: "any kind of vinegar you like, four cups veal or chicken stock, a package of active dry yeast, any spices you like, a bottle of Champagne, and Vialone Nano rice."

"Is that something Mork and Mindy ate? Vialone Nanu Nanu?" my comedian cracked, laughing hysterically at his own joke.

I was frustrated, but I couldn't blame the students. They were familiar with Arborio, radishes, and oranges, but even to aspiring cooks, ingredients like nettles, blood oranges, green garlic, mizuna, rose geranium, and Vialone Nano rice were completely foreign.

"Come on up and check out the ingredients," I urged.

Reluctantly, the students shuffled forward and stood around the large teaching island at the front of the room. They cautiously investigated the ingredients now displayed on the wooden countertop. I picked a leaf from the rose geranium plant and rubbed it between my fingers, inhaling its intense rosy perfume. I encouraged the students to do the same. I sliced small wedges of blood orange and grated a few spoonfuls of grana padano for everyone to taste. Finally, they were exploring, smelling, tasting, touching the unfamiliar ingredients, and I started to see some lightbulbs come on.

"Okay, it's time to come up with a menu. Make believe you're standing in front of your refrigerator. You're going to cook with what you have. Allow these new and unusual ingredients to stir your creative juices. You'll thank me in the end, I promise you!"

nettle and spinach frittata

¼ pound nettles
1 tablespoon extra-virgin olive oil
8 green onions, thinly sliced
1 garlic clove, minced
¼ pound baby spinach
Kosher salt and freshly ground black pepper
6 large eggs
½ cup grated grana padano cheese
½ cup ricotta cheese
1 tablespoon unsalted butter

1 Wearing gloves, remove the stems from the nettles, then rinse in cold water and spin dry.

2 Preheat the oven to 350°F. In a large frying pan, heat the oil over medium heat. Add the green onions and garlic and cook, stirring occasionally, until soft, about 3 minutes. Add the nettles and spinach and cook, turning them with tongs, until they are soft but still bright green, 3 to 4 minutes. Season with salt and pepper and let cool.

3 In a medium bowl, whisk together the eggs until blended. Add the grana padano and ricotta and whisk until well mixed. Don't worry that small pieces of ricotta will still be visible in the mixture. Season with ½ teaspoon salt and a good pinch of pepper, then add the cooled nettle mixture and stir until combined.

4 In a 9½-inch ovenproof nonstick frying pan, melt the butter over medium-high heat. Add the egg mixture and stir gently until it begins to set and is bubbling slightly around the edges, about 30 seconds. Reduce the heat to medium-low and cook until the frittata is set around the edges and on the underside but the center is still wet, 4 to 5 minutes. Transfer the pan to the oven and cook the frittata until completely set, 7 to 10 minutes.

5 Remove from the oven and run a heat-resistant rubber spatula around the edge of the pan to loosen the frittata. Invert a serving plate over the pan, invert the pan and plate together, and then lift off the pan. Cut into wedges and serve warm or at room temperature.

serves 4 to 6

For the next twenty minutes, my now-focused students looked over their lists and jotted down ideas. Occasionally someone would come up to look at the nettles or smell the green garlic. At the end of the allotted time, they were eager to share what they had recorded.

"Spinach frittata with grana padano. Or maybe we wilt the nettles in there, too, so perhaps a nettle and spinach frittata?" a brave cook ventured.

"How about a squash risotto using that 'nanu nanu' rice?" someone else offered.

"What about adding some squash blossoms?" another student chimed in.

"I love the idea of adding the squash blossoms," I said, agreeing with last suggestion. "They'll not only contribute a vibrant orange color but also a nice peppery flavor that will give the risotto a little kick. Now, what about the rose geranium?"

The class looked stumped, until a shy voice offered, "I was thinking of somehow scenting a cake with the rose geranium leaves, but I'm not sure how to do that."

"That's perfect," I responded. "I'll make a deal with you. I just wrote a recipe for a rose geranium cake. If you set up all of the ingredients, I'll demonstrate how to make it."

"I was thinking about the rose petals. Could we infuse a simple syrup with the roses and then use it to make a rose petal sorbet? It would be really cool to douse the sorbet in bubbles just before serving. Can I make that?" my confident front-row student asked.

I couldn't believe that this was the same class that twenty minutes earlier had sat dumbfounded by the ingredients I'd pulled from my basket. Now I was hearing creative ideas and fielding a flurry of questions. Excitement filled the air. They were getting it. I felt encouraged and more relaxed. Maybe this wouldn't be my last class after all (see recipes on pages 175, 178, 181).

sparkling rose petal sorbet

1 cup sugar
  Petals from 12 pesticide-free large, strongly
  perfumed red roses, plus more for garnish
1 bottle (750 ml) Champagne or sparkling wine,
  chilled

1 In a saucepan, combine the sugar, petals from the 12 roses, and 1 cup water; bring to a boil over high heat, stirring to dissolve the sugar. Remove from the heat and pour into a heatproof bowl. Let cool, then cover and refrigerate overnight.

2 The next day, strain the syrup through a fine-mesh strainer, pressing on the petals with the back of a spoon. Measure the rose syrup. For each cup of rose syrup, add 2 cups Champagne and stir together. Chill the remaining Champagne.

3 Transfer the syrup mixture to an ice cream maker and freeze according to the manufacturer's directions. Store the finished sorbet in an airtight container in the freezer until serving. It tastes best if eaten within 2 days.

4 Scoop the sorbet into glasses. Pour a dash of Champagne over each; garnish with rose petals.

serves 6

farmers' market risotto with squash blossoms

Italians have traditionally cooked with squash blossoms, often stuffing them with mozzarella and anchovy and then frying them until golden, but they remain a novel ingredient in the United States. Their peppery flavor and vibrant color add pizzazz to many dishes. Here, they are used in a creamy summer risotto.

1½ pounds mixed summer squashes with blossoms attached, such as pattypan and zucchini

3 cups chicken stock (page 276)

2 tablespoons extra-virgin olive oil

1 small yellow onion, minced

1½ cups risotto rice, such as Arborio, Vialone Nano, or Carnaroli

½ cup dry white wine, such as Sauvignon Blanc
Kosher salt and freshly ground black pepper

2 tablespoons chopped flat-leaf parsley

1 tablespoon unsalted butter, at room temperature

¾ cup grated grana padano or parmigiano-reggiano cheese

1   Remove the blossoms from the squashes. Cut the squashes crosswise into ¼-inch-thick slices. Cut the blossoms crosswise into thirds.

2   In a medium saucepan, combine the stock and 3 cups water and bring to a boil over high heat. Move the pan to a back burner over low heat and keep the liquid just below the boiling point. Place a ladle in the pan.

3   In a large, heavy soup pot, heat the oil over medium heat. Add the onion and cook, stirring often, until soft, 8 to 10 minutes. Add the squash slices and cook, stirring occasionally, for 1 minute. Add the rice and cook, stirring, until the rice is coated with the oil, the edges of the rice kernels are translucent, and a white dot appears in the center of each kernel, about 3 minutes. Add the wine and cook, stirring, until the wine evaporates, about 1 minute.

4   Add ¼ teaspoon salt and a ladle of the hot stock and stir the rice constantly, wiping it from the bottom and sides of the pot. When most of the liquid has been absorbed but the rice is still loose, add another ladle of the stock and cook, stirring, until most of the liquid has been absorbed. Continue to add the stock, a ladle at a time, and cook, stirring constantly, until most of the liquid has been absorbed before adding more. The rice is ready when it is just beyond the chalky stage, 18 to 22 minutes total. If you run out of stock before the rice is done, add hot water.

5   Remove from the heat and stir in a ladle of stock (or hot water), the parsley, the butter, the squash blossoms, and half of the cheese. Season with salt and pepper. Cover the pot and let sit for 5 minutes.

6   To serve, uncover, stir, spoon into warmed individual bowls, and sprinkle with the remaining cheese, dividing it evenly.

serves 6

rose geranium cake

The less common rose geranium is worth seeking out at your local nursery. At Chez Panisse, we used the leaves to scent ice cream, sorbet, sugar, and crème anglaise. The memory of that floral flavor inspired this cake.

24 rose geranium leaves
1 cup unsalted butter
1½ cups granulated sugar
1 cup whole milk
3 cups all-purpose flour
1 tablespoon baking powder
½ teaspoon kosher salt
1 teaspoon vanilla extract
3 large eggs
3 large egg whites
1½ cups heavy whipping cream
   Powdered sugar for flavoring cream and dusting
   Raspberries for garnish

1   To infuse the butter for the cake, rub 6 of the geranium leaves between your palms to release their oils, then wrap the leaves around the butter. Wrap in plastic wrap and refrigerate overnight.

2   To infuse the sugar for the cake, rub 4 of the geranium leaves between your palms to release their oils, then combine them with the granulated sugar in an airtight container. Let stand at room temperature overnight.

3   The next day, in a saucepan, combine the milk and 4 of the geranium leaves, place over medium heat, and heat until small bubbles appear along the edges of the pan. Remove from the heat and let steep for 1 hour. Strain the milk through a fine-mesh strainer into a clean bowl.

4   Remove the infused butter 30 minutes before you are ready to make the cake. Preheat the oven to 350°F. Butter a 10-inch springform pan with 2-inch sides. Rub the remaining 10 leaves between your palms to release their oils and arrange them on the bottom of the pan, distributing them evenly.

5   In a bowl, whisk together the flour, baking powder, and salt and set aside. Add ½ cup water and the vanilla to the infused milk and stir to mix.

6   Unwrap the butter and remove and discard the leaves. Remove the leaves from the sugar and discard. In a mixer fitted with the beater, combine the butter and infused sugar and beat on medium-high speed until ivory in color and fluffy, 1 to 2 minutes. Add the eggs, one at a time, beating well after each addition. Then add the egg whites and beat until incorporated. On medium-low speed, add the flour mixture in three batches alternately with the milk mixture in two batches, beginning and ending with the flour mixture and beating after each addition until well mixed.

7   Pour the batter into the prepared pan. Bake the cake until golden, 45 to 50 minutes. Let cool in the pan on a cooling rack for 20 minutes. Run a thin knife blade along the inside edge of the pan to loosen the cake, then unclasp the latch and lift off the sides. Invert a cooling rack on top of the cake, and then invert the cake and rack together. Lift off the pan bottom.

8   Just before serving, in a bowl, whisk the cream until soft peaks form. Add the powdered sugar to taste and whisk to mix well.

9   Transfer the cake to a cake plate, bottom side up, and dust the top with powdered sugar, then peel off the geranium leaves. Serve wedges with the whipped cream and raspberries on the side.

serves 10

MY EXPERIENCE AT TANTE MARIE'S COOKING SCHOOL confirmed my passion for teaching. In the winter of 1992, when Let's Get Cookin', a well-known cooking school and cookware store, invited me to teach a demonstration class, I was honored. I was also biting my nails: the thought of demonstrating dishes in front of an audience made me nervous.

I planned a seasonal winter menu with lots of citrus and sent it to Phyllis, the owner, along with the recipes and the shopping list.

WINTER WINE COUNTRY DINNER
Citrus Salad with Mint and Red Onions
Beef Kefta with Star Anise and Blood Oranges
Tangerine Granita with Candied Kumquats
Lemon Verbena Elixir

Phyllis called me a few days before the class. "Joanne, we're in trouble. I'm having the hardest time finding kumquats, Cara Cara and blood oranges, and star anise."

Having fun being back in the classroom.

"No problem, I'll get what we need here in San Francisco and bring everything with me," I assured her.

My unique citrus and spices, as well as items like arugula, Sweet 100 cherry tomatoes, chanterelles, green garlic, mesclun, and Padrón peppers weren't readily available at the grocery store like they are now. Thankfully, I knew how to track everything down.

I arrived at Let's Get Cookin' armed with shopping bags full of fresh produce and everything else we'd need for the class. Because the tangerine granita needed time to freeze, I immediately got started making it. Then, mimicking the Chez Panisse aesthetic, I arranged a giant bowl of bright citrus on the countertop. It made me feel a little more at home and gave me confidence. I closed my eyes and breathed deeply. You can do this, I assured myself.

The class was packed and buzzing with energy as I started my first dish, the citrus salad. While demonstrating how to peel the Cara Cara oranges with a knife, leaving only the flesh, I explained my fondness for their sweet, almost cherry-like flavor. I repeated the technique with the grapefruit and blood oranges.

As I reached the crimson flesh of the blood orange, a chorus of "wows" rose from the crowd. They'd never seen such a variety of citrus, being accustomed to only the navel oranges sold year-round at the grocery store. I wonder what they'll think of the kumquats, I thought, as I began slicing the small orange ovals into thin disks.

"What are those?" a women in the front row asked.

"Kumquats. You will love them. They're a challenge to eat whole, but I want you to try them," I said, passing a basket around. The reaction was comical. I watched faces pinch and lips pucker as the sweet-tart fruits burst in their mouths.

"You can see why I like to slice them and toss them in a salad, right?"

I placed rounds of deep red blood orange, pale yellow and soft pink grapefruit, and bright orange Cara Cara on a large white plate. I added fuchsia rings of red onion, tiny gold-orange circles of kumquat, and vibrant wedges of lime and leaves of spearmint. The result was a stunning burst of color. I smiled proudly at my masterpiece (see page 184).

For the dressing, I whisked together fruity olive oil and a touch each of honey, vinegar, and blood orange juice. I grated blood orange zest with a Microplane grater and added it along with salt and pepper. I drizzled the dressing over the salad and passed out samples to my salivating students.

"I've never eaten anything so gorgeous," one student said, staring admiringly before taking a taste.

"It's a work of art, but it's also absolutely delicious!" someone else exclaimed.

I was relieved that the demonstration was going so well. "Now, let's make *kefta*!" I announced. I knew I was in trouble as soon as the word crossed my lips. A sea of curious faces stared up at me, so I immediately explained, "*Kefta* is heavily spiced ground beef or lamb, or a combination of the two, wrapped around skewers and grilled. It's a traditional Moroccan street food, but I'm giving it a little California twist." (See recipe on page 186.)

citrus salad with mint and red onions

When I first began frequenting farmers' markets, it seemed as if I discovered a new type of citrus each visit. Beyond the standard Valencia and seedless oranges of my childhood, there were Cara Cara and blood oranges, pink grapefruits and kumquats—the varieties seemed endless. United in this citrus salad, they're a kaleidoscope of colors and a mouth-watering mélange of flavors.

1 pink grapefruit

1 yellow grapefruit

2 Cara Cara or navel oranges

2 blood oranges

½ small red onion, cut into thin rings

¼ cup extra-virgin olive oil

2 tablespoons freshly squeezed orange juice

1 tablespoon white balsamic vinegar

2 teaspoons honey

Kosher salt and freshly ground black pepper

8 kumquats, thinly sliced crosswise and seeded

2 tablespoons chopped fresh mint, plus small leaves for garnish

Lime wedges for garnish

1 Grate 1 teaspoon zest from one of the grapefruits and 2 teaspoons zest from one or two of the oranges. Set the zest aside.

2 Using a sharp knife, cut a thin slice off both the stem end and the blossom end of each grapefruit and orange to reveal the flesh. Stand a grapefruit upright on a work surface. Using a small, sharp knife, and working from the top to the bottom of the fruit, cut off the peel and white pith in wide strips, following the contour of the fruit. Invert the fruit and trim away any white pith on the opposite end. Repeat with the remaining grapefruit and all 4 oranges. Then cut the fruits crosswise into ¼-inch-thick slices and remove any seeds.

3 Arrange the citrus slices, alternating the colors, on a serving platter. Strew the onion evenly over the top. Set aside.

4 In a small bowl, whisk together the grapefruit and orange zests, then whisk in the oil, orange juice, vinegar, and honey to make a vinaigrette. Season with salt and pepper.

5 Drizzle the vinaigrette evenly over the citrus and onion slices. Scatter the kumquats over the top and sprinkle with the chopped mint. Garnish with the lime wedges and mint leaves.

serves 6

beef kefta with blood oranges

3 blood oranges
½ star anise pod
1 tablespoon coriander seeds
1½ teaspoons cumin seeds
½ teaspoon ground ginger
½ teaspoon ground cinnamon
1½ pounds ground beef
½ cup finely grated yellow onion
2 garlic cloves, minced
2 teaspoons *harissa*
3 tablespoons chopped cilantro,
   plus sprigs for garnish
2 tablespoons chopped flat-leaf parsley
   Kosher salt and freshly ground black pepper
6 large handfuls of salad greens
   Couscous for serving (optional)

DRESSING
¼ cup freshly squeezed blood orange juice
1 tablespoon Champagne vinegar
2 tablespoons white balsamic vinegar
1 teaspoon *harissa*
3 tablespoons extra-virgin olive oil
   Kosher salt and freshly ground black pepper

1 Soak 12 thick, square bamboo skewers in water to cover. Grate enough zest from the blood oranges to yield 1½ teaspoons. Set the zest and the oranges aside separately.

2 In a frying pan, toast the star anise, coriander seeds, and cumin seeds over medium-high heat until fragrant, 30 to 60 seconds. Transfer to a spice grinder, let cool, and then grind finely.

3 Transfer the spices to a large bowl and add the ginger, cinnamon, beef, onion, garlic, harissa, chopped cilantro, parsley, 2 teaspoons salt, ½ teaspoon pepper, and 1 teaspoon of the reserved orange zest. Mix well with a wooden spoon.

4 Drain the skewers. Dampen your hands with cold water and divide the mixture into 12 egg-size portions. Working with 1 portion and 1 skewer at a time, press the mixture firmly around the skewer, forming it into a rough sausage shape 4 to 5 inches long and 1 to 1¼ inches wide. Transfer to a baking sheet, cover, and refrigerate.

5 Using a sharp knife, cut a thin slice off the ends of each blood orange to reveal the flesh. Stand an orange upright on a work surface. Using a small knife, cut off the peel and white pith in wide strips, following the contour of the fruit. Holding the orange over a bowl, cut along each side of the membrane between the segments, letting each segment drop into the bowl. Repeat with the remaining oranges. Discard any seeds. Set the segments aside.

6 To make the dressing, in a small bowl, whisk together the orange juice, Champagne vinegar, balsamic vinegar, harissa, the remaining ½ teaspoon orange zest, and the oil. Season with salt and pepper.

7 Heat an outdoor grill to medium (350°F to 450°F), or preheat a ridged cast-iron stove-top grill pan over medium heat. Arrange the skewers directly over the fire or on the pan. Grill the skewers, turning as needed, until golden on all sides, 6 to 7 minutes.

8 Meanwhile, in a bowl, toss the salad greens with half of the dressing, then arrange the greens on a platter. When the skewers are ready, remove them from the grill and arrange on top of the dressed greens. Spoon the remaining dressing and the orange segments over the kefta and garnish with cilantro sprigs. Serve with couscous if you like.

serves 6

First, I toasted star anise, cumin, and coriander in a hot, dry frying pan. As the spices heated up and unfurled their sweet, smoky flavor, my students breathed in the exotic aroma. They then watched as I ground the spices, mixed them gently into the ground beef with other spices and seasonings, and shaped the mixture around thick, square bamboo skewers. I placed the *kefta* on the grill and started on my vinaigrette.

"I'm using those gorgeous blood oranges again, combining their bright juice and zest with some vinegar and *harissa*, a hot chili paste used in North African cooking. It will lend a blooming heat to our vinaigrette."

The excitement in the room was palpable. I knew that some of it was due to the intoxicating aroma of the *kefta* charring on the grill. Everyone seemed eager for a taste. But the students also seemed genuinely excited about all of the new ingredients I'd introduced that day: *harissa*, star anise, coriander, blood oranges, kumquats, Cara Caras. It was fun to witness a roomful of students discovering new flavors and ingredients.

× ● ×

IT WAS AN EXHILARATING TIME to be living, cooking, and teaching in Northern California. As the California food revolution pushed forward, restaurants like Chez Panisse were responsible for bringing a plethora of new ingredients to the market. Chefs demanded new varieties of produce and farmers responded. Growers like Tom Chino of Chino Farms and Bob Cannard of Green String Farm were cultivating previously unavailable fruits and vegetables. But volume was limited. Restaurants had first dibs and bought almost everything the farmers grew. When savvy home cooks tasted these newly obtainable ingredients at restaurants, they wanted a way to get their hands on them, too. This led to the proliferation of farmers' markets, which started to pop up throughout the Bay Area.

Not only was fresh produce more abundant, but more and more foreign ingredients were showing up on store shelves, too. Everyone seemed to be traveling, especially people I knew through culinary circles, and they weren't going only to Europe. They were also heading to Mexico, Morocco, Thailand, Japan, and more and then returning home with intriguing new ingredients, techniques, and gadgets, from spices, oils, and pastas of all shapes and colors to cured meats, dried beans and seeds, and grains. Ingredients like *harissa*, Chioggia beets, *ras el hanout*, pancetta, preserved lemons, and alpine strawberries were beginning to show up on restaurant menus.

As restaurant chefs incorporated these ingredients, methods, and tools into their repertoire, I set out to sample as much of this new world of flavor as possible. Inspired by what I had tasted, I'd experiment with introducing these new elements into my cooking and then my classes. It pleased me that my students were invariably receptive to these bold, global flavors.

"Has anyone ever tried a granita?" I asked my students, who were now, after having tasted the *kefta*, riveted on my every word.

"A what? Granite?" a gentleman asked.

"No, a granita! It's like a flavored slush. Tonight I'm making one with tangerine juice, but the possibilities are limitless. You can make a granita with any juice or fruit purée."

This frozen dessert was yet another new discovery for my class. I did a quick demo, showing them how easy it was to mix sugar and water with citrus juice, transferred it to a shallow pan, and placed the pan in the freezer. "Now, you scrape it with a fork every thirty minutes for two hours," I instructed.

"Two hours?" someone mumbled. "We won't be out of here until eleven o'clock!"

"Don't worry. I have a batch in the freezer already. I also candied some kumquats to spoon over the top," I added, as I scooped orange crystals of granita into bowls. "The sweet, tangy kumquats are a perfect counterpoint to the tart tangerine granita. You'll love it." And they did (see page 190).

I turned my attention to the final recipe for the class, an elixir made with lemon verbena, a recipe that I'd gotten from Alberto Gaburro, an older gentleman whom I'd met on a recent trip to the Veneto. I placed lemon peel, grappa, sugar, and lemon verbena in a jar and stirred until the sugar dissolved.

"This is the last obscure ingredient I'll introduce you to this evening," I promised, as I passed the fragrant lemon verbena leaves around for everyone to smell. "Now we just have to wait eight to ten days for the elixir to be ready," I joked.

"I'm only kidding!" We all laughed as I pulled a jar from the freezer and poured them each a small glass of the elixir. They swooned. Whether it was the refreshing citrus flavor, the strong, intoxicating grappa, or the combined impact of the day's discoveries, I'll never know.

lemon verbena elixir

This bright, lemony elixir is the cure for all that ails you. Okay, maybe not quite, but it is immensely refreshing and restorative. I like to keep it in the freezer and serve it ice-cold. It also makes a great host or hostess gift.

    4 lemons
    1 bottle (1 liter) grappa or 100 proof vodka
 1½ cups sugar
    2 ounces fresh lemon verbena leaves (about 1 cup)

1 Using a vegetable peeler, peel the lemons in wide strips, removing only the colored portion. If some white pith comes away with the peel, remove it by scraping it off with a paring knife.

2 In a large jar, combine the lemon peels, grappa, sugar, and lemon verbena leaves. Stir the mixture until the sugar dissolves. Cover and let sit at room temperature for 8 to 10 days.

3 After 8 to 10 days, strain the contents of the jar through a fine-mesh strainer and discard the solids. Transfer to a bottle and cap tightly. Serve at room temperature, lightly chilled, or over ice. Store in a cool, dry, dark place, or you can even store it in the freezer. It will keep for up to 1 year.

makes 1 generous liter

tangerine granita with candied kumquats

I once knew a chef who had a kumquat bush in his backyard for years and didn't realize the fruits were edible until he saw them thinly sliced on a salad. The little sweet-tart orange orbs were bursting with flavor, just waiting to be picked.

CANDIED KUMQUATS
24 kumquats
1 cup sugar

TANGERINE GRANITA
1 cup sugar
2 tablespoons grated tangerine zest
2 cups freshly squeezed tangerine juice

1 To make the candied kumquats, halve the kumquats lengthwise, removing and discarding the seeds as you go. Line a baking sheet with parchment paper.

2 In a small heavy saucepan, combine 1 cup water and the sugar and bring to a boil over high heat, stirring until the sugar dissolves. Reduce the heat to medium-low, add the kumquats, and simmer until the kumquats are tender and translucent, about 10 minutes.

3 Remove from the heat and, using a slotted spoon, transfer the kumquats to the parchment-lined pan. Return the pan to high heat, bring the syrup to a boil, and boil until reduced to ¾ cup, 3 to 5 minutes. Remove from the heat.

4 In a bowl, combine the kumquats and syrup and let cool completely.

5 To make the granita, combine 1 cup water and the sugar in a saucepan and bring to a boil over high heat, stirring until the sugar dissolves. Remove from the heat, add the tangerine zest and tangerine juice, stir well, and let cool.

6 Pour the mixture into a shallow 9- by 13-inch baking dish. Place in the freezer and freeze until ice crystals begin to form in the mixture, 1½ to 2 hours. Remove from the freezer, scrape the mixture with a fork to break up the ice crystals completely, and return the mixture to the freezer. Repeat this process every 30 minutes, making sure to break up the mixture thoroughly each time, until the mixture is the consistency of frozen slush, about 2 hours. The granita tastes best if eaten right away, though it can be held for up to 3 days in an airtight container in the freezer.

7 To serve, spoon the granita into dessert bowls and garnish with the candied kumquats and a drizzle of the syrup.

serves 8

IN 1993, THE FERRY PLAZA FARMERS MARKET opened on the Embarcadero in downtown San Francisco. I shopped there every week, learning something new each visit.

"This looks like a persimmon," I said to the farmer overseeing the stand, holding up a round orange fruit with sturdy green leaves, "but it's a different shape and it's firm."

"That's right," the farmer replied. "The one you most commonly find is the Hachiya, an oval persimmon. It's the type that is the texture of jelly when it's ripe. I bet you've used Hachiyas to make persimmon pudding at Christmas, right?"

"Exactly! So, what are these?"

"These are Fuyu persimmons, and you eat them when they're firm, just like this," he said, gently squeezing a round, squat persimmon. "My favorite way to eat them is peeled, cut into wedges, and tossed into a salad with fresh ripe figs and pears and maybe some toasted nuts."

After years of working closely with restaurant chefs, the farmers selling this new produce were well informed on how to best use each ingredient and offered a wealth of information. Here I was, a formally trained chef, learning each week from my local

My favorite place on Earth, the Ferry Plaza Farmers Market.

Making a salad with autumn's bounty.

farmers. In turn, the markets provided an opportunity for small-scale farmers to sell directly to consumers, enabling them to prosper. It was a win-win situation.

"Have you ever eaten a Muscat grape?" my new farmer friend asked me.

"No, but to be honest, I've never cared much for those overly sweet grocery store grapes. They just taste like sugar. Can I try one?"

"Of course, please!"

The Muscats were floral, with a delicately sweet, yet spicy flavor. "Here's what you do," my farmer urged. "Halve and seed them and add them to that salad I was telling you about. What I like to do is take a little of my late-harvest Riesling, reduce it by half, and add some extra-virgin olive oil and white wine vinegar for a wine-friendly salad dressing." I couldn't wait to try it that night. I placed a couple of big Muscat clusters in my bag and slung it over my shoulder. (See recipe on page 194.)

I continued on through the market and couldn't believe my eyes when I spotted a stall displaying the most beautiful array of wild mushrooms I'd ever seen: Pristinely clean egg-yolk-yellow chanterelles, black *trompettes de la mort* (trumpets of the dead), and buff-colored hedgehogs. I had encountered some of these mushrooms at Chez Panisse and in restaurants, but I had never seen them available for sale to the public. Cultivated mushrooms were available at the grocery store, but even those were relatively expensive and still considered "fancy."

Foragers were unique contributors to the food scene. They practiced the lost art of scavenging for rare and unusual wild edible plants, berries, nuts, barks, and, most commonly, mushrooms. What had started as a hobby for many of them had turned into a successful commercial business, as they regularly worked closely with restaurants that highly valued their exceptional finds. I was thrilled to see those same foragers now broadening their reach, making their prized ingredients available to eager cooks like me.

With a bit of guidance from the expert forager manning the stall, I selected a few handfuls of meaty, earthy wild mushrooms. As I happily marched home, I began concocting in my head a recipe for a warm wild mushroom salad to showcase their natural beauty (see page 197). The more I thought about my salad idea, the faster I walked.

autumn salad with figs, grapes, pomegranate, and persimmon

Renaissance paintings depict these sensual fruits, but when I was growing up, figs, persimmons, and pomegranates never made an appearance in our fruit bowl. I'm pleased to say times have changed. During the brief window in autumn when all of these fruits ripen at the same time, I celebrate the glorious harvest with this colorful salad.

½ cup pecan or walnut halves

1 small pomegranate, quartered

½ cup late-harvest Riesling

1½ tablespoons white wine vinegar

3 tablespoons extra-virgin olive oil
    Kosher salt and freshly ground black pepper

2 large heads frisée, leaves separated

1 Fuyu persimmon, stem end discarded
    and thinly sliced

1 red Bartlett pear, halved, cored, and
    thinly sliced

6 figs, stems trimmed and halved lengthwise

1½ cups Muscat grapes, halved and seeded

1 In a small frying pan, toast the nuts over medium heat, shaking the pan occasionally, until they are fragrant and have taken on some color, 3 to 4 minutes. Pour onto a plate and let cool.

2 Drop the pomegranate quarters into a bowl of cold water. Using your fingers, gently separate the seeds from the membrane and pith. The membrane and pith will float to the surface and the seeds will sink to the bottom. Discard the spent quarters and the membrane and pith, then scoop up the seeds and set them aside on paper towels to dry.

3 In a small saucepan, bring the Riesling to a boil over high heat and boil until reduced to 2 tablespoons. Transfer to a small bowl and let cool for 2 minutes. Whisk in the vinegar and oil and season with salt and pepper to make a dressing.

4 In a large bowl, combine the frisée, persimmon, pear, and figs. Add the dressing and toss gently to coat evenly. Divide the salad evenly among salad plates. Garnish with the pomegranate seeds, grapes, and nuts.

serves 6

wild mushroom bruschetta salad

I'm not much of a forager myself—it's too hard to extract the burrs from my corkscrew curls. All kidding aside, I'm ever so grateful to the skillful purveyors who make wild mushrooms so readily available. This simple bruschetta showcases the beautiful earthiness of the wild fungi.

5 tablespoons extra-virgin olive oil, plus more
   for drizzling
1 tablespoon freshly squeezed lemon juice
1 teaspoon grated lemon zest
1 small shallot, minced
   Kosher salt and freshly ground black pepper
1½ pounds fresh porcini or other wild mushrooms,
   stem ends trimmed and cut in half
2 garlic cloves, peeled but left whole
6 slices coarse-textured bread, such as Tuscan,
   toasted
8 cups arugula
6-ounce chunk grana padano cheese

1 In a bowl, whisk together 4 tablespoons of the oil, the lemon juice and zest, and the shallot to make a vinaigrette. Season with salt and pepper. Set aside.

2 Heat a large frying pan over high heat. Add the remaining 1 tablespoon oil to the pan, then add the mushrooms and cook, stirring occasionally, until golden brown and softened, 8 to 10 minutes. Season with salt and pepper. Remove the pan from the heat.

3 Using the whole garlic cloves, rub each bread slice on one side, coating it lightly. Place 1 slice of toast on each individual plate, drizzle the slices with oil, and sprinkle with salt.

4 Put the arugula in a bowl, drizzle with the vinaigrette, and toss to coat evenly. Divide the mushrooms evenly among the plates, placing them on top of the bread. Top with the arugula, dividing it evenly. Using a cheese shaver or a vegetable peeler, shave the cheese over the tops of the salads.

serves 6

CHAPTER 9

WANDERLUST

WARNING: ALTERATION, ADDITION OR MUTILATION OF ENTRIES IS PROHIBITED. ANY UNOFFICIAL CHANGE WILL RENDER THIS PASSPORT INVALID.

NAME
JOANNE TENANES SEE PAGE 5
BIRTH DATE
AUG. 2, 1952
BIRTHPLACE
MASSACHUSETTS, U.S.A.
HEIGHT
5 FEET 4 INCHES
HAIR
BROWN
EYES
BLUE
WIFE
X X X
ISSUE DATE
MAY 1, 1972
CANCELED
NEW APPLICATION
JUN 24 1977
MINORS
X X X
EXPIRATION DATE
APRIL 30, 1977
Joanne Tenanes
SIGNATURE OF BEARER

IMPORTANT: THIS PASSPORT IS NOT VALID UNTIL SIGNED BY THE BEARER. PERSONS INCLUDED HEREIN MAY NOT USE THIS PASSPORT FOR TRAVEL UNLESS ACCOMPANIED BY THE BEARER.

WHERE ARE YOU OFF TO NOW, my wandering gypsy?" my father asked.

I climbed onto my bicycle, glanced over my shoulder at him, and grinned. Then I was off, pedaling purposefully into the sunshine.

From the moment I could toddle, I loved to roam. Whether I was walking across the freshly mowed twelve-foot-wide strip of grass that separated our house from the Ritters' place next door, traipsing down the block to swim in the Richiedis' pool, or riding my fat-tired, green-striped, hand-me-down bicycle to Look Park, I couldn't be pinned down.

On a road trip with my family when I was ten years old, the familiar question, what do you want to be? circled the car. My father looked over at me and asked, "Joey, what do you want to be when you grow up?"

You should've seen the look on his face when I replied proudly, "I want to be a bus driver."

"A bus driver?" Dad was puzzled.

My well-traveled passport was completely full by the time it expired.

"I want to drive on every road in the world," I replied in earnest.

I was always out and about as a kid. I was never content to stay at home and play. When I was about as tall as my father's waist, he started calling me his "wandering gypsy." Dad had me all figured out: he understood my need to explore. My father was a man of few words, so when he did speak, everyone took note. That he gave me this sweet nickname made me feel like the most special person in the world.

When I was old enough to drive, my favorite afternoon activity was riding around with my friend Karen, exploring roads new to us and trying to get lost. A decade later, I ventured out on what was then my biggest new road. I drove straight across the United States, landed in California, and never looked back. Dad had planted the seed with his term of endearment. This wandering gypsy was going to see the world. I loved the adventure, the thrill of newness that traveling gave me. It inspired me and fed my soul.

In 1990, my Australian friend Gwenda Robb, whom I'd met when I was teaching with Madeleine Kamman in France, came to visit San Francisco. At the time, I was busy cooking at Chez Panisse by day and teaching at Tante Marie's Cooking School by night. I invited her to a class one evening.

As I drove Gwenda back to her hotel that night, she asked, "Would you be interested in coming to Australia to teach? I think Aussies would love your classes."

My heart was doing backflips, but I played it cool. "Yeah, sure, I'd be interested," I said in a collected voice, thinking nothing would ever come of the conversation.

"Great, I'll see what I can do."

A few weeks later a fax arrived.

> *Hi Joanne,*
>
> *Your Aussie friend here. Are you free in August? I've set up twenty-eight classes for you. You'll start in Sydney with six classes, go on to Perth, Brisbane, Melbourne, and then at the end, you and I can drive south to Adelaide. Maybe we can even squeeze in a trip to the Barossa to taste some wine and ride bikes on the Riesling Trail? Oh, almost forgot, the folks at Hayman Island invited you to come and have a few leisure days there. What do you say, mate?*
>
> *Kisses,*
>
> *Gwenda*

I couldn't believe my eyes. I wrote back immediately. "Will I get to see kangaroos and koala bears, too?"

⨉ ● ⨉

I GOT OFF MY QUANTAS FLIGHT, jet-lagged and unsure of where I was. But I soon felt like a rock star when a black town car, courtesy of Gwenda, whisked me away to my hotel. After a good night's sleep, we drove the next morning through the Yarra Valley en route to my first event. There, in front of the TarraWarra Estate Winery, was a troop of kangaroos chomping on vines. I squealed. It doesn't get more Down Under than that, I thought to myself. It was the perfect welcome.

It didn't take long for me to fall madly and hopelessly in love with Australia, the people, the vibrant mix of cultures, the trendy Asian- and Mediterranean-inspired food, and the extraordinary Riesling and Shiraz wines. I got to know culinary legends like Maggie Beer, Stephanie Alexander, Tetsuya, Gay Bilson, and Janni Kyritsis. I tasted foods I'd never encountered before: smoked kangaroo tail, Anzac biscuits, damper on a stick, Balmain bugs, Lamingtons, Vegemite on toast, and hamburger with beetroot. I'm happy to say I graciously passed on the witchetty grubs. I learned to say toe-mah-toe and always to call the first meal of the day brekkie. And if that wasn't enough, I got my wish and held a koala.

Inspired by my years at Chez Panisse, I was excited to teach what I'd learned about fresh, seasonal cooking—about taking the best ingredients and preparing them simply to bring out their natural flavors. I was on the cusp of creating my own cooking style, taking classic techniques and recipes and employing a personal twist to make them my own: serving shaved raw root vegetable chips with roasted carrot hummus (see page 205) or making risotto with farro instead of rice.

Words like *local*, *sustainable*, and *seasonal* that were commonplace in California were new to Australians, and no farmers' markets had been established anywhere in the country. My students were fascinated by the California food revolution and the concepts that I was introducing. I was a new voice bringing an innovative approach to food and cooking, and the Aussies literally ate it up. It was a perfect fit. I returned year after year to travel the vast country and to teach new, fun recipes.

After a few years of teaching annually in Australia, food writer and friend Lauraine Jacobs invited me to teach in New Zealand. At the time, New Zealand, like Australia, was fairly isolated from innovations in the food world. My teaching was a breath of fresh California air to the Kiwis.

I traveled the country from the northern tip of the northern island down to the southern tip of the southern island, educating eager students about California cuisine. My repertoire of simple, rustic recipes included pork riblets braised with aged balsamic vinegar (see page 206), creamy coconut and citrus sorbet (see page 209), and panna cotta with Greek yogurt, toasted walnuts, and local honey (see page 210). These dishes opened their eyes to new uses for ingredients, some familiar and some not yet seen in New Zealand. And that stunning island nation wowed me with phenomenal Bluff oysters; young, tender lamb; green-lipped mussels; and extraordinary Sauvignon Blanc and Pinot Noir.

On my first visit to New Zealand, I planned to teach the students how to make a *tagine* of lamb with artichokes. When I got to the cooking school and looked at the ingredients set out on the counter for me, I found a can of artichoke hearts sitting next to the lamb.

"What's this for?" I wondered aloud.

"Your *tagine*," my teaching assistant replied.

"I need fresh artichokes."

"We don't have fresh artichokes." I'd forgotten I wasn't in California, the land of abundant produce. I made do with what we had.

The next year when I returned to teach, the artichoke incident fresh in my memory, I taught a recipe that I'd developed using canned artichokes along with grape leaves, lemon zest, and shaved parmigiano-reggiano. The combination was vibrant, briny, and zesty and a total hit when served on top of crostini (see page 205).

Sailing in the Sydney Harbour with a friend.

✕

farro risotto with caramelized onions and madeira

Risotto, the classic northern Italian rice dish, gets a tasty makeover when prepared with farro in place of rice. Delightfully earthy and chewy, with the familiar creaminess of risotto, it's an innovation worth trying.

2 cups chicken stock (page 276)
2 tablespoons extra-virgin olive oil
2 red onions, halved through the stem end and thinly sliced
2 cups semipearled farro (emmer)
¾ cup dry Riesling
Kosher salt and freshly ground pepper
1 tablespoon unsalted butter
3 tablespoons madeira (optional)
1 cup grated parmigiano-reggiano cheese
¼ cup canola oil
3 shallots, thinly sliced and slices separated

1   In a saucepan, combine the stock and 2 cups water and bring to a boil over high heat. Move the pan to a back burner over low heat and keep the liquid just below the boiling point. Place a ladle in the pan.

2   In a large, heavy saucepan, heat the olive oil over medium heat. Add the onions and cook, stirring occasionally, until light golden and very soft, 30 to 40 minutes. Add the farro and cook, stirring constantly to coat the grains with oil and "toast" them, about 2 minutes. Add the wine and cook, stirring, until the wine evaporates, about 1 minute.

3   Add ½ teaspoon salt and a ladle of the hot stock and stir the farro constantly, wiping it from the bottom and sides of the pot. When most of the liquid has been absorbed but the farro is still loose, add another ladle of the stock and cook, stirring, until most of the liquid has been absorbed. Continue to add the stock, a ladle at a time, and cook, stirring often, until most of the liquid has been absorbed before adding more. The farro is ready when it is tender, 25 to 30 minutes total. If you run out of stock before the farro is done, add hot water.

4   Remove the farro from the heat and stir in a ladle of stock (or hot water), the butter, the madeira (if using), and half of the cheese. Cover and let sit for 5 minutes.

5   Meanwhile, in a small frying pan, heat the canola oil over medium-high heat until it ripples. Test the oil with a shallot slice; if it sizzles on contact, the oil is ready. Working in batches, add the shallots and fry until golden brown, 1 to 2 minutes. Using a slotted spoon, transfer the shallots to paper towels to drain and immediately sprinkle with salt.

6   To serve, uncover, season with salt and pepper, stir, and spoon into warmed individual bowls. Sprinkle the risotto with the remaining cheese and the shallots.

serves 6

roasted carrot hummus with vegetable chips

ROASTED CARROT HUMMUS

¾ pound carrots, peeled and cut into 1-inch pieces
    Kosher salt
1½ tablespoons extra-virgin olive oil
 2 tablespoons tahini (sesame paste), well stirred
 1 teaspoon firmly packed light brown sugar
½ teaspoon ground cumin
    Pinch of red chile flakes, or to taste

    Variety of root vegetables, such as unpeeled turnip and radishes, plus trimmed and peeled parsnip, carrot, red beets, and yellow beets

1 Preheat the oven to 375°F. Put the carrots on a sheet of parchment paper. Sprinkle with salt, drizzle with oil, toss to coat evenly, and then wrap loosely in the parchment, sealing the edges. Place on a baking sheet. Bake until tender, 30 to 40 minutes. Open the parchment and continue to roast for 5 minutes. Let cool completely, then transfer to a food processor. Add the tahini, brown sugar, cumin, and chile flakes, and process until smooth, scraping down the sides of the bowl. Add a little water if needed to thin. Transfer to a bowl and season with salt.

2 To make the chips, have ready 2 bowls of ice water. Using a mandoline, cut the turnip, parsnip, radishes, and carrot into paper-thin slices and add them to one bowl. Cut the beets in the same way and add them to the second bowl. Let stand for 15 minutes. Pat the vegetable slices dry on towels and arrange on a platter. Serve with the hummus.

serves 6

crostini with artichokes and grape leaves

Fresh artichokes weren't available the first time I taught in New Zealand, so I had to make do with a can of brined artichoke hearts. The resulting crostini were such a hit, this remains one of my favorite go-to appetizers.

 6 whole artichokes hearts in brine, well drained and very coarsely chopped
 4 grape leaves in brine, well drained, stems removed, and very coarsely chopped
½ cup green olives, such as picholine or Castelvetrano, pitted
 1 garlic clove, minced
½ teaspoon grated lemon zest
 6 to 8 shavings parmigiano-reggiano cheese
1½ tablespoons extra-virgin olive oil
 1 tablespoon freshly squeezed lemon juice
    Kosher salt and freshly ground black pepper
16 slices coarse-textured bread, about 2 inches in diameter, toasted or grilled
    Lemon wedges for garnish

1 In a bowl, stir together the artichokes, grape leaves, olives, garlic, and lemon zest. Transfer the mixture to a cutting board and chop together until the mixture is coarsely chopped. Return the mixture to the bowl, add the cheese, oil, and lemon juice and stir gently to mix. Season with salt and pepper.

2 To serve, spread the mixture on the toasted bread, dividing it evenly, and arrange on a platter. Garnish with the lemon wedges.

makes 16 crostini; serves 8

skillet riblets with balsamic

I grew up eating my mom's over-the-moon grilled spareribs dripping with spicy home-made barbecue sauce. My updated version features a rosemary-infused balsamic vinegar and red wine glaze in place of the sauce, but the tender meat, falling right off the bone, is just like Mom's.

2 racks baby back ribs or St. Louis–cut spareribs, about 4 pounds total weight, halved lengthwise by the butcher
Kosher salt
1 tablespoon extra-virgin olive oil
2 garlic cloves, crushed
1 cup dry red wine, such as Cabernet Sauvignon
½ cup peeled, seeded, and chopped tomatoes (fresh or canned)
¾ cup high-quality balsamic vinegar, preferably aged
3 rosemary sprigs
Large pinch of red chile flakes
3 cups low-sodium beef broth
5 cups water
1½ cups coarse-grind polenta
3 tablespoons unsalted butter

1 Cut the ribs into 2- or 3-rib sections, then either sprinkle them with salt or immerse them in a brine made in a ratio of 2 teaspoons salt to 1 cup water. Cover and refrigerate overnight.

2 The next day, if you have brined the ribs, discard the brine and pat the ribs dry. In a large frying pan, heat the oil over medium-high heat. Working in batches to avoid crowding, add the ribs and brown, turning them occasionally, until golden, 10 to 12 minutes. Using tongs, transfer the ribs to a platter. Reserve 1 tablespoon of the fat in the pan; pour off and discard any remaining fat.

3 Return the pan to medium heat. Add the garlic and cook, stirring occasionally, until light golden, 30 to 60 seconds. Add the wine, tomatoes, and vinegar, bring to a boil, and boil for 1 minute. Add the rosemary, chile flakes, and the ribs, meat side down, then pour in the broth, which should almost cover the meat. Bring to a boil, reduce the heat to medium-low, cover, and simmer, turning occasionally, until the meat is tender and almost falling off the bone, about 1 hour.

4 While the ribs are cooking, cook the polenta. In a saucepan, bring the water to a boil over high heat. Slowly add the polenta in a fine shower while whisking constantly. Season with 1 teaspoon salt and continue to whisk until the mixture begins to bubble. Reduce the heat to medium-low and simmer, stirring often with a wooden spoon, until the polenta is thick, no longer tastes grainy, and if you stand the wooden spoon in the center of the pot, it remains almost upright, 15 to 20 minutes. Remove from the heat, season with salt, cover, and set aside until serving.

5 When the ribs are done, uncover the polenta, add the butter, and stir well. Place over medium heat and heat, stirring occasionally, for 5 minutes to heat through. At the same time, using tongs or a large slotted spoon, transfer the ribs to a plate. Strain the sauce through a fine-mesh strainer into a clear glass bowl or measuring pitcher, then skim off any fat from the surface with a large spoon. Return the sauce to the frying pan, place over medium-low heat, bring to a simmer, and reduce if needed to thicken to a syrupy consistency. Return the ribs to the sauce and turn them gently to coat evenly.

6 To serve, spoon the polenta into warmed individual bowls, dividing it evenly. Top with the ribs and their sauce.

serves 6

citrus coconut sorbet

This ice-cold tropical treat is a delightfully refreshing dessert. Served in frozen navel orange "bowls," the playful presentation is nearly as popular as the sorbet itself.

3 navel oranges
½ cup freshly squeezed lime juice
½ cup freshly squeezed lemon juice
1 cup canned coconut milk
⅔ cup sugar

1 Cut 1 orange in half crosswise and squeeze the halves to yield ½ cup juice. Set the juice aside. Cut the remaining 2 oranges in half crosswise, squeeze the juice from them, and reserve the juice for another use. Check to see if the halves will stand upright. If not, cut a thin slice off the bottom. Put the orange halves in the freezer.

2 To make the sorbet, in a bowl, combine the ½ cup orange juice, the lime and lemon juices, the coconut milk, and the sugar and stir until the sugar is completely dissolved. Transfer the mixture to ice-cube trays and freeze overnight.

3 The next day, transfer the frozen cubes to a high-powered blender and process until smooth and the consistency of sorbet.

4 To serve, place a frozen orange half on each dessert plate and scoop the sorbet onto the halves, dividing it evenly.

serves 6

greek yogurt panna cotta with walnuts and honey

When I first created this recipe, Greek yogurt was pretty hard to come by. Thankfully, it's available almost everywhere nowadays. The yogurt lends a lovely tanginess to the rich, creamy, subtly nutty panna cotta. If you like, substitute 1½ cups of almond milk for the walnut half-and-half.

WALNUT HALF-AND-HALF

- 1 cup walnuts
- 1 tablespoon honey
- Pinch of kosher salt

PANNA COTTA

- 1 envelope (2½ teaspoons) unflavored gelatin
- 1½ cups walnut half-and-half (above)
- ½ cup sugar
- 1 vanilla bean, split lengthwise
- 1½ cups plain Greek yogurt
- ¾ cup walnut halves
- ½ cup honey

  Boiling water for unmolding

1 To make the walnut half-and-half, combine the walnuts in a small bowl with water to cover and let sit at room temperature for 2 hours.

2 Drain and rinse the walnuts, then transfer to a blender. Add 2 cups water, the honey, and the salt and blend until very smooth, about 2 minutes. Strain through a fine-mesh strainer into a measuring pitcher. You should have 2 generous cups. Measure 1½ cups to use for the panna cotta. Reserve the remainder in an airtight container in the refrigerator for another use.

3 To make the panna cotta, put 2 tablespoons water in a small bowl, sprinkle the gelatin over the water, and let stand for 5 minutes.

4 In a saucepan, combine the walnut half-and-half and sugar. Using a sharp knife, split the vanilla bean pod lengthwise, then scrape the seeds from the pod and add to the pan with the pod. Place over medium heat and bring to a simmer, stirring to dissolve the sugar. Remove from the heat and stir in the gelatin mixture.

5 Remove the vanilla bean pod from the walnut mixture and discard. Spoon the yogurt into a medium bowl, then slowly add the warm walnut mixture while whisking gently to combine thoroughly. Divide the yogurt mixture evenly among eight ½-cup ramekins. Cover and refrigerate until set, at least 3 hours or up to overnight.

6 In a small frying pan, toast the walnuts over medium heat, shaking the pan occasionally, until they are fragrant and have taken on some color, 3 to 4 minutes. Pour onto a plate and let cool.

7 In a saucepan, combine the toasted walnuts, honey, and 1 to 2 tablespoons water over medium heat, stir well, and warm slightly, about 1 minute. Remove from the heat and let cool completely.

8 Just before serving, fill a bowl with boiling water. Run a small, thin-bladed knife around the inside rim of each ramekin to loosen the panna cotta. Dip a ramekin into the boiling water up to the rim for 1 second, invert a dessert plate over the ramekin, invert the ramekin and plate together, and lift off the ramekin. You may have to tap and shake the ramekin or use a small knife to loosen the panna cotta. Repeat with the remaining ramekins.

9 Top each serving with honey and walnuts.

serves 8

Teaching my students how to make spinach pasta in Tuscany.

"CAN WE MEET FOR COFFEE? I'm here in San Francisco," Pia Scavia said in her melodious Italian accent.

I'd never met Pia Scavia before. She'd just gotten off a plane from Milan and was armed with a pile of Tasting Italy brochures that boasted grand villas with cavernous kitchens and outdoor pizza ovens. She wanted to know if I could help her fill her cooking classes.

As we sat drinking cappuccino, we realized that we had a lot in common, namely a love for food and travel. Pia told me all about Tasting Italy's kitchen-centric vacations. She spoke passionately about visiting gorgeous destinations and immersing oneself in the country's culture and cuisine. Then, as she cocked her head and raised her eyebrows, she announced, "I think you should come teach in my program, maybe in the Veneto in northern Italy?" I didn't need any convincing. I booked an Alitalia flight that very day.

The memory of the cypress-lined lane that led to our home for the week, La Foresteria, the sprawling historic villa owned by Count Serego Alighieri, a direct descendant of Dante, will stay with me forever.

On arrival, I greeted my students with glasses of prosecco to celebrate the start of our Italian adventure together. Everybody sipped in silence, which made the atmosphere seem oddly formal. Oh no, do I have a group of duds? I wondered fearfully. Finally, the bubbles kicked in, and a flurry of conversation erupted. I breathed a sigh of relief.

Excitement continued to build as I handed out our itinerary for the week. Plans for our excursion to Venice had the group giddy. We would ride a gondola, lunch at a friend's villa on the Grand Canal, shop the outdoor Rialto vegetable and fish markets, sip coffee at Caffè Florian in Piazza San Marco, and visit a couple of *bacari*, Venetian wine bars, for *cicchetti*, the local equivalent of Spanish tapas. I was just as excited as my students.

When we weren't off seeing the sights, we spent our days in the villa's expansive kitchen. We cooked dishes inspired by northern Italian classics, focusing on local ingredients and my personal penchant for vibrant, fresh flavors. We made *piadine,* grilled flatbread piled high with peppery arugula and whispers of shaved taleggio (see page 215), and a green Caprese salad with creamy mozzarella, sugar snap peas, asparagus, and fresh mint and oregano from the garden. Crowded around the huge kitchen island, we rolled sheets of pasta by the yard, as small clouds of flour rose from surface. Steps away, pots of salted water bubbled away wildly, making the air so humid that we had to step through the tall, arched doorway to cool off in the courtyard. Each afternoon, we sat at a table that overlooked the lush Italian countryside and feasted on the fruits of our labor. I had to pinch myself. Was this really my job? Empty wine bottles and clean plates were signs of the day's success.

green caprese salad

Wandering the outdoor Rialto market in Venice one spring with my students, I was inspired to incorporate fresh, green produce in place of the tomatoes often used in this classic Italian salad. Thus, my favorite spring salad was born.

1½ pounds fava beans in the pod
　　Kosher salt and freshly ground black pepper
6 ounces asparagus, tough ends removed and
　　cut on the diagonal into 1-inch lengths
1 cup shelled fresh English peas
1 pound *mozzarella di bufala* cheese, sliced
1 tablespoon chopped fresh mint
2 teaspoons chopped fresh savory (optional)
1 teaspoon chopped fresh oregano
¼ cup extra-virgin olive oil
1½ cups young, tender salad greens

1 Remove the fava beans from their pods and discard the pods. Bring a saucepan of water to a boil, add the favas, and boil for 30 seconds. Drain, let cool, then peel away the outer skin from each bean. Set the beans aside in a bowl.

2 In a saucepan, bring 2 cups salted water to a boil. Add the asparagus and cook until almost tender, 3 to 5 minutes. Using a slotted spoon, transfer to the bowl with the favas. Add the peas to the boiling water, cook for 30 seconds, drain, and add to the asparagus. Let cool completely.

3 Arrange the mozzarella on a platter. Scatter the vegetables over the cheese. Sprinkle with the herbs. Drizzle with the oil and sprinkle with salt and pepper. Scatter the salad greens over the top.

serves 6

piadine with arugula, cherry, and pistachio salad

This is hands-down one of my favorite creative Italian dishes. It combines two things that I love: pizza and salad. The crisp flatbread is traditional, but the ingredients on top are uniquely my own; you'd never find this combination in Italy, but that's what makes it fun!

PIADINE DOUGH
- 2 teaspoons active dry yeast
- ¾ cup plus 1 tablespoon warm (110°F) water
- 2 cups unbleached bread flour
- ½ teaspoon kosher salt

- 1½ tablespoons freshly squeezed lemon juice
- 2 tablespoons extra-virgin olive oil
- Kosher salt and freshly ground black pepper
- 5 cups loosely packed arugula
- ½ cup fresh mint leaves
- ½ cup cilantro leaves
- ½ cup fresh basil leaves
- 1½ cups cherries, halved and pitted
- ½ cup salted roasted pistachios

1 To make the dough, in a large bowl, combine the yeast, ¼ cup of the warm water, and ¼ cup of the flour and stir to mix. Let the mixture sit at room temperature until bubbles are visible, about 30 minutes.

2 Add the remaining 1¾ cups flour, remaining ½ cup plus 1 tablespoon warm water, and the salt and, using a wooden spoon, stir until the dough comes together in a rough mass.

3 Lightly flour a work surface, turn the dough out, and knead until smooth, 7 to 8 minutes. Shape the dough into a ball, place in an oiled bowl, cover with plastic wrap, and let the dough rise in a warm place (about 75°F) until double in volume, 1 to 1½ hours.

4 Thirty minutes before you are ready to bake, place a pizza stone on the lowest rack in the oven and preheat the oven to 500°F or to the highest temperature possible.

5 To make the dressing, in a bowl, whisk together the lemon juice and olive oil. Season with salt and pepper and set aside.

6 Lightly flour a work surface and turn the dough out. Divide it in half and form each half into a ball. Flatten and stretch 1 dough ball into a circle 12 to 13 inches in diameter and ⅛ to ¼ inch thick. If the dough will not stretch to this size, let it rest for 5 minutes and try again.

7 Lightly flour a pizza peel (or a rimless cookie sheet) and transfer the dough circle to the peel. Lightly brush the dough to within ½ inch of the edge with olive oil. Using fork tines, puncture the dough in several places (this will prevent the dough from forming big bubbles in the oven). Slide the dough circle onto the pizza stone and bake until golden and crisp, 8 to 10 minutes.

8 Meanwhile, in a bowl, combine half each of the arugula, mint, cilantro, basil, cherries, and pistachios. Drizzle with half of the dressing, then toss to coat evenly.

9 Using the peel, remove the piadina from the oven and slide it onto a wooden serving board. Top with the salad and fold it in half. Repeat with the remaining dough and salad ingredients. Cut each piadina into thirds to serve.

makes 2 piadine; serves 6

My first culinary tour of the Veneto had gone off without a hitch. Well, almost. In Venice, a tipsy midwestern student of mine fell into the Grand Canal. Two *gondolieri* had to fish him out with their oars. He was soaking wet when we arrived at the door of the iconic Harry's Bar to have one of Italy's most famous cocktails, the Bellini, a mixture of prosecco and white peach juice. We were almost home before his clothes had fully dried.

⚸ ● ⚸

DESPITE HAVING ALMOST LOST A STUDENT to a Venetian canal, I was asked to return to Italy time and again to lead culinary tours. On a trip to the Piedmont region, I took my group truffle hunting. Master truffle hunter Martino insisted that he pick us up at midnight to hunt during the harvest moon. I had some crazy notion that truffle hunting meant we'd get decked out in plaid Burberry and gracefully wander the woods in search of the prized fungi. In reality, we spent the night chasing two dogs, Sheila and Gussy, as they barked incessantly and ran wildly up and down muddy hills in a forest filled with pricker bushes. I was so caked in mud by the time we arrived back at our villa after the hunt that I had to throw away my shoes and jacket. Even more disappointing, those barking dogs hadn't found a single truffle.

But the next morning, Martino returned to our villa with a surprising gift. As soon as I opened his van door, I was bowled over by the sexy, musky scent of truffles. Martino's dogs had in fact found truffles, but he wanted to keep their location secret. He had gone back after he dropped us off to let the dogs work their magic. That afternoon, we shaved four golf ball–size truffles over our homemade fettuccine. Doused in pungent olive oil, it was a meal I'll always remember.

In Piedmont, I loved taking my students shopping at the outdoor market in the small town of Nizza Monferrato. We bought anchovies for *bagna cauda*, bunches of cardoons, bags of freshly ground polenta, artisanal cheeses, and impossibly fresh fruits. One morning, I was inspired to make *mostarda*.

"You're making mustard?" a student questioned, her southern accent sounding particularly thick next to the Italian voices dancing in the air.

"Well, like mustard, *mostarda* is a condiment, but it is more similar to chutney. It is made with fresh or dried fruit and mustard essence and is very trendy in the States right now. See the gorgeous apricots, plums, and nectarines? We'll use those," I explained.

We made a simplified version of *mostarda* that day using the stone fruits and adding sharp mustard along with sugar and vinegar. The result was sweet, spicy, and assertive. In the evening, we served it alongside roasted duck breast, and it cut through the richness of the duck just as I had hoped it would. That *mostarda* was an example of my Italian fusion cuisine at its finest. I was taking inspiration from Italy's best produce, drawing ideas from its culture and cuisine, and creating a dish that was at once Italian, yet distinctly my own.

The Nizza market was close to our villa, so we went there often. On another visit, we found perfectly ripe fresh figs.

"How do you know they're ripe?" asked a student. "We never see figs in Boston."

Taking a break from teaching in Italy. Cooking with a nonna in Italy, with my friend Brett Jackson at my side.

⚸

"See the cracks along the side. That shows me they're bursting with sweetness and flavor," I instructed.

We bought a bunch of figs, and when we got back "home," we filled them with fresh, creamy goat cheese, wrapped them in paper-thin slices of prosciutto, and grilled them. The salty cured meat melted around the plump fruits and turned crisp at the edges. The result was simple and delicious (see page 220).

Home in Piedmont was La Villa Hotel, a four-century-old gem surrounded by fruit trees and vineyards and tucked into a rolling hillside near the small town of Mombaruzzo. Living together for a week in a stunning villa and cooking together with like-minded, food-loving people was a dream. But it wasn't all romance and glamour.

The work I put into every trip was tedious and time-consuming. The various tasks—organizing travel arrangements, working with the language barrier, writing recipes, planning meals and shopping—would often make my head spin. Perhaps the hardest part was managing the personalities in a house harboring fourteen strangers. Sometimes, everyone clicked. Other times, results were wild and crazy.

On one trip, the water main in Mombaruzzo broke. It didn't take long to realize that cooking classes were practically impossible without water. It was like camping. By the third day of no water, the troops were getting restless. The weather was hot and sticky, and everyone was anxious to shower. But there was absolutely nothing I could do. When a photographer came knocking at the door, I almost didn't open it. Weeks before, I had arranged for him to take a class photograph, and I had forgotten all about it until he arrived. To this day, every time I look at that photograph, I laugh. Our hair was matted to our heads, tensions were running high, and we certainly weren't saying "cheese" for his camera.

⤫ ● ⤫

FOR MY TUSCANY TOURS, we stayed at the idyllic Villa il Leccio in Strada. Just down the road was the little village of Panzano, where we went to visit my friend Dario Cecchini, the most famous butcher in all of Italy, if not the world. Antica Macelleria Cecchini isn't an ordinary butcher shop. Along one wall is a table set with Dario's salted and spiced *porchetta* served with chili jam, orange-scented olives, house-made salami, crostini topped with spiced *lardo*, and jugs of Dario's homemade Chianti. We'd stand around for hours sampling Dario's goods as he recited Dante and sang.

Late one afternoon, I decided that we should make a quick run to Dario's to grab some chicken breasts for our afternoon class. After thirty minutes of photographs with Dario, kisses from Dario, Dario reciting Dante, and laughing and partying, one of my students disappeared into the walk-in refrigerator with one of the shop's butchers. She came back out with lipstick smudged all around her lips. We were just there for some chicken and somehow found ourselves in the middle of a Tuscan love affair.

Later that day, we stuffed those chicken breasts with shredded fontina and sweet dried figs (see page 222). As the stuffed breasts cooked, the melting cheese oozed out from their sides, becoming crisp and charred against the pan. A drizzle of aged balsamic on top pulled

the whole dish together. The entire group grinned throughout the meal that evening. Was it the quality of our cooking or thoughts of the tryst in the walk-in? I'll never know.

My culinary tour to Cinque Terre sold out within minutes of the posting and rightfully so. We walked from town to town, including along the Via dell'Amore (Path of Love) from Riomaggiore to Manarola, taking in magnificent views of the aquamarine Italian Riviera. In Monterosso, we learned how to make *focaccia al formaggio* at Focacceria Il Frantoio. We ate so much of the soft, puffy warm dough filled with melted cheese that all we could muster for dinner was a salad of thinly shaved fennel, sweet dried fruit, and prosciutto ribbons.

Another day, I hired a boat for the group. We went out on the Mediterranean, where we drank prosecco and ate seafood cooked on a tiny grill the captain fired up for us. I relished the fresh grilled calamari and halibut skewers as I baked in the sunshine and gazed at the crystal blue waters from which the seafood had just come. A few people decided to go for a swim. I won't mention whether or not bathing suits were involved. What happens in the Mediterranean after eighteen bottles of prosecco stays in the Mediterranean.

Throughout my Italian travels, I continually discovered new ingredients and techniques, adjusting them to create dishes that were my own. Italy was feeding me valuable lessons about food, and I was eating them up.

fennel, prune, and grana padano salad with prosciutto

After eating so much focaccia in Monterosso, this combination of sweet prunes, bitter frisée, bright fennel, and salty prosciutto was truly perfection.

2 teaspoons crushed fennel seeds
¼ cup extra-virgin olive oil
1 tablespoon freshly squeezed lemon juice
  Kosher salt
2 heads frisée, leaves separated
2 bulbs fennel, trimmed, halved, and very thinly sliced crosswise
3- to 4-ounce chunk grana padano cheese
15 prunes, pitted and sliced
6 thin slices prosciutto, serrano ham, or duck prosciutto, halved lengthwise

1 In a frying pan over medium-high heat, toast the fennel seeds, shaking the pan, until aromatic, 15 to 30 seconds. Add the oil and stir together. Remove from the heat and let sit for 20 minutes.

2 Strain the oil through a fine-mesh strainer into a bowl; discard the seeds. Whisk the lemon juice into the oil. Season with salt.

3 Add the frisée and fennel to the dressing and toss to coat evenly, then transfer to a large serving bowl. Using a cheese shaver or vegetable peeler, shave the cheese over the salad. Scatter the prunes over the vegetables and cheese, then twist each ribbon of prosciutto and arrange on top.

serves 6

grilled prosciutto-wrapped figs with goat cheese and thyme

A little trattoria in the town of Alba in the Piedmont region of Italy serves these bites of heaven. I ate there with my students, and they begged to re-create the irresistible stuffed figs at our villa. We did, with great success.

3 ounces fresh goat cheese
1 tablespoon chopped fresh thyme
2 teaspoons grated lemon zest
6 black Mission figs, stems removed and
    halved lengthwise
12 thin slices prosciutto
¼ cup extra-virgin olive oil, plus more for brushing
2 tablespoons balsamic vinegar
1 tablespoon freshly squeezed lemon juice
    Kosher salt and freshly ground black pepper
5 cups baby arugula

1 Heat a grill to medium (350°F to 450°F). In a small bowl, stir together the goat cheese, thyme, and lemon zest.

2 Put 1 tablespoon of the goat cheese mixture on the cut side of each fig half, then wrap each with a prosciutto slice. Brush the figs lightly with oil.

3 In a large bowl, whisk together the vinegar and lemon juice, then whisk in the oil to make a vinaigrette. Season with salt and pepper and set aside.

4 Arrange the figs on the grill rack over the fire and grill, turning, until light golden, 4 to 5 minutes. Move the figs to a cooler area of the grill and cook, turning as needed, until the prosciutto is crisp and the figs are soft, 5 to 6 minutes.

5 Just before the figs are ready, add the arugula to the vinaigrette and toss to coat evenly. Divide the arugula evenly among individual salad plates. Carefully remove the finished figs from the grill, and top each bed of greens with 2 or 3 fig halves.

serves 4 to 6

chicken breasts stuffed with dried figs and fontina

Only the Italians could take five simple ingredients and turn them into such a mouth-watering dish. Rich with creamy fontina cheese and sweet dried figs, this stuffed chicken breast just may be your new favorite weeknight dinner. Be sure to enjoy the crisp, charred cheese that inevitably bakes onto the pan— it's my favorite part!

12 dried figs, sliced

6 ounces Italian fontina cheese, coarsely shredded
   Kosher salt and freshly ground black pepper

6 boned chicken breast halves with skin attached

1 tablespoon extra-virgin olive oil

⅓ cup aged balsamic vinegar

1 Preheat the oven to 375°F. In a bowl, stir together the figs, cheese, and ½ teaspoon salt, mixing well.

2 To make a pocket in each chicken breast, using a small, sharp knife, cut a horizontal slit 1 inch long into the thickest part of the side of the breast. Using a sawing motion, continue to cut into the chicken to the opposite side of the breast, being careful not to cut all the way through. To stuff the breast, slip your index finger into the pocket to open it up slightly, then stuff one-sixth of the cheese-and-fig mixture into the pocket. Season the outside of each breast with salt and pepper.

3 In a large ovenproof frying pan, heat the oil over medium-high heat. Place the chicken breasts, skin side down, in the pan, and sear the chicken until the skin is golden brown, 2 to 3 minutes. Turn and continue to cook on the second side until light golden, about 2 minutes. Transfer the pan to the oven and cook until an instant-read thermometer inserted into the thickest part of a chicken breast registers 165°F, 12 to 15 minutes.

4 Remove the pan from the oven and, using tongs, transfer the chicken breasts to a platter. Be careful when grasping the handle of the pan as it will be very hot! Tent loosely with foil and let rest for 10 minutes.

5 Cut each chicken breast against the grain into slices ½ inch thick, and fan the slices on a warmed individual plate. Drizzle each chicken breast with a scant 1 tablespoon vinegar.

serves 6

halibut and squash ribbon skewers with pistachio-mint salsa verde

I could eat this rustic Italian green sauce every night of the week. Drizzled over skewers lined with elegant ribbons of zucchini and cubes of halibut, this dish is visually dazzling. But the salsa verde is just as tasty with any fish, poultry, meat, or vegetable.

PISTACHIO-MINT SALSA VERDE
½ cup packed fresh mint leaves
½ cup packed flat-leaf parsley leaves
1 garlic clove, minced
3 tablespoons extra-virgin olive oil
¼ cup salted roasted pistachios, coarsely chopped
1 teaspoon grated lemon zest
1½ tablespoons freshly squeezed lemon juice
   Kosher salt and freshly ground black pepper

1 tablespoon chopped fresh mint
1 tablespoon chopped fresh oregano
1 tablespoon chopped chives
1 teaspoon chopped fresh thyme
3 tablespoons extra-virgin olive oil
   Kosher salt and freshly ground black pepper
1½ pounds skinned halibut fillets, cut into
   1- to 1¼-inch cubes
4 medium zucchini (about 1½ pounds total
   weight)

1 To make the salsa verde, combine the mint, parsley, and garlic on a cutting board and chop finely together. Transfer to a small bowl, add the oil, pistachios, and lemon zest and juice, and stir well. Season with salt and pepper and set aside.

2 In a medium bowl, combine the mint, oregano, chives, thyme, and 2 tablespoons of the oil and stir together. Season with salt and pepper. Add the fish and stir gently to coat evenly.

3 Using a vegetable peeler or mandoline, slice a zucchini lengthwise into long, paper-thin ribbons until you reach the core with the seeds, then rotate the zucchini and repeat to cut more ribbons. Continue in this manner until only the core with the seeds remains. Discard the core and repeat with the remaining zucchini.

4 Heat an outdoor grill to medium-high (about 450°F), or preheat a ridged cast-iron stove-top grill pan over medium-high heat. Have ready metal skewers or bamboo skewers that have soaked in water to cover for 30 minutes.

5 In a bowl, toss the squash ribbons with the remaining 1 tablespoon oil until well coated. Alternately thread the halibut cubes and squash ribbons onto the skewers, weaving each ribbon over and under to create a wave effect. Season the loaded skewers with salt and pepper.

6 If using an outdoor grill, arrange the skewers directly over the fire. If using a stove-top pan, arrange the skewers on the pan. Grill the skewers, turning once, until the halibut has light golden grill marks, about 2 minutes on each side.

7 Transfer the skewers to a platter or individual plates and accompany with the salsa verde.

serves 6

❧

*Teaching
at Blanche Fleur
in Provence.*

~~~~~~~

✕

IN ITALY, I TAUGHT COURSES in the Veneto, Piedmont, Tuscany, Sardinia, Umbria, and the Cinque Terre and I enjoyed nearly every moment. But after five years, this wandering gypsy was ready for a new challenge. I set my sights on picturesque Provence.

When Carla Cavila Magnelli, my assistant, and I found Blanche Fleur, a tranquil country estate in the Châteauneuf-du-Pape area of the Rhône valley, we struck gold. Marie Claude, the owner, welcomed my group with typical Provençal hospitality, a glass of Tavel rosé, and almond, anchovy, and fennel toasts (see page 228). Nestled between two rivers, surrounded by white flowers, and complete with its own chapel, it was the perfect venue.

"Will we be having croissants and café au lait every morning?" a student asked.

"Mais, bien sûr!" I said. "But of course!"

I channeled my inner mademoiselle as we shopped the outdoor markets of Saint-Rémy-de-Provence, the hilltop village of Gordes, and canal-laced L'Isle-sur-la-Sorgue, picking up anything and everything that spoke to us: rose garlic, a bundle of fresh savory and thyme, purple-tinged young artichokes, fresh goat cheese, hand-picked ripe red tomatoes, bunches of lavender, and green-gold virgin olive oil that smelled of freshly mown grass. I loved watching my students' excitement build as we strolled around the market stalls, cameras clicking in an effort to capture the moment in time. I wanted to tell them, "Put your cameras away. You'll never forget this experience."

The very first thing I taught my students to make was *anchoïade*, a Provençal sauce not fit for the timid. We mashed garlic, anchovies, wine vinegar, parsley, and olive oil in a mortar to make a coarse paste. The bold aroma wafted through the air, awakening all of our senses. I came up with an idea to add almonds and serve it atop wedges of roasted cauliflower (see page 231). It was the perfect first taste of Provence.

Next, I showed the group how to make mayonnaise. "If we add some finely minced garlic, what do we have?" I asked, subtly gauging the cooking knowledge of my new group.

"Aioli!" someone blurted out.

We added walnuts to the aioli, and served it with asparagus (see page 232).

With some of the basics out of the way, it was time to move on to the classic French dish everyone envisioned mastering in Provence: the soufflé. My bravest students volunteered to whip the egg whites in a large, ancient copper bowl. I showed them that holding two balloon whisks in one hand would cut whisking time in half. They eagerly took notes and mentally put a copper bowl at the top of their Christmas lists; the others sipped rosé. We added the pillowy egg whites to a lavender and lime soufflé base and gracefully slipped the dish into the oven (see page 233).

Minutes later, the students pulled the puffy, featherlight soufflé out of the oven to a round of enthusiastic applause. My students beamed with pride, having mastered the always-intimidating quintessential French dish. We quickly carried the soufflé outside to a spot between the kitchen garden and the shimmering turquoise pool, where we happily ate light, aromatic mouthfuls as we watched the sun slowly sink in the sky.

almond, anchovy, and fennel toasts

This recipe comes from my dear winemaker friend Amy Lillard, proprietor of La Gramière in Provence. It takes me back to an enchanted evening with my students, eating dinner under the stars in the middle of Amy's vineyards.

¾ cup almonds or walnuts

1 teaspoon fennel seeds

6 anchovy fillets, soaked in cold water
   for 5 minutes and patted dry

8 mint sprigs, plus small leaves for garnish

1 teaspoon grated orange zest

¼ cup freshly squeezed orange juice

¼ cup extra-virgin olive oil, or as needed
   Kosher salt

½ baguette, thinly sliced and toasted

1 In a small frying pan, lightly toast the nuts over medium heat, shaking the pan occasionally, until they are fragrant and have taken on a little color, 2 to 3 minutes. Pour onto a plate and let cool.

2 Return the pan to medium heat. Add the fennel seeds and toss and stir until light golden and fragrant, about 1 minute. Transfer to a spice grinder, let cool, then grind coarsely.

3 In a food processor, combine the nuts, fennel seeds, anchovies, mint, and orange zest and juice and pulse until the mixture is chunky. With the food processor running, slowly add the oil and continue to process until well mixed and coarse textured. If the mixture is too thick to spread, add a little more oil. Transfer to a bowl and season with salt.

4 Spread the paste onto the baguette slices and arrange on a platter. Garnish with mint leaves.

serves 10

whole roasted cauliflower with almond anchoïade

I used to cut a head of cauliflower into florets for roasting. Then I saw cooks in the south of France roast the cauliflower whole. It makes a strong statement on any dinner table and is delicious cut into wedges and served with anchoïade, *a sauce of anchovies, garlic, olive oil, and vinegar, over the top.*

1 head cauliflower
2 tablespoons extra-virgin olive oil
½ teaspoon kosher salt

ALMOND ANCHOÏADE
⅓ cup blanched almonds
5 salt-packed whole anchovies, or 10 oil-packed
   anchovy fillets
2 garlic cloves, coarsely chopped
2 tablespoons unsalted butter, at room temperature
½ cup extra-virgin olive oil
1½ teaspoons aged red wine vinegar
2 tablespoons finely chopped flat-leaf parsley
1 teaspoon red chile flakes
   Kosher salt and freshly ground black pepper

1 Preheat the oven to 450°F. Lightly oil a rimmed baking sheet.

2 Remove and discard the leaves from the cauliflower. Core the cauliflower, leaving the head intact, and discard the core. Place the cauliflower, core side down, on the prepared baking sheet. Drizzle the oil over the top of the cauliflower and sprinkle with the salt.

3 Roast the cauliflower until tender when pierced and golden on top, 1 to 1¼ hours. Remove from the oven and let cool briefly.

4 To make the anchoïade, toast the nuts in a small frying pan over medium heat, shaking the pan occasionally, until they are fragrant and have taken on some color, 3 to 4 minutes. Pour onto a plate and let cool.

5 If using salt-packed anchovies, fillet each anchovy, discarding the spine. For both types of anchovies, soak the fillets in cold water for 5 minutes, rinse under cool running water, and pat dry with paper towels.

6 In a food processor, combine the almonds, anchovies, garlic, and butter and pulse until smooth. Transfer the mixture to a bowl and gradually whisk in the oil and vinegar. Stir in the parsley and chile flakes and season with salt and pepper. Set aside.

7 To serve, cut the cauliflower into wedges, place a wedge on each individual plate, and spoon the anchoïade around each wedge.

serves 4 to 6

warm asparagus salad with toasted walnut aioli

Homemade mayonnaise is one of my favorite things to teach students to make. They're always amazed to see the emulsion occur before their eyes. Loaded with garlic and meaty walnuts, it becomes a bold aioli fit to dress this warm asparagus salad.

TOASTED WALNUT AIOLI
- ½ cup walnut halves
- ½ cup extra-virgin olive oil
- ½ cup canola, corn, or safflower oil
- 1 large egg yolk
- 2 or 3 garlic cloves, mashed to a paste
- 1 to 2 teaspoons freshly squeezed lemon juice
  Kosher salt and freshly ground black pepper

- 3 large eggs
- 1¼ pounds asparagus, tough ends removed
- 2 tablespoons extra-virgin olive oil
  Lemon wedges for garnish

1 Preheat the oven to 375°F. To make the aioli, spread the walnuts on a rimmed baking sheet and toast in the oven until fragrant and light golden, about 7 minutes. Pour onto a plate to cool. In a blender, pulse the cooled walnuts several times until finely chopped. Leave the oven on.

2 In a liquid measuring cup, combine both oils. In a small bowl, whisk together the egg yolk and 1 tablespoon of the combined oils until an emulsion forms. Drop by drop, begin adding the remaining oil to the emulsion while whisking constantly. Continue in this manner until about half of the oil has been added. You can then add the second half slightly faster, yet still in a very fine, steady stream, continuing to whisk constantly until all of the oil has been incorporated. Do not add the oil too quickly and be sure that the emulsion is homogeneous before adding more oil. Whisk in the garlic, lemon juice, salt, and pepper to taste. Add the walnuts, then whisk in ⅓ to ½ cup warm water to make a sauce that is almost pourable. It should be the consistency of thick heavy cream. Cover and refrigerate until serving.

3 Bring a saucepan filled with water to a boil over high heat. With a slotted spoon, lower the eggs, one at a time, into the boiling water. Reduce the heat to medium and cook the eggs for 8 minutes. Meanwhile, ready a bowl of ice cubes and water.

4 When the eggs are ready, using the slotted spoon, transfer them to the ice water. When they are cool enough to handle, after about 1 minute, remove them from the water, tap them on a work surface to crack them all over, and return them to the ice water for 5 minutes. Remove them from the water again, peel them, cut into quarters lengthwise, and set aside.

5 Ten minutes before serving, place the asparagus on a rimmed baking sheet and drizzle with the oil. Roll the asparagus to coat evenly with the oil, then arrange in a single layer. Roast until tender but still bright green, 7 to 8 minutes.

6 Transfer the asparagus to a platter and drizzle with the aioli. Garnish with the eggs and lemon wedges.

serves 6

lavender lime soufflé

⅔ cup sugar
1 tablespoon dried unsprayed culinary lavender
5 large eggs, separated
¼ teaspoon cream of tartar
  Pinch of kosher salt
1 teaspoon grated lime zest
⅓ cup freshly squeezed lime juice
2 tablespoons unbleached all-purpose flour
1 tablespoon unsalted butter
  Powdered sugar for dusting

1 Preheat the oven to 375°F. In a food processor, combine the sugar and lavender and process to a fine dust. Using a mixer fitted with the whisk, beat the egg whites and cream of tartar on medium-high speed until foamy, then slowly add ⅓ cup of the lavender sugar and the salt and beat to stiff peaks. Transfer to a clean bowl and set aside.

2 Using a clean bowl, fit the mixer with the beater and beat the egg yolks and remaining lavender sugar on medium speed until creamy, about 1 minute. Add the lime zest and juice and the flour and beat just until incorporated. Using a rubber spatula, gently fold one-third of the egg whites into the lime mixture, then fold in the remaining whites just until incorporated.

3 In a 10-inch ovenproof frying pan, melt the butter over medium-low heat, swirling to coat the pan evenly. Add the batter and cook until the edges begin to set and bubble lightly, about 2 minutes. Transfer to the oven and bake until the soufflé is puffed and golden brown, 7 to 11 minutes. Do not open the oven door for the first 7 minutes. Serve immediately, dusted with powdered sugar.

serves 6

escarole, pear, marcona almond, and manchego salad

These were some of my favorite ingredients to use when teaching in Spain's La Rioja region. Although you wouldn't typically see them combined in this manner, I find the sweet pears, buttery manchego cheese, and salty Marcona almonds play perfectly against the bitter greens.

1½ tablespoons white wine vinegar
1 teaspoon almond, walnut, or hazelnut oil
¼ cup extra-virgin olive oil
  Kosher salt and freshly ground black pepper
1 small head escarole, leaves separated
  and torn into 1½-inch pieces
2 heads Belgian endive, leaves separated
2 celery stalks, thinly sliced on a sharp diagonal
1 green Bartlett or Comice pear, halved, cored,
  and thinly sliced lengthwise
½ cup roasted Marcona almonds
3-ounce chunk aged manchego cheese

1 In a small bowl, whisk together the vinegar and both oils to make a vinaigrette. Season with salt and pepper.

2 To serve, in a large salad bowl, toss together the escarole, endive, and celery. Add the pear slices and almonds, drizzle with the dressing, and toss to coat evenly. Using a cheese shaver or vegetable peeler, shave the manchego over the top.

serves 6

WORD SPREAD ABOUT THE QUALITY OF MY TRIPS, and in 1996, I was awarded the first ever International Association of Culinary Professionals (IACP) Cooking Teacher Award of Excellence. Former students began to approach me again and ask, "I've done the Veneto, Provence, and Tuscany tours. What about a class in Spain or Morocco?"

Under the guise of a "research" trip, I spent a week with close friends Ángel Perez Aguilar; his wife, María Angeles Alonzo; and Ignacio Tricio, in northwestern Spain's La Rioja region. La Rioja is famous for its exquisite wines, long, complex history, stunning scenery, quaint villages, and explosive tapas scene, so I was ecstatic to have an excuse to visit.

I told my friends my dilemma. "I need a new destination for my cooking tours."

"That's no problem," Ángel said. "We can organize a course for you here."

"Where will we cook? Who will be my assistant?"

"At my restaurant, of course," he replied matter-of-factly.

"And I can be your assistant," said Ignacio, a friend who just happened to be in the travel business.

I couldn't believe that the thought had not already occurred to me. They were correct: Ángel and María Angeles's restaurant, La Vieja Bodega, which stands in the heart of La Rioja,

On a street in southern Spain.

×

was perfect, plus lovely accommodations were available in the nearby tiny town of Casalarreina, where a sixteenth-century monastery had been converted into a hotel.

Less than a year later, I returned with a group of students. In the first class, my chefs-in-training gathered to review the recipes I had assembled. I assigned tasks, and they peeled, chopped, and whisked their way through the hours. We cooked lamb chops over vine cuttings in an *asador*, a wood-fired grill, and roasted *piquillo* peppers over white-hot coals. I taught them to make *tortilla española*, with tender chunks of potato wrapped in the embrace of fresh eggs, and they went crazy for the spicy-hot tomato sauce we spooned on the top (see page 236). We made a salad of juicy pears, Marcona almonds, and shards of manchego cheese (see page 233). And for the main course, we spent hours preparing a velvety white bean, chorizo, and pork stew, which we drizzled with smoked *pimentón* oil (see page 239). Maybe it was all of the bold, new flavors, or perhaps there was a full moon that night. Whatever the cause, the energy in the air at our first dinner in La Rioja was electric.

Ángel, María Angeles, and Ignacio shared the true La Rioja with us. They introduced us to friends like Javier and Marina, a brother and sister team who make olive oil at Lectus. It wasn't an ordinary tour. They planned a hayride into the middle of their olive orchards, where we helped gather olives for crushing. We were all completely captivated as we watched fresh golden yellow olive oil emerging from the press. When my students took their first taste, their eyes revealed the pleasure.

Toward the end of our visit, Javier and Marina passed out their handmade chocolates filled with olive oil and sprinkled with flake salt.

Someone questioned, "Why does each box contain seven chocolates?"

Javier replied, "You'll need one for every day of the week!"

Late into the night, we wandered the streets of two La Rioja villages, Haro and Logroño, known for their tapas bars, pretending to be Spaniards and trying to blend in with the magnificent culture for just a few hours. We made the rounds of tapas bars, where we drank rich red Tempranillo wine and recounted all the funny, exciting, fascinating things we'd experienced that day. Everyone was sad that the evening had to end, and the bus ride back to our hotel was silent until a couple of people began singing to lighten the mood. The rest of us soon joined in and together we sang Beatles' songs all the way back to Casalarreina, our pitch-imperfect voices disappearing into the dark.

The last night in La Rioja was a surprise for both me and the students. Ángel, María Angeles, and Ignacio arranged for all of the new friends we'd met during our journey to share an evening of dinner and dancing. They even arranged for a band that specialized in American songs from the 1960s and 1970s. We danced and sang until we were hoarse, the sun threatening to rise before we made it to our beds.

It was an adventure you would never find in a travel guide. As a teacher and travel enthusiast, there's nothing more delicious I can offer my students than the opportunity to visit exotic destinations and immerse themselves in the food and culture. I was certain no one would ever forget that journey to Spain, including me.

spanish tortilla with spicy sauce

SPICY TOMATO SAUCE

1 tablespoon extra-virgin olive oil

2 tablespoons minced yellow onion

1 garlic clove, minced

1 cup peeled, seeded, and chopped tomatoes

¼ cup dry white wine

1 tablespoon tomato paste

Large pinch of red chile flakes

2 tablespoons chopped flat-leaf parsley

Pinch of sugar

1 to 2 teaspoons sherry vinegar

Kosher salt and freshly ground black pepper

TORTILLA

1½ pounds russet potatoes, peeled

1¼ cups extra-virgin olive oil

8 large eggs

Kosher salt and freshly ground black pepper

Flat-leaf parsley leaves for garnish

1 To make the sauce, heat the oil in a frying pan over medium heat. Add the onion and garlic and cook, stirring, until soft, about 7 minutes. Add the tomatoes, wine, tomato paste, chile flakes, parsley, sugar, and ¾ cup water and stir well. Reduce the heat to low and simmer, uncovered, for 15 minutes to blend the flavors. Remove from the heat and let cool slightly. Transfer to a blender and process until a smooth purée forms. Season with vinegar, salt, and pepper to taste. Set aside.

2 To make the tortilla, insert the tip of a small knife into a potato and twist the knife to cut the potato into ¼-inch-thick chips. You do not want perfect slices—you want them to be uneven so that there will be space between them as they cook. Repeat with the remaining potatoes.

3 In a large nonstick frying pan, heat the oil over medium heat. Add the potato slices one at a time to prevent sticking. There should be space between the slices because of the angles and the way they were cut. Cook slowly, lifting and turning the potatoes occasionally, until they are tender but not brown, 8 to 10 minutes. The potatoes will remain separate rather than form a "cake." You may have to do this in two batches.

4 Meanwhile, crack the eggs into a large bowl, season with salt and pepper, and beat with a fork until slightly foamy.

5 Using a slotted spoon, transfer the potatoes to the eggs, pressing down on the potatoes so they are completely covered with egg. Drain off the oil from the pan and set aside 3 tablespoons. Discard the remaining oil or reserve for another use.

6 In a large frying pan, heat 2 tablespoons of the reserved oil over medium-high heat until very hot. Add the potato mixture and, using a rubber spatula, spread the mixture evenly in the pan. As the edges set, loosen them with a fork to allow the uncooked egg to flow underneath. Continue to cook until the tortilla is almost set and the bottom is golden brown, 6 to 10 minutes.

7 Remove the pan from the heat, invert a flat plate a little larger than the pan on top, and invert the pan and plate together. Lift off the pan, return it to medium heat, and add the remaining reserved oil. Slide the tortilla, browned side up, into the pan. Cook, shaking the pan to prevent sticking, until the egg is cooked through, 4 to 6 minutes longer.

8 Remove the pan from the heat and slide the tortilla onto a serving plate. The tortilla and tomato sauce can be served hot or at room temperature. Cut the tortilla into wedges and spoon the tomato sauce over the top. Garnish with the parsley.

serves 6

braised pork with shell beans and pimentón garlic oil

I love good braised pork—the tender meat melting in my mouth and flooding it with rich flavor. This version takes on a Spanish flair with spicy chorizo and pimentón. *If fresh shell beans are unavailable, use 2 cups of cooked white beans.*

    2 tablespoons extra-virgin olive oil
3½ pounds boneless pork shoulder or butt, trimmed
    of fat and cut into 1½-inch pieces
    1 yellow onion, minced
      Kosher salt and freshly ground black pepper
1½ cups peeled, seeded, and diced tomatoes
    (fresh or canned)
    3 garlic cloves, minced
    1 bay leaf
    2 pounds fresh shell beans, such as cranberry
      or cannellini, shelled
    ½ pound dry Spanish chorizo, sliced

PIMENTÓN GARLIC OIL
    3 tablespoons extra-virgin olive oil
    1 teaspoon sweet Spanish paprika *(pimentón)*
    ½ teaspoon sweet smoked Spanish paprika
      (pimentón de la Vera)
    2 garlic cloves, thinly sliced
      Kosher salt

1 In an 8-quart dutch oven or other large, heavy pot, heat the oil over medium-high heat. Add the pork and onion, season with salt and pepper, and cook, stirring occasionally, until the pork is golden on all sides, 8 to 10 minutes.

2 Add the tomatoes, garlic, bay leaf, and 4 cups water and bring to a boil over high heat. Reduce the heat to low and simmer gently, uncovered, for 1 hour. Add the beans and chorizo and continue to simmer, adding more water if the pan begins to dry, until the pork and beans are tender, 30 to 40 minutes.

3 Meanwhile, make the pimentón garlic oil. In a small frying pan, heat the oil over low heat, add both paprikas and the garlic, and heat gently for about 30 seconds to infuse the oil. Do not let the garlic or spices take on color. Remove the pan from the heat.

4 When the pork and beans are tender, remove and discard the bay leaf. Ladle the stew into warmed individual bowls and drizzle the pimentón garlic oil over the top.

serves 6

I GOT OFF THE PLANE and stepped into the sultry mid-October heat. As we rode in the van through the old part of Marrakech, past the ancient medina (town center), I recalled my first trip here in the early 1990s. It was now 2011, and I'd returned with my latest troop of culinary hopefuls in tow. I was curious to see how much Morocco had changed. I peered out my window and spotted camels with Berber blankets strapped to their backs alongside the road. Nothing has changed, I thought to myself, and I was grateful.

To me, Morocco is nothing short of magical. The sights, the sounds, the flavors, the smells stimulate all of my senses. I hadn't been on the ground for an hour before I heard the call to prayer emanating from the speakers of a mosque in the medina. Five times a day, the deep, almost haunting voice wound its way through the air and into my core, reverberating long after the call had finished. It was a reminder that yes, I was back in Morocco. Suddenly it felt like I'd never left, or perhaps it was that Morocco had never left me.

Jnane Tamsna, a private estate just outside of Marrakech, was our tranquil oasis for the week. Surrounded by olive and orange trees, blooming jasmine and palms, I once again fell in love.

Bahija Lafridi, the chef and cooking teacher, came to meet us dressed in her chef's jacket, white apron, and white head scarf. She greeted us in English mixed with Berber and French, bursting with enthusiasm. I knew immediately that we would be friends.

The first morning, after a breakfast of fresh mint tea, luscious fruit, freshly squeezed orange and grapefruit juice, and homemade *khboz* (wheat flatbread), we headed to the souk (marketplace) in the medina. Nowhere is the spirit of Marrakech more alive than in the souk. Snake charmers and water sellers called to us; everywhere we turned there were more colors, sounds, movements. The atmosphere was so frenzied that our senses could not process everything. I was distracted. I could only imagine how my students felt, experiencing the souk for the first time.

With my sister-in-law, Kathy, on my first trip to Morocco. Shopping in Marrakech, a favorite pastime.

×

"Stay close," I called to them. "If you don't, you might end up with a monkey on your shoulder or a snake wrapped around your neck!" That got their attention. They laughed, but I'd been here before and knew it was true.

Led by my wonderful friend and guide, Abdou Mahmoudi, we traveled deeper into the souk. He and I spouted facts about the market, but my students didn't hear a word. No one's eyes were on us. They were busy photographing piles of preserved lemons, mounds of spices and olives, colorful shoes, rugs, and baskets while simultaneously trying to keep up and navigate the labyrinthine streets. After stopping for lunch at La Terrasse des Épices, a trendy rooftop café, we headed back to the tranquility of Jnane Tamsna, a welcome breath of fresh air and quiet after the captivating chaos of the souk.

That afternoon, we met in the kitchen for our first cooking class. Bahija already had everything set out on a big marble island: cutting boards, lots of different spices, bowls of vegetables, dried and fresh fruits, almonds, honey, and a knife for each student.

"We'll be making a *tagine* today, and everyone will be making his or her own," Bahija announced.

The students looked at me, puzzled. I explained, "*Tagine* has two meanings. This conical terra-cotta vessel in front of me is a *tagine*. Remember, I showed you a selection of these pots in the souk today? It's also the name of the stew that you're going to make in the *tagine* pot. Don't worry, this isn't a pottery class."

I stood back and let Bahija teach them the basic steps of preparing a chicken *tagine*. Unlike in my classes in Italy or Provence, there were no recipes. It was up to each student to decide what to include in his or her *tagine*. Options both sweet and savory abounded: preserved lemons, dried fruits, olives, ginger, cilantro, artichokes, tomatoes, and almonds. The combinations were countless. I watched my students overcome their timidity and get creative.

It was tough for me to stand back and let Bahija teach. I was used to being in charge. A few times I had to bite my tongue to keep from interrupting her lesson. I needed something to do, so I grabbed a pen and paper to draft recipes for my students to take home. I knew they'd be eager to replicate these exotic dishes once they returned to their own kitchens.

Once the *tagines* were assembled, we took them outside to cook them over individual wood-fired braziers set along the ground. In no time at all, dinner was ready. A long table was set for us outdoors. Exotic music was playing, incense was burning, and the light of a thousand candles illuminated the central courtyard. A gentle breeze stirred the date palms and olive trees that arched over our table, with stars and the nearly full moon flickering between the branches against the clear night sky. A fountain, the centerpiece of the courtyard, trickled with water. Rose petals floated in the crystalline pool. I felt like I'd stepped into paradise.

For the next several hours, we dined on a myriad of unique *tagines*: one perfumed with orange blossom water and studded with apricots and almonds; another with preserved lemons, sweet peppers, and tomatoes; yet another sweet with quince, raisins, and ginger. My students smiled with joy and pride.

Every evening as I drifted off to sleep, I'd digest the day's events, my mind spinning with new recipe ideas. Everywhere I travel, I draw inspiration from the local restaurants, markets, purveyors, and friends I encounter. From this trip to Marrakech, I'd return home with a recipe for spiced walnuts from my new chef friend Bahija and an idea for modern, open-faced burgers based on the *merguez* sausages I'd learned to make at Al Fassia, a restaurant run by women. From a market-stall vendor in the souk, I picked up a tip for perfecting preserved lemons and a secret ingredient to take my *ras el hanout* spice mixture to the next level.

But the true mark of a successful trip is more than returning home with new recipes and a camera full of photos. It is taking the spirit of Marrakech, of Provence, of Tuscany, of La Rioja, of Sydney home, too, and injecting some of its magic into our everyday lives. Although my classes are focused on food, they're really about much more than that. They're about living life to the fullest each day, about exploring, appreciating, and learning from foreign lands and cultures. I am thankful every day that I get to travel the world for a living. I know my dad was proud of his wandering gypsy.

dandelion and kale salad with marrakech-spiced walnuts and preserved-lemon dressing

MARRAKECH-SPICED WALNUTS

1 tablespoon unsalted butter
1 teaspoon *ras el hanout*
Small pinch of cayenne
½ teaspoon kosher salt
1½ tablespoons firmly packed light brown sugar
1 cup walnuts, toasted and kept warm (page 232, step 1)

2 tablespoons freshly squeezed lemon juice
¼ cup extra-virgin olive oil
½ preserved lemon, homemade (page 279) or purchased, pulp discarded and peel minced
Kosher salt and freshly ground black pepper
1 small bunch young dandelion greens, trimmed
½ bunch kale, stems removed and leaves torn
12 kumquats, thinly sliced crosswise and seeded

1 Preheat the oven to 375°F. To prepare the walnuts, line a baking sheet with foil. In a small saucepan, melt the butter over medium heat. Add the ras el hanout, cayenne, salt, brown sugar, and

1½ teaspoons water and stir until the sugar has melted and the mixture bubbles and looks foamy on top, 1 to 2 minutes. Add the warm walnuts and toss until evenly coated.

2 Pour the walnuts onto the prepared baking sheet, spread them in a single layer, and return them to the oven for 5 minutes. Remove from the oven and, using a spoon, toss the walnuts. Return the walnuts to the oven for 5 minutes longer. They should be coated with the glaze and golden. Remove from the oven and let cool completely. Break apart any walnuts that have stuck together.

3 In a small bowl, whisk together the lemon juice, oil, and preserved lemon and season with salt and pepper.

4 In a large salad bowl, combine the dandelion greens, kale, and kumquats. Drizzle with the dressing and toss. Add the walnuts.

serves 6

salmon tagine with preserved lemons and walnut chermoula

Wild salmon takes an exotic turn in this Moroccan-inspired dish. One of the easiest and fastest tagines imaginable, it's topped with a nutty, herbal chermoula sauce for a flavor experience that's nothing short of extraordinary. Look for preserved lemons in a Middle Eastern or well-stocked grocery store, or make them yourself.

WALNUT CHERMOULA

1½ teaspoons ground cumin

1 teaspoon sweet paprika

½ teaspoon ground turmeric

¼ teaspoon cayenne

2 garlic cloves, minced

½ cup chopped cilantro

½ cup chopped flat-leaf parsley

¼ cup freshly squeezed lemon juice

¼ cup extra-virgin olive oil

½ teaspoon kosher salt

¼ teaspoon freshly ground black pepper

¾ cup chopped toasted walnuts

1 tablespoon ground cumin

Large pinch of red chile flakes

2 tablespoons freshly squeezed lemon juice

2 tablespoons extra-virgin olive oil

⅓ cup chopped cilantro

1 garlic clove, minced

1¼ teaspoons kosher salt

¼ teaspoon freshly ground black pepper

2 pounds skinned wild salmon fillets, any pin bones removed, then cut into 2-inch pieces

2½ cups drained diced canned tomatoes

1 green or red bell pepper, seeded and thinly sliced lengthwise

1½ preserved lemons, homemade (page 279) or purchased, pulp discarded and peel thinly sliced

1   To make the chermoula, in a blender or food processor, combine the cumin, paprika, turmeric, cayenne, garlic, cilantro, parsley, lemon juice, oil, salt, and pepper and process until smooth. Transfer the mixture to a bowl, stir in the walnuts, and set aside.

2   In a small bowl, combine the cumin, chile flakes, lemon juice, oil, cilantro, garlic, ¾ teaspoon of the salt, and the pepper and mix well. Put the salmon in a bowl, sprinkle with the spice mixture, and rub the mixture evenly into the salmon pieces. Cover and refrigerate for 1 hour.

3   In a medium bowl, combine the tomatoes and the remaining ½ teaspoon salt and mix well. Place half each of the tomatoes, bell pepper, and preserved lemons on the bottom of a tagine or heavy stew pot. Place the salmon on top. Top with the remaining bell pepper, followed by the remaining preserved lemons, and then the remaining tomatoes.

4   Place over high heat and bring to a boil. Reduce the heat to medium and simmer, uncovered, until the peppers are tender and the salmon is almost cooked through but still slightly pink in the center, about 15 minutes.

5   To serve, spoon the salmon and vegetables into warmed individual soup bowls and top each serving with a spoonful of the chermoula.

serves 6

moroccan-style lamb burgers with cucumber-ginger yogurt

Of all the places I've traveled, Morocco is the most energizing and intoxicating. Whenever I long to be back in that magical land, I make these boldly spiced lamb burgers, my updated version of the merguez *sausage I learned to prepare at Al Fassia restaurant in Marrakech. The pork in the recipe adds richness but use all lamb if you like.*

CUCUMBER-GINGER YOGURT

1 cup plain Greek yogurt

½ English cucumber, peeled, halved lengthwise, seeded, and cut into ¼-inch dice

1 teaspoon grated lemon zest

1½ tablespoons peeled and grated fresh ginger

1 garlic clove, minced

Kosher salt

LAMB BURGERS

1¼ pounds ground lean grass-fed lamb

½ pound ground pork

6 garlic cloves, minced

1½ tablespoons sweet paprika

1½ teaspoons ground cumin

1½ teaspoons kosher salt

1 teaspoon freshly ground black pepper

½ teaspoon ground cloves

½ teaspoon ground cinnamon

¼ teaspoon freshly grated nutmeg

1½ teaspoons *harissa*

¼ cup chopped cilantro, plus sprigs for garnish

6 slices coarse-textured bread, toasted

1 To make the yogurt, in a bowl, combine the yogurt, cucumber, lemon zest, ginger, and garlic and stir to mix well. Season with salt. Cover and refrigerate until serving. You should have about 1½ cups.

2 In a food processor, combine about one-fourth of the lamb, the pork, and the garlic and process until finely ground. Add the paprika, cumin, salt, pepper, cloves, cinnamon, nutmeg, and harissa and pulse several times until well mixed. Add the remaining lamb and the chopped cilantro and pulse a few times until well mixed.

3 To test for seasoning, heat a small frying pan over medium heat. Shape a walnut-size piece of the meat mixture into a small, thin patty, add to the pan, and cook, turning once, until done, about 3 minutes. Let cool slightly, taste, and adjust the seasoning of the meat mixture with salt, pepper, or other spices or harissa if needed.

4 Heat a grill to medium to medium-high (350°F to 450°F). Divide the meat mixture into 6 equal portions and shape each portion into a patty ¾ to 1 inch thick.

5 Place the patties on the grill directly over the fire and cook, turning once, for 3 to 5 minutes on each side for medium-rare.

6 To serve, place a toasted bread slice on each plate, then place a burger on each bread slice. Top the burgers with some of the yogurt and garnish with cilantro sprigs.

serves 6

COPITA
TEQUILERIA Y COMIDA

Maestra de Cocina – Joa

Jicama & cucumber w

SMALL PLATES

Chips & Two Seasonal Salsas - 5

Guacamole - 9
Avocado, chile serrano, cilantro, onion
$2 add queso cotija

Papas Bravas - 7
Roasted & fried Kennebec potatoes, fried jalapeños, cumin-arbol
chile dusted, avocado crema

Mexico City Style Quesadillas - 11
Filled with yukon potatoes & green chorizo, Toluca style, cuitlacoche
corn truffle, epazote, serrano chile, goat cheese, queso Oaxaca, lime
crema, queso fresco

Trio of Tamalitos - 12
Roasted butternut squash, queso fresco, rainbow swiss chard, slow
roasted chicken with pipián; slow cooked pork nejo Zihuatanejo
style, tomato-habanero salsa

Chicory and Citrus Salad - 11
Mixed chicory, local citrus, avocado, pommegrante seeds, spiced
pepitas, honey & cumin vinaigrette

Tortilla Soup - 9
With roasted chicken, seasonal vegetables, avocado, cotija ch
tortilla strips

CHAPTER 10

the

AGAVE GIRLS

**Y**OU MAKE ME YOUR MARGARITA, and I'll make you mine. Then we'll see whose is better," I challenged my friend and restaurant industry titan Larry Mindel as we cruised along the coast of southern Mexico on his boat sharing a week of much needed vacation.

"Deal," Larry said, thumbing through my latest cookbook, *Tequila*. "Tequila is my favorite spirit."

"Mine, too!" I agreed.

I carefully measured two ounces of 7 Leguas *blanco* tequila, an ounce of freshly squeezed lime juice, a half ounce of agave nectar, and three-quarters ounce of water. My competitive self was sharpening her claws. I did not want to lose.

I loaded the shaker half full with ice, covered it, and shook it vigorously until my fingers felt numb and frost coated the metal cup. I strained my margarita into a chilled glass with a single large ice cube and garnished it with a lime wheel.

Larry was also just finishing his margarita, which he called "the Lorenzo." We exchanged glasses. On the count of three, we each sampled the other's drink. Larry's version was delicious and packed quite a punch. It was less sweet and more acidic than mine and with a heftier dose of tequila.

I watched out of the corner of one eye as Larry sipped my magical concoction. "This is the best margarita I've ever had," he said, grinning with pleasure. I'll leave the story right here. Larry tells a very different version, but tequila does that to people.

× • ×

The bar at my restaurant, Copita Tequileria y Comida, in Sausalito, California.

×

WHAT LARRY AND I HAD IN COMMON was our love of 100 percent blue agave tequila. Just give us the good stuff, please! No *mixto*! No headaches! No, thank you! When I say I love tequila, I use the term *love* loosely. A more accurate expression is I appreciate tequila. I'm proud to say that I never had a single shot of Jose Cuervo tequila in college or the infamous hangover it provides. I've also never stepped foot inside a Señor Frog's, the shot-slamming Mexican bar-and-grill chain popular with wild spring breakers.

My appreciation for tequila started several years ago on a trip to the Yucatán, when you could buy a great bottle for a few pesos, and it grew from there. Then, a few years ago, I was invited to the legendary *tequileria* Tommy's in San Francisco for the launch of Corzo, a new tequila sold in a sexy square bottle. The crowd was predominantly male. I was one of just a handful of women. Is tequila a man's drink? I wondered, as I circled the room surveying the women. Nope. My conversations that evening revealed that women were just as passionate as men about tequila.

That very night, I decided to start a club called Agave Girls for women who appreciate tequila. I hosted our first event at Tres Agaves (now known as Tres) restaurant and *tequileria* in San Francisco. I extended invitations to forty-five women and almost fell to the floor when nearly one hundred women showed up. Tequila was clearly a female libation, too. I followed that first Agave Girls meeting with a few more successful events and word spread. People were contacting me from Dallas, Miami, New York, and even the Philippines wanting to start their own chapters.

"What about writing a book about tequila?" my literary agent Doe Coover asked.

I loved the idea. At that point, I'd written fifteen cookbooks geared toward Mediterranean cuisine. What's another cookbook? I thought. It'll be easy. All I had to do was explain how tequila was made, invent a bunch of cocktails, and write a few Mexican recipes.

I started my research with a few trips to Jalisco with fellow tequila lover and friend Eric Rubin. We visited several distilleries and learned all about the tequila-making process.

All was going well until I realized that writing cocktail recipes was not all that easy, especially when you're a chef and not a bartender! Instead of fumbling my way through, I solicited help from the experts. I found the top tequila-focused bartenders across the nation and asked them to share their favorite tequila cocktail recipes. Next, in the name of research, I tasted every single cocktail recipe to find the ones worthy of a spot in my book. Tough job, I know.

When it came to writing the food recipes, I was nervous. Sure, I'd gone to Mexico numerous times and explored its culture and cuisine, but I was certainly no Diana Kennedy or Rick Bayless. Ultimately, I decided to stay true to myself. *Tequila* didn't need to be a reference book for authentic Mexican cuisine. I focused instead on my style of cooking, presenting clean, fresh flavors with Mexican flair—dishes like Gazpacho with Drunken Prawns and a tequila-infused riff on tiramisu I called Tequilamisu. The recipes were fun, festive, and flavorful, and the book was well received.

Larry intently perused *Tequila* as he finished my contest-winning margarita, "This truly is the best margarita I've ever tasted," he repeated. "If I ever find a location to open a Mexican restaurant, would you be my partner?"

I'd just finished two, maybe three margaritas, so I boldly replied, "Sure!" I had never told anyone that deep down in my soul I aspired to open my own restaurant. It was at the top of my bucket list, but only if the right partner came along. Larry was definitely the right partner.

copita margarita

To create the perfect margarita for Copita, we took the same mix of lime juice and agave nectar and tested it with fifty different 100 percent agave blanco tequilas. When I tasted the winning combination, I knew we'd struck gold. It's a smooth, refreshing, sweet-tart sip of liquid sunshine. Double the recipe if you like.

2 ounces tequila *blanco* (made from 100 percent blue agave)
½ ounce agave nectar
1 ounce freshly squeezed lime juice
Ice for the cocktail shaker, plus 1 ice cube, 1¾ inches square
1 thin lime wheel

1 In a cocktail shaker, combine the tequila, agave nectar, lime juice, and ¾ ounce water, then fill the shaker half full with ice. Cover and shake vigorously until you see frost form on the outside of the shaker, about 5 seconds.

2 Place the ice cube in a highball glass and strain the margarita into the glass. Garnish with the lime wheel.

serves 1 very happy margarita lover

LARRY MINDEL HAD A RÉSUMÉ as long as my arm. He had opened nearly one hundred extraordinarily successful restaurants, including Chianti in Los Angeles, Prego in San Francisco, the Il Fornaio group of restaurants up and down the West Coast, Poggio in Sausalito, and more. I'd have been crazy to pass up the opportunity to achieve a lifelong goal with the help of such an accomplished partner. But at the same time, the thought of opening a restaurant was totally daunting.

A couple of months passed and the restaurant conversation vanished into a haze of tequila. Then one morning the phone rang.

"Joanne, I found the perfect place for us," Larry's voice announced on the line.

"A place? A place for what?" I asked.

"A Mexican restaurant? Remember? The margarita competition?" Larry urged.

A cloud lifted and the day came floating back to me. Beaming hot Mexican sun. Larry's boat undulating beneath my feet. Ice melting in a cluster of empty margarita glasses. Mention of a restaurant. A Mexican restaurant. Larry was calling about the restaurant!

"When do you want to talk?" I managed.

We stepped into an empty restaurant in Sausalito, just across the Golden Gate Bridge from San Francisco. It wasn't a big space; if it had been, I might have turned around and walked right back out the door. Instead, it was about eighteen-hundred square feet, with a long bar on one side and a huge open fireplace, and it seemed intimate and charming. Despite the room's dark and dusty state, I immediately felt at home. I could tell there was something magical here. Larry was right.

"Do you like it? Can you see yourself here? What do you think if we make this fireplace into a huge rotisserie for roasting chickens? Love the floors, don't you?" Larry had a million questions. It was the most excited I'd ever seen him.

With a twinkle in my eye, I responded with a question of my own. "What if we extended the bar and made a ceviche, salsa, and guacamole station at the end, so cooking would be visible from the dining room?" With that, I think he knew I was sold.

"Yes!" Larry replied. "I've always loved live cooking in a restaurant. We can probably get about ten seats at the bar and another forty in the dining room. It's small, but I think we can make it work. I almost forgot. Last night when I couldn't sleep, I got up and read your *Tequila* book again. I came up with a name: Copita. What do you think?"

"Copita," I repeated, to test how the name sounded when I said it. "It means 'little cup' in Spanish. It's perfect."

Larry and I were on the same page. We didn't waste any time transforming the space into our Copita: terra-cotta waxed walls, hand-painted Mexican tiles in twilight blue and white

I've learned so much from my friend and restaurant partner, Larry Mindel.

✕

surrounding the fireplace, sea foam green translucent tiles lining the bar, dark wooden floors, a blue-and-white hand-embroidered Oaxacan tapestry above the long banquette, and, centered on the wall at the entry, a commissioned painting of a *jimador*, the man who tends the agave fields, by artist Jay Mercado. To give the restaurant the light, bright atmosphere we desired, we removed the entire front wall and replaced it with folding glass doors. The indoor-outdoor space blended seamlessly. The feel of the restaurant was just right.

We were ready to open, aside from one minor detail: we hadn't yet found an executive chef. It was a small issue that kept me up all night every night. Larry and I both understood the importance of finding just the right person for the job. We were looking for a perfect fit in terms of personality, passion, culinary skill, and work ethic. And try as we might, we just hadn't found anyone will all those qualities.

We knew exactly what we did want and what we didn't want. No heaping platters of Tex-Mex beans, rice, and gloppy cheese. We intended to dispel the public's perception that Mexican food meant a cheap, overstuffed burrito. Our goal was to serve seasonal, modern Mexican food with authentic flavors. We would even source much of our fresh produce from our own organic garden in the Sausalito hills. The Chez Panisse spirit was alive and well in this budding restaurateur.

After countless interviews, we finally hired an executive chef. We were relieved and optimistic. We then turned our attention to the equally important position of sous chef. We hired Dilsa Lugo on the spot after we tasted her delicate homemade tortillas. She had learned to cook at her mother's side in Cuernavaca, Mexico, and now ran a successful catering company. You could taste the love in her simple, nurturing food. And as much as she loved to cook, she also loved to garden. Dilsa was absolutely perfect except for one thing: she didn't have a stitch of restaurant experience. We didn't care; we wanted her food in our kitchen.

Dilsa's lack of experience wasn't a problem until a week before we were set to open. Suddenly our executive chef quit. We were already receiving an inordinate amount of press, and the pressure was too much for him to handle.

"Everything happens for a reason," Larry said calmly. "We have a week to pull it together."

Meanwhile, I was panicking. It wasn't as if Dilsa could step into the executive chef role. Despite her incredible culinary prowess, she was in no position to run a restaurant kitchen.

"I'll do it!" I said, with a mask of false bravado. Inside I was terrified.

We opened our doors on Cinco de Mayo 2012 to throngs of people. I hadn't worked the line since my Chez Panisse days more than twenty years earlier. I didn't know a thing about ordering, scheduling, costing out a dish, or reading a P&L (profit and loss statement, as I learned). This was not the job I'd signed up for. I had lovely visions of myself walking around in fashionable clothing, schmoozing with customers, ensuring they were enjoying the Copita experience, maybe even sipping a margarita alongside my guests. Instead, I was in my white chef's coat and working twelve hours a day making ceviche, guacamole, and salsa. I was in way over my head.

Our little fifty-five-seat restaurant was bustling, serving about five hundred diners daily. People loved Copita and traveled from all over the San Francisco Bay Area—and even from around the United States—to see for themselves what all the buzz was about. But my role was killing me.

"We need a chef!" I appealed to Larry.

This time we hired a handsome Latino chef with a broad smile and a roving eye. A few days into the job he asked if we could pay him in cash so that he wouldn't have to pay alimony to his ex-wife. That was our first clue he wasn't going to work out. The second had to do with that roving eye. So long, Casanova. And back into the kitchen I went.

"Okay, now what do we do?" I asked Larry, praying he had a solution.

"When one door closes, another opens," he told me confidently.

I was glad Larry had faith because I didn't, especially when chef number three was a bust, too. This time we'd hired a qualified chef with goals that matched ours: to serve fresh, seasonal food using the produce from our organic garden in the Sausalito hills. The problem was his Mexican cooking skills were limited and, with a kitchen full of Mexican cooks, he wasn't a good fit. At least he was smart enough to understand that and leave on his own.

"Welcome to the restaurant business!" Larry said, still not breaking a sweat. He was used to this, having run restaurants for almost his entire life. I, on the other hand, was in a state of panic. Why in the world did I think I needed to run a restaurant? Damn that bucket list and those margaritas!

I had worked every single day for five straight months. I hadn't spent more than a few exhausted minutes with my husband, Joe, that entire time. I missed my life before Copita. My back ached, my head throbbed, and I thought I might develop an ulcer from all my worrying. This was not the glamorous restaurant-owning life I'd envisioned.

Someone must have been looking out for me (I like to think it was my Grampa Sears) because just as I reached the depths of my despair, we found Gonzalo. Gonzalo Rivera was born in Gridley, a rural town in Northern California, to Mexican immigrant parents. He grew up with his mother, father, siblings, aunts, uncles, cousins, and grandmother. Together they traveled up and down the West Coast as migrant workers, picking citrus and apricots in Southern California, onions and garlic in the Central Valley, grapes in California wine country, cherries in Oregon, and pears and apples in Washington. Gonzalo learned to love food through his grandmother's eyes, as he helped her make the tamales that she sold in the fields to other migrant workers. After high school, Gonzalo studied cooking at the California Culinary Academy and went on to work with award-winning chef Michael Mina. Gonzalo's dream came true when he moved to Mexico to become executive chef for Michael's restaurant NEMI and later for Capella Hotels and Resorts. It was during this time that he polished his Mexican cooking skills through studying the regional foods of the country. We brought him back home to California to be our executive chef at Copita. He truly was the answer to my prayers.

"Gonzalo, what do you think about doing Mexican french fries?" I asked one day. "I'm thinking we roast them, then deep-fry them until they're gold and crispy. We could toss them with lime zest, cumin, and some hot chiles. What kind of chiles do you think would be best?" I asked, energized by our spur-of-the-moment recipe creation.

"Árbol chile would give the hot you're looking for," Gonzalo replied. "We could also dust some sliced jalapeños with flour and fry them with the potatoes. And an avocado *crema* for dipping."

"Sounds amazing! I can't wait to try them." Those *papas bravas* have been a staple on our menu since that day (see page 258).

Me, at Copita.

spiced papas bravas with avocado crema

When my first true collaboration with Gonzalo yielded these irresistible Mexican fried potatoes, I knew we'd found the right chef for Copita. Crisp, golden, and spicy on the outside and insanely tender on the inside, they are a constant fixture on the menu. If they ever disappeared, our loyal patrons might revolt.

SPICE MIX

1½ teaspoons cumin seeds
½ teaspoon árbol chile powder
1½ teaspoons kosher salt
1½ teaspoons grated lime zest

3 pounds Kennebec, russet, or other baking potatoes
Olive oil for drizzling
Kosher salt and freshly ground black pepper
1 cup sour cream
1 avocado, halved, pitted, peeled, and coarsely chopped
1 small garlic clove, minced
1 to 2 teaspoons freshly squeezed lime juice
1 cup all-purpose flour
4 jalapeño chiles, thinly sliced crosswise
Canola oil for deep-frying
Maldon sea salt for finishing
Cilantro sprigs for garnish
Lime wedges for garnish

1 To make the spice mix, toast the cumin seeds in a small frying pan over medium heat, shaking the pan occasionally, until they are fragrant and have taken on some color, 30 to 60 seconds. Pour into a spice grinder, let cool, then grind finely.

Transfer to a bowl and stir in the chile powder, salt, and lime zest. Set aside.

2 Preheat the oven to 400°F. Place the potatoes in a single layer in a baking pan, drizzle with the olive oil and 2 tablespoons water, and season with salt and pepper. Cover with foil, place in the oven, and cook until tender, 40 to 50 minutes. Remove from the oven, let cool, and cut into rough 1½-inch chunks.

3 Meanwhile, make the avocado crema. In a blender, combine the sour cream, avocado, garlic, and 1 teaspoon lime juice and process until smooth. Transfer to a serving bowl and season with salt. Taste and adjust with more lime juice if needed. Set aside.

4 Put the flour in a bowl and season with salt and pepper. Add the chile slices, toss to coat evenly, and then lift out the slices, shake off the excess flour, and transfer to a small bowl.

5 Pour the canola oil to a depth of 3 inches into a deep, heavy-bottomed saucepan and heat to 375°F. Working in batches, add the potatoes and fry until golden and crisp, 2 to 3 minutes. Add some of the chile slices about 1 minute before the potatoes are ready and fry them as well until golden and crisp. Using a slotted spoon, transfer the potatoes and chile slices to paper towels to drain, then transfer to a bowl and keep warm. Repeat with the remaining potatoes and chile slices.

6 Sprinkle the spice mix over the potatoes and chiles and toss to coat evenly. Transfer to a serving bowl, sprinkle with the Maldon sea salt, and garnish with the cilantro sprigs and lime wedges. Serve with the avocado crema for dipping.

serves 6

Coctel Mixto · 15
Maine lobster, bay scallops, Gul
orange, chile, and avocado

Classic · 13
Lime marinated Gulf of Mexic
serrano, and cilantro

Bay Scallop Agua de Chile ·

WORKING WITH GONZALO was a true collaboration. Finally, I had someone who spoke the same food language. No egos involved; just ideas bouncing from one to the other. *This* was the restaurant experience I'd signed on for. I enjoyed coming to Copita each day, cooking and creating with Gonzalo.

"What about putting *elote* on the menu?" I asked one day, referring to seasoned corn on the cob, a popular street food in Mexico. "We served it last summer before you were here, but we were so insanely busy, we couldn't keep up with the demand. Gonzalo, I know you can pull it off."

The next morning, cases of gorgeous just-picked Brentwood corn arrived at Copita. Gonzalo had it all figured out. The first step was to roast the ears of corn in their husks. When we got an order for *elote*, he showed the cooks how to grill the corn on the *comal* (flat griddle), turning it occasionally, until half of the kernels were golden brown. This process gave the corn its distinctly chewy quality, just like the *elote* sold on the streets in Mexico. But that was just the beginning!

Next, Gonzalo demonstrated how to pull the husks back and tie them into a little handle. He brushed the corn with melted butter and smeared it with homemade mayonnaise. Finally, he sprinkled the corn with ground árbol chile, crumbled *cotija* cheese, chopped

elote with chipotle crema

When the first hint of fresh sweet corn hits the markets at the start of summer, it means the return of elote *to the Copita menu. The popular Mexican street food is also one of Copita's most popular appetizers. Guests are known to share the first ear, then order another just for themselves!*

6 ears corn in the husk
¼ teaspoon árbol chile powder
1 teaspoon guajillo chile powder
¼ teaspoon kosher salt
2 tablespoons unsalted butter, melted
Chipotle Crema (page 277)
½ cup crumbled *cotija* cheese
3 tablespoons chopped cilantro
3 tablespoons minced red onion
6 large lime wedges

1 Heat a grill to medium. Cut ½ inch off the top of each ear of corn. Place the corn directly over the fire and grill, turning occasionally, until the husk is golden, about 20 minutes.

2 In a small bowl, stir together both chile powders with salt.

3 When the corn is ready, peel back the husk on each ear to expose the kernels and remove and discard the silk. Arrange the ears on a large platter and brush on all sides with the butter. Using a spoon, drizzle the chipotle crema in a zigzag pattern onto the top of each ear. Sprinkle with the cheese, cilantro, and onion and then with the chile powder mixture. Garnish with the lime wedges.

serves 6

cilantro, and minced red onion, and then finished with a spritz of lime juice. The flavor was spicy, rich, and sweet, all in one bite. I'd never tasted *elote* this good, not even in Mexico.

"*Muy rico!*" Gonzalo and I said at the same time and laughed.

That first summer Gonzalo was with us, we sold out of *elote* every night. Even after summer had passed and the season for corn was over, people kept asking, "When can we have that heavenly *elote* again?"

⚹ ● ⚹

I SAY THIS WITHOUT EXAGGERATION: working with Gonzalo was a blessing. I had found my cooking soulmate and could finally breathe again.

When autumn rolled around, it was time to put some hearty, comforting dishes on the menu. Several years earlier, when I was working on my cookbook *You Say Tomato*, I'd written a recipe for braised chicken with tomatoes, vinegar, and spices. It was a riff on chicken adobo, and although it was good, something wasn't quite right. I showed the recipe to Gonzalo to get his opinion.

spiced chicken with vinegar

2 teaspoons *each* ancho chile powder and dried oregano

1 teaspoon *each* ground cumin and dried thyme

½ teaspoon ground cinnamon

¼ teaspoon *each* ground cloves and ground allspice

6 garlic cloves, minced

3 cups peeled, seeded, and chopped tomatoes

1 tablespoon extra-virgin olive oil

1 chicken, 3½ to 4 pounds, cut into 8 serving pieces

1 large yellow onion, minced

¼ cup cider vinegar

Kosher salt and freshly ground black pepper

1 In a blender, combine the chile powder, oregano, cumin, thyme, cinnamon, cloves, allspice, garlic, and tomatoes and process until smooth. Set aside.

2 In a large frying pan, heat the oil over medium heat. Add the chicken in a single layer and cook, turning once, until light golden, 10 to 12 minutes. Transfer the chicken to a plate.

3 Drain off all but 1 tablespoon of the fat from the pan and return the pan to medium heat. Add the onion and cook, stirring, until soft, about 7 minutes. Add the vinegar and simmer until reduced by half, about 2 minutes. Add the tomato mixture and simmer for 5 minutes. Reduce the heat to low, return the chicken to the pan, cover, and simmer until the chicken is easily pierced with a fork, 35 to 40 minutes.

4 Transfer the chicken to a plate and tent with foil. Raise the heat to high and simmer the sauce until thickened, about 5 minutes. Season with salt and pepper, then spoon over the chicken.

serves 6

"You're close, but let's work on it together. I think we can make this a real winner," he grinned.

Using my recipe as a starting point, we added some ground ancho chile, allspice, and oregano. Gonzalo's few, subtle changes resulted in a deep, rich, warmly spiced chicken adobo, so delicious and comforting that each bite was like being wrapped in a tender hug. We immediately put it on the menu.

It was fun to be the student again. I was learning so much from Gonzalo, and not just about Mexican flavors, spices, and regional cuisine but also about friendship, teamwork, and life in general. We complemented each other perfectly, found real joy in collaborating, and created countless memorable dishes together.

× • ×

THE DAYS GOT SHORTER, the rains came, and temperatures grew colder. Winter was upon us in Sausalito. Farmers' markets were filled with heaps of bright red pomegranates and piles of brightly colored citrus fruits. Blood oranges, Meyer lemons, Cara Cara oranges, and kumquats had returned.

"What do you think about a ceviche with blood orange juice and pomegranate seeds?" Gonzalo asked me one day. He knew that one of our rules was never to put a dish on the Copita menu that I hadn't tasted.

"I love both of those things, pomegranates and blood oranges. You don't have to ask me twice. Let's make it right now."

As we "cooked" the fresh-caught sea bass in lime juice, I looked over at Gonzalo. His head was bent in concentration as he sectioned blood oranges and seeded pomegranates. He was a true perfectionist. I thanked my lucky stars for bringing this guy into our kitchen.

We added the blood orange juice, pickled red onion, cilantro, and serrano chiles.

"Something's missing!" Gonzalo announced.

"How about some grated blood orange zest? Maybe even a splash of *blanco* tequila? Does that sound crazy?" I proposed, thinking the acidity of the *blanco* would balance the sweetness of the citrus and pomegranate nicely.

We took another taste. "So much better," we agreed in unison.

I ate that ceviche every day that winter, until blood oranges and pomegranates vanished from the markets. That's how satisfying and flavorful our creation was (see page 264).

× • ×

"OKAY, YOU MIGHT THINK I'M CRAZY, but I want to do pork belly tacos," I told Gonzalo as we husked the tomatillos. "I'm embarrassed to say that I've never cooked pork belly, but don't you think it would make a great taco? How are you at making pork belly?"

Gonzalo grabbed his stomach with both hands, "You mean this pork belly?" he chuckled. I gave him a playful shove. All kidding aside, it turned out Gonzalo was a pork belly master. He took my taco idea and ran with it.

When I walked into the kitchen the next day, Gonzalo called me over as he did most mornings. "I have something for you to try."

He handed me a plate with two warm handmade corn tortillas topped with crispy fried pork belly drizzled with a *pipián* mole sauce and finished with a tangle of pickled red onions (see page 266).

"What do you think?" he asked eagerly, watching me chew.

"Gonzalo, you nailed it!" was all I could manage. I had to have another bite. The pork belly didn't taste fatty at all, just rich and creamy with a crisp, crackling exterior. The spicy sweetness of the *pipián* sauce and the acidity of the pickled onions pushed it over the top. I never dreamed anything could taste so good.

"These tacos are out-of-this-world delicious," I gushed. "I could eat a half dozen every day. I'll have to restrain myself, or I'll be the one with the pork belly." We both laughed.

Working the room at Copita.

ceviche with blood oranges and pomegranate

In the winter, when juicy blood oranges and pomegranates are in season, I eat this bright-flavored ceviche for lunch almost every day—no kidding.

1 pound skinned sea bass or halibut fillets
1 cup freshly squeezed lime juice
¼ cup tequila *blanco*
1 tablespoon agave nectar
¼ cup freshly squeezed blood orange juice
2 teaspoons grated blood orange zest
1 cup pomegranate seeds (page 194, step 2)
½ cup pickled red onions (page 279)
¼ cup finely chopped cilantro
½ to 1 serrano chile, seeded and minced
2 avocados, halved, pitted, peeled, and diced
Kosher salt
Tortilla chips for serving

1 Check the fish fillets for pin bones and, using needle-nose pliers or tweezers, pull each bone straight out. Cut the fillets into ½-inch pieces and transfer to a medium bowl. Add the lime juice, stir to mix, and let sit for 30 minutes.

2 Drain the fish, capturing the lime juice in a bowl. Return the fish and half of the lime juice to the original bowl. Add the tequila, agave nectar, orange juice and zest, pomegranate seeds, onions, cilantro, and half of the serrano chile to the fish and lime juice and stir together to mix well. Add the avocados, season with salt, and stir gently just until mixed. Taste and adjust the seasoning with lime juice, salt, and additional minced chile.

3 Transfer the ceviche to a serving bowl and accompany with tortilla chips.

serves 8

fried pork belly tacos with pipián sauce

I had never cooked pork belly myself when I asked Gonzalo to help me come up with a pork belly taco for the Copita menu. Rich and creamy with a crisp, crackling exterior, his creation blew me away. With a tomatillo-laced, nutty pipián *sauce and pickled red onions on top, I can only describe this taco as out of this world.*

PORK BELLY
¼ cup kosher salt
¼ cup sugar
2 tablespoons cider vinegar
½ celery stalk, chopped
½ yellow onion, chopped
1 small carrot, peeled and chopped
1 tablespoon black peppercorns, coarsely crushed
1 tablespoon coriander seeds, coarsely crushed
2-pound piece pork belly, skin removed

Rice bran oil for deep-frying
12 corn tortillas
Pipián sauce (page 278), warmed
Pickled red onions (page 279)
Chopped cilantro for garnish

1   To make the pork belly, combine in a saucepan the salt, sugar, vinegar, celery, onion, carrot, peppercorns, coriander seeds, and 8 cups water. Place over high heat and bring to a boil, stirring to dissolve the salt and sugar. Remove from the heat and let cool to room temperature.

2   Using a sharp knife, score the fatty side of the pork in a crosshatch pattern, cutting about ½ inch deep. Place the pork belly in a 9- by 12-inch baking pan and pour the cooled liquid over it. Cover the pan with parchment paper and then with foil and refrigerate overnight.

3   Preheat the oven to 350°F. Remove the parchment and transfer the pan to the oven. Braise the pork belly until the meat is tender and can be easily pierced with a thin skewer, 3 to 4 hours.

4   Line a rimmed baking sheet with parchment paper. Remove the baking pan from the oven and transfer the pork belly to the prepared baking sheet. Lay a piece of parchment paper the size of the baking sheet on top of the pork belly, then set a second baking sheet on top of the paper. Place a brick or other heavy object, such as a couple of large cans of tomatoes, on top of the second baking sheet. Refrigerate for about 5 hours.

5   Remove from the refrigerator and lift off the weight(s), the top baking sheet, and the parchment. Transfer the pork belly to a cutting board and cut into ½-inch cubes. Place the cubes in a bowl and set aside until using.

6   To deep-fry the pork belly, pour the rice bran oil to a depth of 2 inches into a deep, heavy-bottomed saucepan and heat to 375°F. Working in batches, add the pork belly and fry until golden and crispy, 3 to 4 minutes. Using a slotted spoon, transfer to paper towels to drain.

7   While the pork belly is frying, place a large nonstick frying pan over medium heat. Working with 2 or 3 tortillas at a time, place them in the pan and heat, turning them as needed, until they begin to blister slightly, 1 to 1½ minutes. Transfer to a plate and cover with a kitchen towel to keep warm.

8   To assemble the tacos, place a couple of tablespoons of the warm sauce on each tortilla, top with some pork, and garnish with the pickled onions and cilantro.

serves 6

WHEN IT CAME TO COPITA'S DESSERT MENU, we decided from the outset that we wanted to keep it simple. We'd feature a few selections, incorporating seasonal flavors and, of course, something chocolate.

The one dessert that's been on the menu since the day we opened our doors is a spiked chocolate milk shake. It blends together spiced Oaxacan chocolate and the richest of chocolate ice creams with guajillo chile, cinnamon, vanilla extract, and a generous splash of tequila *añejo*. Poured into an ice-cold glass, it is as good as it sounds. It's the richest, most decadent milk shake you'll ever taste, and it leaves you feeling all warm and fuzzy.

And it's better than any shake you ever sipped in your childhood because of the, well, tequila. Only I would find a way to add tequila tastefully to a milk shake. They don't call me the Agave Girl for nothing.

oaxacan chocolate milk shakes

1½ cups whole milk

1½ cups heavy whipping cream

⅔ cup sugar

4 cinnamon sticks, each about 3 inches long

6 ounces bittersweet chocolate, finely chopped

2 teaspoons minced chipotle in adobo sauce

7 large egg yolks

Pinch of guajillo chile powder

½ teaspoon pure vanilla extract

¼ cup tequila *añejo*

10 ice cubes

1 In a saucepan, combine the milk, cream, sugar, and cinnamon sticks, place over medium heat, and heat, stirring, until small bubbles appear along the edges of the pan and the sugar has dissolved. Cover and set aside off the heat to steep for 2 hours.

2 Put the chocolate and chipotle in a heatproof bowl and set aside. In a bowl, whisk the egg yolks until blended. Return the steeped milk mixture to medium heat to warm. Slowly drizzle the milk mixture into the egg yolks while whisking constantly. When all of the milk mixture has been incorporated, pour the milk–egg yolk mixture back into the saucepan. Place over medium heat and cook, stirring constantly, until the mixture thickens and coats the back of the spoon, 2 to 4 minutes. Do not boil.

3 Remove from the heat and strain through a fine-mesh strainer set over the bowl containing the chocolate. Add the chile powder and vanilla then whisk until the chocolate has melted and the mixture is smooth. Cover and refrigerate until well chilled.

4 Pour the chilled custard into an ice cream maker and freeze according to the manufacturer's directions. Transfer the ice cream to an airtight container and store in the freezer until you are ready to make the milk shakes. You'll have about 1 generous quart; plan to use it within 1 week.

5 To make the milk shakes, in two equal batches, combine the ice cream, tequila, and ice cubes in a blender. Process until the ice cubes are completely incorporated, 1 to 1½ minutes. Stir together the two batches, mixing well. Pour into glasses to serve.

serves 6 to 8

⚜

I'M FINALLY LIVING THE RESTAURANT LIFE I envisioned, spending my evenings in cute outfits, tasting with Gonzalo and our sous chef, and wandering from table to table connecting with guests and asking "How is everything?" with a genuine smile on my face. It feels like it took an eternity, but at long last I'm right where I want to be at Copita.

I've learned a lot from my experience opening a restaurant. I've learned that things constantly need fixing, whether it's the dishwasher or a relationship, and as soon as you fix one problem, another one arises. I've learned who my real friends are and also that people aren't perfect, especially me. I've learned the importance of patience and honesty. But above all, I've learned to cherish the love and support that I have at home, because without it, none of this would be possible.

Opening a restaurant is the hardest thing I've ever done in my life. But anytime I've had doubts or wanted to throw in the towel, my people have been there for me: Joe, to offer a listening ear, sage advice, a shoulder to cry on, and plenty of love. My mom, to love, support, and believe in me like only a mother can. And Larry, to teach, reassure, and guide me through the gauntlet of restaurant ownership and to point out when I'm doing something right or just plain wrong.

"Would you do it over again?" Larry asked me one day.

"In a heartbeat," I replied sincerely, "especially if I have a chef with a heart and soul like Gonzalo and a generous teacher and partner like you!"

I often think back to that day on Larry's boat and wonder if Copita would be here without that friendly margarita competition. I'd like to think so, but I'm far from sure, which is yet another reason why tequila will always be my favorite spirit.

The original
Agave Girl.

epilogue

My life on
camera.

✕

"AND THAT'S A WRAP!" my coproducer, director, and friend Paul Swensen calls out proudly. The team immediately sings out a celebratory whoop. We've just finished filming *Joanne Weir Gets Fresh*, the ninth iteration of my PBS cooking show. I look around my kitchen-cum-television studio and smile gratefully at the crew of cameramen; sound experts; lighting technicians; grips; my hair and makeup savior, Chris; my culinary director and the culinary team; my wonderful assistant, Karen Alvey; and Paul.

For the past six weeks, my kitchen, living room, and dining room have been taken over by enormous cameras, lights on cumbersome metal scaffolding, microphone booms, audio monitors, a jib, viewing screens, and many more gadgets whose function I can't even venture to guess. For weeks now, we've been putting in twelve-hour days cooking and filming. We are all relieved to be finished. A sense of pride and accomplishment flitters about the room. As I stand at the center of it all, I take a moment to soak everything in.

When I stop to think about it, I can't believe this is where life has taken me. If you had told nine-year-old Joey, who'd just rescued an explosion of baking soda–filled cookies from the oven, that she would one day host her own television cooking program, she would have laughed at the suggestion, her mop of curly red hair bouncing wildly along with her giggles. Even when I moved across the country to pursue cooking seriously by studying with Madeleine Kamman, I never could have imagined the culinary career I have now.

What I do know is that food, beyond its obvious nutritional necessity, has always been vital to my well-being. My life's most vivid memories all center on food: lunch under Grampa Sears's maple tree, Mom's tomato sandwich, my first slurp of Chez Panisse oysters and mignonette, Madeleine's three grains of salt, noshing on *kefta* in the bustling souk in Marrakech. Scents, flavors, even sounds in the kitchen have the ability to transport me back in time.

I'm often asked in interviews who has influenced me the most in the kitchen, and I always reply the same way: my mother, my teacher Madeleine Kamman, and my mentor Alice Waters. And although it is true that these three strong, inspiring women are at the top of the list, many more people have influenced me over the years and will continue to do so. From my very first cooking instructor Leo Romero to the farmers at the market to Gonzalo and Dilsa at Copita, I gather knowledge and inspiration from nearly everyone I encounter. I firmly believe that I am the person I am today because of a combination of all those people and of life's unique occurrences, both big and small.

⌗ ● ⌗

WHAT IF MY DAD HADN'T called me his wandering gypsy? What if I hadn't found that fly in the wine bottle? What if I'd never eaten at Chez Panisse? What if I hadn't challenged Larry Mindel to a margarita contest? All of these seemingly small incidents have combined to shape who I am today: chef, teacher, restaurateur, cookbook author, television personality, travel guide, daughter, wife, friend.

It is sometimes overwhelming to be all of those things all of the time. But then I remember how bad I am at being still. I have an insatiable drive to do more, see more, create more, live more. If things are too quiet, if the pace is too slow, I get scared. I'm constantly seeking out the next creative project. Whether it is tasting new varietals for Joanne Weir Wines, developing recipes for the restaurant or a magazine contribution, conducting a radio interview, or filming my show, I like to be busy.

Not long ago, I spent a few days working in the kitchen at Chez Panisse. I had a rare free weekend between trips to New York to meet with my editors and Arizona to teach a few cooking classes. Most people would relish the downtime, but not me. I decided I needed to be in the kitchen where it all began. I'd been to the restaurant just a month earlier to film a segment with Alice for my television show, and Alice and the cooks encouraged me to return again soon.

My experience at Chez Panisse had been so profound that I never worked in another restaurant until I opened my own, Copita, decades later. Chez Panisse grabbed my soul on the first day and never let go. Its philosophy inspires my cooking to this day. It felt so good to be back in that familiar, energizing environment and to be welcomed like one of the family. You may think I'm crazy to opt for a weekend of backbreaking labor over a weekend of free time, but that is who I am.

Dad had my number all those years ago: I was not born to stay put. I've followed my heart (and my nose) for my entire life, and they've led me on the most incredible journey around the globe. I'm excited to see what's next, because clearly this kitchen gypsy has no intention of slowing down any time soon.

With Alice Waters in the garden at the Edible Schoolyard Project at Martin Luther King Middle School in Berkeley, California.

⌗

basic recipes

VEGETABLE STOCK

10 cups chopped vegetables or vegetable trimmings, such as onions, leeks, carrots, celery, tomatoes, potatoes, mushrooms, green beans, squashes, garlic, fennel, eggplant, cabbage, and greens

1 yellow onion, coarsely chopped

1 carrot, peeled and coarsely chopped

12 flat-leaf parsley sprigs

3 thyme sprigs, or ¼ teaspoon dried thyme

1 bay leaf

1 In a large stockpot, combine the vegetables, onion, carrots, parsley, thyme, and bay leaf. Add water to cover by 3 inches and bring to a boil over high heat. Immediately reduce the heat to medium-low and simmer gently until the stock smells good and has a good flavor, about 45 minutes. As the level of the liquid decreases in the pot, replenish it with water to maintain the original level.

2 Strain the stock through a fine-mesh strainer into a large bowl. If not using immediately, let cool, then transfer to 1 or more airtight containers and refrigerate for up to 5 days or freeze for up to 2 months.

MAKES 8 TO 12 CUPS

CHICKEN STOCK

5 pounds chicken parts, such as backs, necks, and wings, trimmed of excess fat

1 yellow onion, coarsely chopped

1 carrot, coarsely chopped

12 flat-leaf parsley sprigs

3 thyme sprigs

¼ teaspoon dried thyme

2 bay leaves

1 In a large stockpot, combine the chicken, onion, carrot, parsley stems, thyme, and bay leaves. Add water to cover by 2 inches and bring to a boil over high heat. Immediately reduce the heat to medium-low, skimming off any foam that rises to the surface. Simmer gently, skimming as needed, until the meat is falling off the bone and the stock tastes very rich, 5 to 6 hours. As the level of the liquid decreases in the pot, replenish it with water to maintain the original level.

2 Scoop out and discard the larger pieces with a slotted spoon, then strain the stock through a fine-mesh strainer into a large bowl. If using immediately, use a large metal spoon to skim off as much of the fat from the surface as possible. If not using immediately, let it cool at room temperature, then cover and refrigerate overnight. The next day, using a spoon, lift off and discard the fat that solidifies on the surface. Transfer the stock to 1 or more airtight containers and refrigerate for up to 5 days or freeze for up to 2 months.

MAKES 8 TO 12 CUPS

FISH STOCK

4 to 5 pounds bones from white, non-oily fish, such as red snapper, halibut, and/or sole

1 cup dry white wine

1 yellow onion, chopped

1 carrot, peeled and chopped

2 bay leaves

3 thyme sprigs, or ¼ teaspoon dried thyme

12 flat-leaf parsley sprigs

1 Clean the fish bones well, discarding any fat or skin. Put the bones in a large stockpot and add the wine, onion, carrot, bay leaves, thyme, parsley, and water to cover. Bring to a boil over high heat, then reduce the heat and simmer for 35 minutes. Using a wooden spoon, mash the bones occasionally during cooking.

2 Strain the stock through a fine-mesh strainer into a large bowl. If not using immediately, let cool, then transfer to 1 or more airtight containers and refrigerate for up to 5 days or freeze for up to 2 months.

MAKES 8 TO 12 CUPS

HOMEMADE MAYONNAISE

½ cup neutral-flavored oil, such as
   safflower, canola, or sunflower
½ cup extra-virgin olive oil
1 large egg yolk
1 teaspoon Dijon mustard
   Freshly squeezed lemon juice
   Kosher salt

In a liquid measuring cup, combine
both oils. In a small bowl, whisk
together the egg yolk, mustard, and
1 tablespoon of the combined oils
until an emulsion forms. Drop by
drop, begin adding the remaining oil
to the emulsion while whisking constantly. Continue in this manner until
about half of the oil has been added.
You can then add the second half
slightly faster, yet still in a very fine,
steady stream, continuing to whisk
constantly until all of the oil has been
incorporated. Do not add the oil too
quickly and be sure that the emulsion
is homogeneous before adding more
oil. Season with lemon juice and salt.
Then, while whisking constantly,
slowly add 1 to 2 tablespoons warm
water to thin slightly. The mayonnaise
will keep in an airtight container in the
refrigerator for up to 10 days.
MAKES ABOUT 1 CUP

VARIATION
MEYER LEMON MAYONNAISE
Use Meyer lemon juice in place of the
regular lemon juice.

POACHED EGGS

   Large eggs
2½ tablespoons white wine vinegar

1   Pour water to a depth of 1 inch
into a large frying pan. Place over
high heat and bring to a boil. Reduce
the heat to low so that the water
simmers very gently and add the
white wine vinegar.
2   One at a time, crack the eggs
into a small ramekin or custard cup
and carefully slide them into the
barely simmering water. Cook until
the white of each egg is firm but
the yolk is still soft and runny, 2 to
2½ minutes. Using a slotted spoon,
lift each egg from the water, briefly
resting the bottom of the spoon
against a paper towel to absorb any
excess moisture.

CHIPOTLE CREMA

1 cup sour cream
1 tablespoon minced chipotle chiles
   in adobo
1 tablespoon freshly squeezed lime juice
1½ teaspoons freshly squeezed
   orange juice
¼ teaspoon kosher salt

In a blender or food processor, combine
the sour cream, chipotle chiles, lime and
orange juices, and salt and process
until smooth.
MAKES ABOUT 1 CUP

MINT CRÈME ANGLAISE

2 bunches mint
2½ cups whole milk
5 tablespoons granulated sugar
½ vanilla bean
5 large egg yolks

1   Using the back of a chef's knife,
bruise the mint stems and leaves well.
In a medium saucepan, combine the
milk, sugar, and mint. Using a sharp
knife, split the vanilla bean pod lengthwise, then, using the tip of the knife,
scrape the seeds from the pod and add
to the pan along with the pod. Place
over medium heat and heat until small
bubbles appear along the edges of the
pan. Immediately remove from the
heat, cover, and let steep for 1 hour.
2   In a medium bowl, whisk the egg
yolks to break them up. Do not allow
any foam to form. Return the steeped
milk mixture to medium heat and heat
again until small bubbles appear along
the edges of the pan. Remove from the
heat and pour through a fine-mesh
strainer into a heatproof pitcher.
Slowly drizzle the scalded milk, a few
tablespoons at a time, into the egg
yolks while whisking constantly. Pour
the egg yolk–milk mixture back into
the saucepan, place over medium heat,
and heat, stirring constantly, until the
mixture thickens and coats the back of
a spoon, 2 to 3 minutes. Do not boil.
To test if it is ready, draw your finger
across the back of the spoon. If your
finger leaves a trail that does not flow
back together, the custard has cooked

to the right point. Alternatively, test the custard with an instant-read thermometer; it should register 170°F. Immediately remove from the heat and pour through a fine-mesh strainer into a clean bowl. Whisk for 2 minutes to cool slightly. Cover and refrigerate until well chilled before using.

MAKES ABOUT 3 CUPS

CHESTNUT HONEY ICE CREAM

3 cups heavy whipping cream
1 cup whole milk
1 vanilla bean
8 large egg yolks
½ cup sugar
5 tablespoons chestnut honey

1 In a large saucepan, combine the cream and milk. Using a sharp knife, split the vanilla bean pod lengthwise, then, using the tip of the knife, scrape the seeds from the pod and add to the pan along with the pod. Place over medium heat and heat until small bubbles appear along the edges of the pan. Immediately remove from the heat, cover, and let steep for 30 minutes.

2 In a bowl, whisk together the egg yolks, sugar, and honey until the sugar dissolves, 3 to 4 minutes. Return the steeped cream mixture to medium heat and heat again until small bubbles appear along the edges of the pan. Remove from the heat and slowly drizzle about one-fourth of the scalded cream mixture, a few tablespoons at

a time, into the egg yolk mixture while whisking constantly. Pour the egg yolk–cream mixture into the saucepan and whisk together with the remaining cream mixture. Place over low heat and cook, stirring constantly with a wooden spoon, until the mixture thickens and coats the back of the spoon, 2 to 3 minutes. Do not boil. Strain through a fine-mesh strainer into a bowl. Whisk vigorously for about 2 minutes to cool slightly, then let cool completely. Cover and refrigerate until well chilled.

3 Pour the chilled custard into an ice cream maker and freeze according to the manufacturer's directions. Transfer ice cream to an airtight container and store in the freezer until serving. The ice cream tastes best if eaten within 1 week.

MAKES 1½ QUARTS

PIPIÁN SAUCE

15 tomatillos, husks removed and cored
3 garlic cloves, peeled but left whole
1½ serrano chiles, stems removed
½ cup pumpkin seeds
½ teaspoon cumin seeds
1 whole clove
1½ teaspoons dried oregano
½ yellow onion, coarsely chopped
½ cup lightly packed fresh cilantro stems and leaves
2 cups chicken stock (page 276) or water Kosher salt
2 tablespoons canola or olive oil

1 Heat a large frying pan over medium-high heat. Add the tomatillos, garlic, and serrano chiles and toss and stir occasionally until nicely charred on all sides, 4 to 5 minutes. Transfer to a blender. Add the pumpkin seeds, cumin seeds, and clove to the same pan and toss and stir until golden, 2 to 3 minutes. Pour the contents of the frying pan into the blender and add the oregano, onion, cilantro, and stock. Process until a smooth sauce forms, then season with salt.

2 Place a medium frying pan over high heat, add the canola oil, and heat until the oil begins to ripple and smoke. Add the sauce, reduce the heat to low, and cook, stirring constantly, until it thickens slightly, 3 to 4 minutes. Remove from the heat. Serve warm.

MAKES ABOUT 3 CUPS

PICKLED RED ONIONS

- 1 red onion, thinly sliced
- ½ cup freshly squeezed lime juice
- 1 teaspoon kosher salt

In a bowl, combine the onion slices, lime juice, and salt. Add water just to cover, then stir together, mixing well. Let sit for 1 hour. To use, scoop out what you need and refrigerate the remainder in the lime-water mixture for up to 2 days.

MAKES ABOUT ½ CUP

QUICK PRESERVED LEMONS

- ¼ cup kosher salt
- 4 lemons, quartered lengthwise

1 In a small saucepan, combine 2 cups water, the salt, and the lemons, place over high heat, and bring to a boil. Reduce the heat to medium and simmer until the lemon peels are tender, about 20 minutes. Remove from the heat and let cool to room temperature.

2 Store the lemons in an airtight container in the refrigerator for up to 1 week. To use, scrape away and discard the pulp and cut the peel as directed in individual recipes.

MAKES 1½ TO 2 CUPS

PIZZA DOUGH

- 2 teaspoons active dry yeast
- ¾ cup plus 2 tablespoons warm (110°F) water
- 2 cups unbleached bread flour
- 2 tablespoons extra-virgin olive oil, plus more for the bowl
- ½ teaspoon kosher salt

1 In a large bowl, combine the yeast, ¼ cup of the warm water, and ¼ cup of the flour and stir to mix. Let the mixture sit at room temperature until bubbles are visible, about 30 minutes.

2 Add the remaining 1¾ cups flour, the remaining ½ cup plus 2 tablespoons warm water, the oil, and the salt and, using a wooden spoon, stir until the dough comes together in a rough mass.

3 Lightly flour a work surface and turn the dough out onto it. Knead the dough until smooth, elastic, and a bit tacky to the touch, 7 to 8 minutes. Shape the dough into a ball. Oil a large bowl, place the dough in the bowl, and turn the dough to coat it on all sides with oil. Cover the bowl with plastic wrap and let the dough rise in a warm place (about 75°F) until doubled in volume, 1 to 1½ hours. (Alternatively, let the dough rise in the refrigerator overnight. The next day, bring the dough to room temperature before continuing.)

MAKES TWO 10- TO 12-INCH PIZZA CRUSTS

CALZONE DOUGH

- 2 teaspoons active dry yeast
- 1 cup warm (110°F) water
- 3 cups unbleached bread flour
- ¾ teaspoon kosher salt
- 3 tablespoons extra-virgin olive oil, plus more for the bowl

1 In a large bowl, combine the yeast, ½ cup of the warm water, and ½ cup of the flour and stir to mix. Let the mixture sit at room temperature until bubbles are visible, about 30 minutes.

2 Add the remaining 2½ cups flour, the remaining ½ cup warm water, the salt, and the oil and, using a wooden spoon, stir until the dough comes together in a rough mass.

3 Lightly flour a work surface and turn the dough out onto it. Knead the dough until smooth, elastic, and a bit tacky to the touch, 7 to 8 minutes. Shape the dough into a ball. Oil a large bowl, place the dough in the bowl, and turn the dough to coat it on all sides with oil. Cover the bowl with plastic wrap and let the dough rise in a warm place (75°F) until doubled in volume, 1 to 1½ hours. (Alternatively, let the dough rise in the refrigerator overnight. The next day, bring the dough to room temperature before continuing.)

MAKES DOUGH FOR 4 MEDIUM CALZONE

acknowledgments

OF ALL OF THE COOKBOOKS I'VE WRITTEN, this one is the nearest and dearest to my heart. But I couldn't have done it alone. Some say it takes a village. I say it takes much more than that.

Thanks to the whole team at Oxmoor House, whose support has been phenomenal. A huge hug and a million thanks to the impassioned Grace Parisi, who brought me to Oxmoor and has supported this project from the beginning. Grace put her heart into cooking her way through the recipes and styling the food, and in the process, we became close friends. Thanks, too, to the editorial director, Anja Schmidt, and to my editor, Betty Wong, who guided me every step of the way and let the book be mine. I couldn't ask for more. Special thanks to Leah McLaughlin for seeing the potential for this Kitchen Gypsy.

A special thanks to everyone at Time Inc. Books, especially Margot Schupf, the publisher. Her insights and guidance helped shape this book, and I am forever grateful.

Thanks to the dream team at Sunset Publishing, especially the incomparable Peggy Northrop, editor-in-chief, and Margo True, food editor. They are two of the brightest, most creative women in the business, and I am happy to have had a chance to work with them. Maili Holiman, creative director, rocks my world! Every time I sent her a photograph I'd salvaged from a box in my garage, she managed to find a place for it in the book, so a big thank-you to her. And a big thank-you to Thomas J. Story, photographer extraordinaire. His creativity and passion for what he does show on every page. Bravo! Thanks to Susan Smith, photo editor, for her keen eye, and to Linda Bouchard, production manager, for keeping all of us organized. Thanks to Ebbe Roe Yovino-Smith and Gary Belinsky for their assistance with photography, and to Emma Star Jensen for supplying props.

Thanks to my perfect editor and friend, Kim Laidlaw, who supported this project wholeheartedly with both enthusiasm and brilliance. There wouldn't be a *Kitchen Gypsy* without Kim. And thanks to copy editor Sharon Silva for her expert eye.

Designer Christy Sheppard Knell is responsible for the book design, and I feel fortunate to have her remarkable work grace my project.

Thanks to the whole PR-savvy team at Dadascope, especially Dana Smith, Rena Ramirez, Moira Bartel, Kat Garen, Elka Karl, and Rebecca Eisenberg.

A big thanks to Yasemin Sussman and Lauren Eastman for helping me with publicity, and to everyone at Andrew Freeman and Company, restaurant and hospitality consultants, for their support every day.

A huge hug, a big thanks, and lots of love to my dear friend Inken Chrisman, who guided me through the process of writing this book and who read every word I wrote. Inken is a talented writer and her insights proved invaluable. Thanks to Ianthe Brautigan for helping to finesse the book proposal.

Thanks to my dear sweet friend Nancy Hopkins, deputy food editor at *Better Homes and Gardens* magazine, who embraced my idea early on and sent me many books to look at for inspiration. I'm forever grateful to the adorable Maritess Tse for her food-styling assistance, and to my diligent team of recipe testers, Jo Singleton, Jean Tenanes, Laura Chamberlain, and Paula Levy. My thanks to Clifford Hashimoto for his extraordinary talent with hair and make-up, to Laura Hunt for raiding her prop closet at a moment's notice, to Robert Schueller of Melissa's produce for turning up with just the right vegetables, and to Justin Marx of Marx Foods for locating a few hard-to-find ingredients. Neil Kamman kindly spent considerable time searching through the archives of his mother, Madeleine, to find materials for my book. Big kiss to Brett Jackson for Madeleine's recipes and most importantly her friendship. And thanks to Paul Swensen for being Paul.

To my family at Chez Panisse, especially my friend and mentor Alice Waters, sweet Mary Jo Thoresen, Christina Mueller, and Jullia Kim, as well as the wonderful Kyle Cornforth at the Edible Schoolyard Project.

And to everyone at my restaurant, Copita: partners Larry Mindel, Amy Svenberg, and Michael Mindel; Gonzalo Rivera; Raul Placencia; and Cassie Corless. Thanks for understanding my breakneck pace and crazy schedule and for continuing to support me.

Life wouldn't be the same if I didn't have Karen Alvey in it. The perfect assistant, she helps me keep everything straight. Karen's diligence astounds me daily, and I would never have been able to complete this book without her.

Let's talk indebtedness. Doe Coover, my agent and dear, dear friend, loved the idea of *Kitchen Gypsy* from the get-go and guided me along this incredible journey to its completion.

I wouldn't have been able to write this book without the encouragement and support of my wonderful family: my mom, John, Becky, Sara, Cory, Nancy, David, Liz, Khari, Gianna, Niki, Jinny, Jack, and Beth. Oh, and of course Molly! When times are tough, I call you. When times are good, I call you. Thanks for always picking up the phone and being there for me. And thanks to you, Dad—I'm still your wandering gypsy. My love to Madeline Ehrlich for guiding me through a personal memoir.

And finally, my special love to Joe. He never says a word when I tell him I've just booked another flight or there's a contract I need him to read, or when I sit at my computer writing until midnight. I couldn't do all the things I do without his unwavering support. And he lets me be me, loving me all the while. This book is for you, Joe.

measurement equivalents

Refer to the following charts for metric conversions as well as common cooking equivalents. All equivalents are approximate.

COOKING/OVEN TEMPERATURES

	fahrenheit	celsius	gas mark
Freeze Water	32°F	0°C	
Room Temp.	68°F	20°C	
Boil Water	212°F	100°C	
Bake	325°F	160°C	3
	350°F	180°C	4
	375°F	190°C	5
	400°F	200°C	6
	425°F	220°C	7
	450°F	230°C	8
Broil			Grill

LENGTH

1 in.	=					2.5 cm.		
6 in.	=	½ ft.	=		=	15 cm.		
12 in.	=	1 ft.	=		=	30 cm.		
36 in.	=	3 ft.	=	1 yd.	=	90 cm.		
40 in.	=					100 cm.	=	1 m.

DRY INGREDIENTS BY WEIGHT

1 oz.	=	¹⁄₁₆ lb.	=	30 g.
4 oz.	=	¼ lb.	=	120 g.
8 oz.	=	½ lb.	=	240 g.
12 oz.	=	¾ lb.	=	360 g.
16 oz.	=	1 lb.	=	480 g.

(To convert ounces to grams, multiply the number of ounces by 30.)

LIQUID INGREDIENTS BY VOLUME

¼ tsp.	=					1 ml.		
½ tsp.	=					2 ml.		
1 tsp.	=					5 ml.		
3 tsp.	=	1 tbsp.	=	½ fl. oz.	=	15 ml.		
2 tbsp.	=	⅛ cup	=	1 fl. oz.	=	30 ml.		
4 tbsp.	=	¼ cup	=	2 fl. oz.	=	60 ml.		
5⅓ tbsp.	=	⅓ cup	=	3 fl. oz.	=	80 ml.		
8 tbsp.	=	½ cup	=	4 fl. oz.	=	120 ml.		
10⅔ tbsp.	=	⅔ cup	=	5 fl. oz.	=	160 ml.		
12 tbsp.	=	¾ cup	=	6 fl. oz.	=	180 ml.		
16 tbsp.	=	1 cup	=	8 fl. oz	=	240 ml.		
1 pt.	=	2 cups	=	16 fl. oz.	=	480 ml.		
1 qt.	=	4 cups	=	32 fl. oz.	=	960 ml.		
				33 fl. oz.	=	1,000 ml.	=	1 l.

EQUIVALENTS FOR DIFFERENT TYPES OF INGREDIENTS

standard cup	fine powder (e.g., flour)	grain (e.g., rice)	granular (e.g., sugar)	liquid solids (e.g., butter)	liquid (e.g., milk)
1	140 g.	150 g.	190 g.	200 g.	240 ml.
¾	105 g.	113 g.	143 g.	150 g.	180 ml.
⅔	93 g.	100 g.	125 g.	133 g.	160 ml.
½	70 g.	75 g.	95 g.	100 g.	120 ml.
⅓	47 g.	50 g.	63 g.	67 g.	80 ml.
¼	35 g.	38 g.	48 g.	50 g.	60 ml.
⅛	18 g.	19 g.	24 g.	25 g.	30 ml.

index

index

index

JOANNE WEIR is a James Beard Award–winning cookbook author, cooking teacher, and host of the PBS series *Joanne Weir Gets Fresh* and *Joanne Weir's Cooking Confidence*. She is also the chef and owner of Copita Tequileria y Comida in Sausalito, California. When she is not teaching in her San Francisco studio kitchen, she is traveling and teaching throughout the world.

⚔ ● ⚔

©2015 by Joanne Weir
Design and food photography ©2015 by Time Inc. Books | 1271 Avenue of the Americas | New York, NY 10020

Sunset is a registered trademark of Sunset Publishing Corporation.

All rights reserved. No part of this book may be reproduced in any form or by any means without the prior written permission of the publisher, excepting brief quotations in connection with reviews written specifically for inclusion in magazines or newspapers, or limited excerpts strictly for personal use.

ISBN-13: 978-0-8487-4603-2
ISBN-10: 0-8487-4603-1
Library of Congress Control Number: 2014954434
Printed in the United States of America.
First printing 2015.

SUNSET PUBLISHING

EDITOR-IN-CHIEF Peggy Northrop
CREATIVE DIRECTOR Maili Holiman
PHOTOGRAPHY DIRECTOR Yvonne Stender
FOOD EDITOR Margo True

KITCHEN GYPSY

EDITOR Kim Laidlaw
SENIOR EDITOR Betty Wong
DESIGNER Christy Sheppard Knell
PHOTOGRAPHER Thomas J. Story
EXECUTIVE FOOD DIRECTOR Grace Parisi
PRODUCTION MANAGER Linda M. Bouchard
COPY EDITOR Sharon Silva
PHOTO EDITOR Susan B. Smith
IMAGING SPECIALISTS Kimberley Navabpour, E. Spencer Toy
ASSOCIATE PROJECT EDITOR Sarah Waller
ASSOCIATE PRODUCTION MANAGER Amy Mangus
PROOFREADER Pat Tompkins
INDEXER Ken DellaPenta

For more acknowledgments, see page 280.

To order additional publications, call 1-800-765-6400 or visit timeincbooks.com
Visit *Sunset* online at sunset.com